# Modelling Global Change

ADVANCES IN ECOLOGICAL ECONOMICS

**General Editor:** Robert Costanza, *Director, University of Maryland Institute for Ecological Economics and Professor, Center for Environmental and Estuarine Studies and Zoology Department, US*

This important new series is designed to make a significant contribution to the development of the principles and practices of ecological economics. As this field has expanded dramatically in recent years, the series will provide an invaluable forum for the publication of high quality work and show how ecological economic analysis can make a contribution to understanding and resolving important problems.

The main emphasis of the series is on the development and application of new original ideas in ecological economics. International in its approach, it will include some of the best theoretical and empirical work in the field with contributions to fundamental principles, rigorous evaluations of existing concepts, historical surveys and future visions. It will seek to address some of the most important theoretical questions and give policy solutions for the ecological problems confronting the global village as we move into the twenty-first century.

Economy and Ecosystems in Change
Analytical and Historical Approaches
*Edited by Jeroen C.J.M. van den Bergh and Jan van der Straaten*

Transition to a Sustainable Society
A Backcasting Approach to Modelling Energy and Ecology
*Henk A.J. Mulder and Wouter Biesiot*

Modelling Global Change
The Art of Integrated Assessment Modelling
*Marco Janssen*

Valuation for Sustainable Development
Methods and Policy Indicators
*Edited by Sylvie Faucheux and Martin O'Connor*

# Modelling Global Change

## The Art of Integrated Assessment Modelling

Marco Janssen
*Bureau for Environmental Assessment, RIVM, The Netherlands*

**ADVANCES IN ECOLOGICAL ECONOMICS**

**Edward Elgar**
Cheltenham, UK • Northampton, MA, USA

Published by
Edward Elgar Publishing Limited
8 Lansdown Place
Cheltenham
Glos GL50 2HU
UK

Edward Elgar Publishing, Inc.
6 Market Street
Northampton
Massachusetts 01060
USA

A catalogue record for this book
is available from the British Library

ISBN 1 85898 763 6
Printed and bound in Great Britain by
MPG Books Ltd, Bodmin, Cornwall

# Contents

# List of Figures and Tables

## FIGURES

# TABLES

# Preface

There is an increasing interest in global change and sustainable development in both policy and science communities. One of the tools to study these phenomena is integrated assessment modelling, that is, the development of integrated frameworks of simplified versions of expert models. They can be used as communication tools in the scientific and policy networks to stimulate scientific research and policy making in the field of global change and sustainable development.

Working at the Dutch National Institute for Public Health and the Environment (RIVM), the home of the integrated assessment models IMAGE (climate change) and TARGETS (global change), I became aware that existing models in the field failed to tackle various crucial parts of the problem, such as the methodological gap between economists and natural scientists, the fact that current integrated assessment models do not deal with the adaptive behaviour of biological and social agents, and the notion of various perspectives among the agents as a way to explicate the many uncertainties surrounding global change. This book can be considered as a box of ideas of applying new methodological developments on various aspects of integrated assessment modelling.

In writing this book, I have greatly benefited from the knowledge and support of many colleagues from the RIVM and colleagues from other institutes and universities. First, I would like to thank Bert de Vries and Jan Rotmans, project leaders of the Global Dynamics and Sustainable Development project, for their stimulating attitude towards my research activities. I am also grateful to Jodi de Greef for sharing his knowledge and for having provoking and clarifying discussions on complexity and complex systems. I thank Pim Martens for his enthusiastic co-operation in applying evolutionary modelling techniques to his malaria model as described in Chapter 9. Furthermore, thanks to the (former) members of the Global Dynamics and Sustainable Development project, the former Center of Mathematical Methods, the IMAGE team, the M development team and the Bureau for Environmental Assessment.

Finally, I would like to thank Robert Costanza and Edward Elgar publishers for giving me the opportunity to publish this book.

# 1. Introduction

## 1.1 THE ISSUE

Human activities have always modified the natural environment. The emergence of the integrated world economy during the last two centuries has especially increased both the intensity and scale of these modifications. Our use of land, water, minerals, and other natural resources has increased more than ten-fold during the past two centuries, and it is expected that future increases in population and development will intensify these pressures. The totality of changes on planet Earth, including all human interventions and alterations, is considered as global change. During the last few decades, we have seen growing acceptance of the insight that the increase in intensity and scale may cause serious harm, leading to increasing risks to human health and wealth.

The fast rate, the global scale, and the intensity of current human-induced changes have not earlier been seen to this degree in history, although concerns about limits to human development have been discussed in earlier times. Plato, for example, lamented in his *Critias* that agricultural activities had transformed the land of Attica. More recently in the history of mankind, almost two centuries ago, Malthus (1798) saw food production as a land-limited resource that could not possibly be increased quickly enough to keep pace with a growing population. The present wave of environmental concerns was stimulated by important publications such as Rachel Carson's *Silent Spring* (1962) and *Limits to Growth* by Meadows *et al.* (1972) and got its place on the international agenda of policy makers with the Brundtland Report (WCED, 1987) and the United Nations Conference on Environment and Development in Rio de Janeiro in 1992.

These policy efforts aim at stimulating sustainable development. Although there is no common definition, a widely accepted interpretation is that of a development meeting the needs of the present population without compromising the ability of future generations to meet their own needs. There are various kinds of approaches in which science may support policy making in order to stimulate sustainable development. An approach which became popular after World War II is the use of mathematical models.

1

Analytical mathematical models have been used in physical sciences for centuries, but due to the rapid development of the computer, mathematical models are being used in a broader range of disciplines to support decision making. These models can be used to order and analyse complex systems; the insights derived from the mathematical models may improve our perception of the complex reality.

Mathematical models have been used to support policy since World War II. The 1950s and 1960s were a relatively stable period of economic growth in the Western World. Technology could seemingly handle any difficulty that came along. Affluence was seen as growing and permanent, and the standard of living, it was believed, would continue to improve for individuals and generations. The world was a place of simple equilibria, linear responses were proportionate to stimuli, and policies could match this linearity. Cost-benefit analysis, optimization, and econometric models seemed to be quite appropriate.

During the 1960s, the image of a stable society changed, due to changes in the intellectual, psychological, and artistic views of the younger generation, accelerated by the Vietnam War, the murder of John F. Kennedy and the renewal of ecological concerns. The oil crises in the 1970s led to a change in the western economic success story. During these decades, we became more aware that reality can show strongly non-linear behaviour and that social, technological, economic and ecological systems may be surprisingly sensitive to internal and external fluctuations, as well as perturbations. Recent examples of surprising changes are the drastic economic, social and political changes in the former Soviet Union and the countries of Central and Eastern Europe, and the nationalistic civil wars in those areas, such as in former Yugoslavia.

Humankind is currently confronted with problems of uncommon complexity. The intensity and scale of the problems have increased, and one has become aware of the unpredictable non-linear behaviour of the global system. Due to the scale of human activities, current decisions about which pathways to follow in the next century are of crucial importance for the well-being of the next generations. More and more we are becoming aware, on the one hand, of our limited understanding of the global system and, on the other hand, of the interdependence of the various activities and consequences in time, place and scale. Intensified efforts by our scientific community are needed to pass on to decision makers the information and insights which are useful to help to balance the risks, while meeting targets for a sustainable development.

A recent development in the efforts to support policy making and the scientific community is the development of integrated assessment models.

The multi- and interdisciplinary approach of 'integrated assessment' endeavours to keep track of how the pieces of the puzzle fit together. Integrated assessment models are one type of tool to support integrated assessment and aim at integrating simplified versions of expert models, so that users can scan the future in an interactive way. But it is not the predictions, the glimpses of the future derived from the electronic oracles, which are of main interest. Because the future is inherently unpredictable at a detailed level, such forecasts are of limited use in decision making. Nevertheless, mathematical models may enrich our insights into the behaviour of complex reality. The improvements of our perception of reality may help us to improve our decision making. It is this notion which is an underlying assumption of the usefulness of the tools which are presented in this book.

## 1.2   THE SCOPE AND OBJECTIVES

Since 1991 I have been working at the National Institute of Public Health and the Environment (RIVM) on integrated assessment modelling, in particular on the global, integrated assessment model entitled TARGETS (Tool to Assess Regional and Global Environmental and health Targets for Sustainability) (Rotmans and De Vries, 1997). TARGETS is intended to be used to perform an analysis and assessment on a global scale of social and economic processes, biophysical processes, and effects on ecosystems and humans from an integrated system dynamics perspective. Furthermore, I have been working on the climate change model IMAGE (Integrated Model to Assess the Greenhouse Effect) (Rotmans, 1990; Alcamo, 1994). IMAGE simulates the dynamics of the global society-biosphere-climate system, and is used to investigate the linkages and feedbacks in the system, and evaluates consequences of climate policies. More information on the models can be found in Chapter 3.

During the development and use of these models, I became aware of the embryonic state of the methodology of integrated assessment modelling. Tools for old problems are used within this new research area; I believe that not all of these tools are equally satisfactory. It might be that the new problems need new tools in order to support decision making in a more satisfactory manner. The existing tools probably result in asking lesser relevant questions being asked, rather than in giving the right insights. This can be explained by what is called the *streetlight effect:* a drunk who has lost his door key looks for it under the street lamp because that is the brightest spot. Many of the tools currently used deeply bias the way modellers perceive the world and, thus, influence the contents and shapes of models: 'If the only

tool you have is a hammer, you tend to treat everything as if it were a nail',
(Maslow, 1966).

It is not my intention to claim to provide the right or the best tools.
Existing tools are examined and new methodological approaches are applied
to various aspects of the problem of global change. In this way, I hope to
contribute to the development of more suitable tools by appropriately
reshaping existing methods for the new kind of problems which have been
recognized during the last decades.

More concretely, I will discuss three methodological issues which are of
importance within the present integrated assessment models or are expected
to be of importance in the next generations of those models. First, a widely
spread modelling paradigm within the integrated assessment modelling
community, especially in economic oriented models, is the use of
optimization. Those models use simple linearized representations of the
global system, excluding important processes. I believe that such models are
of limited use, as the inclusion of processes is essential in modelling global
change. Therefore, I will analyse the sensitivity of the present optimization
approach and provide a new direction of optimization oriented studies in
integrated assessment modelling by applying heuristic search algorithms on
advanced simulation models.

Second, in current modelling efforts, uncertainty is represented as a
statistical artefact using educated guesses of ranges of parameter values. As a
moderate step to improve the consistency of educated guesses and to make
uncertainty explicit, I propose to use plural qualitative and quantitative
descriptions of reality to explain partly the uncertainty rooted in subjective
judgement. Some illustrative case studies are performed on quantifying
various perspectives of reality.

Third, the present generation of integrated assessment models is dominated
by a mechanistic world view. Studies often aim to understand the mechanisms
to control the system. I believe that this view is limited in understanding the
ever changing, evolving, and adapting global system. An evolutionary
modelling approach is proposed as a useful alternative, regarding some
exemplary parts of the global system as an organism, instead of a machine.
By applying recent developments in mathematics and computer science on
evolutionary modelling, some case studies are worked out to illustrate the
possible benefits of such an approach.

## 1.3   STRUCTURE OF THE BOOK

In the next chapter, the field of global change is discussed by giving a brief overview of the main issues of the changing global system. In Chapter 3, an overview is given of the emerging field of integrated assessment. Methodological concerns in the integrated assessment community are discussed, as well as prominent integrated assessment models in the field of global climate change.

The methodological backbone of this book is presented in Chapter 4. It discusses a number of methodological problems of integrated assessment modelling. A general discussion is given about what methodological contributions are made in this book; these are worked out in Chapters 5 - 9.

As an illustration of the problems in the present use of optimization, I have applied optimization to a mathematical dynamic system of global climate change in Chapter 5. In Chapter 6, exploratory optimization oriented experiments have been applied with the TARGETS model. The experiments mainly focus on global energy policies meeting climate change targets, taking account of the uncertainties in economic and technological development. In particular the consequences of delayed responses are illustrated.

The initial allocation of emission rights is discussed in Chapter 7, in which perspectives are used to quantify subjective uncertainties in weights of 'equal' sharing. Furthermore, the egalitarian concept of emission debts is presented.

Two case studies are worked out, focusing on adaptive behaviour of social agents, as well as adaptation of biological agents. Chapter 8 presents a study which aims at modelling learning and adaptive behaviour of social agents, a concept which is called 'The Battle of Perspectives'. An example is worked out for the global climate change problem. A malaria case-study in Chapter 9 deals with modelling the adaptation of mosquitoes and parasites. Special attention is given to development of resistance and adaptation of these agents to climate change.

After the concluding remarks, the book closes with a discussion of possible avenues for the near future of integrated assessment modelling of global change.

# 2. Global Change

## 2.1  INTRODUCTION

The history of humankind is a continuing record of interactions between peoples' efforts to improve their well-being and the environments ability to sustain these endeavours. Environmental constraints led to innovations and social development, as well as social stagnation and human suffering. Several ancient cultures collapsed because the increase of affluence and population led to an over-exploitation of the natural environment (Ponting, 1992); some examples are the Mesopotamians (±2000BC), the Mayas (800 AD) and the Polynesians on Easter Island (16th century). While the interactions throughout most of history were on a local scale, during the last decades mankind has become aware that the increasing complexity and scale of the interactions have increasingly been leading to a need for new environmental management. This century, people became aware of various new threats for mankind, such as climate change, acid rain, ozone depletion, resource exhaustion, limits to the availability of food and unpolluted fresh water. In this chapter, I will give a brief overview of the state-of-the-art knowledge of global change. This overview is meant to show the non-informed reader the range of problems which may be analysed in assessing global change. The tools discussed in this book will only be applied to a small subset of these issues (for example climate change, energy, and malaria), and are applied within the context of integrated assessment, an emerging scientific field within the global change research.

I will briefly describe the human and environmental system and related issues based on a number of state-of-the-art publications on the various subjects. This is meant to give only a rough overview of the various issues related to global change and certainly not a complete picture. For those who are interested in a more complete overview, I refer to for example Clark and Munn (1986), UNEP (1992; 1997), WHO (1992b), White *et al.* (1992), Graedel and Crutzen (1993), Seitz (1995) and Brown (1995, 1996).

## 2.2    THE HUMAN SYSTEM

### Population and Health

About 8000 BC, there were approximately 5 million people in the world; this grew to about 200 million in about 1 AD, and 500 million in 1650. The recent period of rapid population increase began in the eighteenth century, growing from a population size of 1000 million in 1800 to more than 5000 million now. Projections of the United Nations show expectations of more than 10 billion people at the end of the next century. This can be explained by changes in demographic and health stages generally described in the theory of health transition (Frenk *et al.*, 1993; Ness *et al.*, 1993; Bongaarts, 1994; Niessen *et al.*, 1997). It describes how populations can go through typical demographic and health stages when they change from living in pre-industrial conditions to having a mortality pattern that is found in the post-modern societies (Omran, 1971) (see Figure 2.1). The early stages are characterized by high fertility levels and a low life expectancy and an epidemiological pattern of infectious diseases. In the last recognized stages, low levels of fertility are dominant, sometimes even below replacement level, life expectancy is high, and diseases are postponed until the last phases of life. The health transition is defined as including all these changes, as well as the changes in the provision and organization of social and health-related services. The changes in fertility and mortality often have different timing, leading to a rapid population growth in the first half of the demographic transition. Also specific sub-populations may find themselves in varying stages of these two processes, depending on their socio-economic and environmental conditions of life. It is assumed that there is a convergence of developmental directions, as societies shift from agricultural-oriented societies to modern industrial economies.

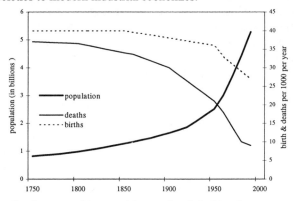

*Figure 2.1: The demographic transition at the global level*

**Economic Activities**

The growth of population and populations' activities caused an emergence of a 'world economy' about two centuries ago. Demands for many goods and services are more and more met by supplies from all over the world, and this trend continues to increase. The volume of the world trade has risen in the past two hundred years by a factor of about 500, leading to a share of one-third of the world's total GNP. The emergence of a global market dominated by many large corporations illustrates the globalization of economic activities. The expanding world economy consists of a number of interrelated human activities that exert pressures on the total environment. Three types of activities are distinguished: agriculture, industry, and services.

**Agriculture**
Humanity has relied solely on hunting, fishing, and gathering food for most of its two million years of existence. Since agriculture appeared about 10,000 years ago, human activities have caused significant changes in land use. In the last century, the mounting demand of growing populations led to an accelerated change in agricultural practices. Increasingly, fragile land has been cultivated more intensively, resulting in environmental damage, especially land degradation. Resources from outside the agricultural system have been imported (water through irrigation, chemical pesticides and fertilizers, fossil fuels energy). This has allowed increased agricultural productivity, although it has undermined the resource base and caused environmental problems.

**Industry**
Industrialization has increased personal incomes and material wealth and improved services, particularly transport and communication. However, industrial practices have various side effects such as pollution and resource depletion. To illustrate, I will discuss the energy problem (Figure 2.2). Before industry developed, human demands for energy were primarily associated with food production. Since some 200 years ago when the industrial revolution started, the energy demand has been increasingly met by fossil fuels replacing renewable resources like water and biomass. Since 1900, world use and production of energy has increased more than tenfold. During the first half of this century, energy production slackened during the First and Second World Wars and the depression of the 1930s. In the 1950s and 1960s, the economy grew rapidly. The inexpensive oil and gas were the basic fuels supporting the economic expansion. However, during the oil crises in the 1970s, the share of oil and gas was reduced somewhat due to higher prices, in favour of an increasing share of coal. In the last decades, people have become aware that the use of fossil fuels has a harmful impact on the environment, which has led to the

desire to limit the use of fossil fuels, by replacing them with traditional alternatives (like biomass and hydropower) or new alternatives (like nuclear and solar energy). Although such a transition might be preferable from an environmental perspective, it is not known what the social and economic consequences will be.

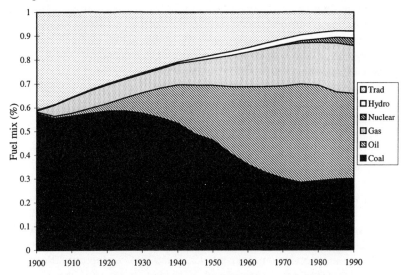

*Figure 2.2: Historical mix of fuels to meet the global energy demand*

**Services**
The service sector is increasing. The service sector has supported industrial activities by, for example, administration and health care. Nowadays, an increasing part of the National Product is produced by non-material production, such as the booming knowledge sector. The expected emergence of an information society becomes imaginable now that the electronic highway finds its place in the (Western) world. Although this sector is less material and energy intensive, it requires a higher quality of these resources, which makes the net effect of an increasing service sector on the environment uncertain.

## 2.3   THE ISSUES WITHIN THE HUMAN SYSTEM

**Population and Health**

Socio-economic development largely determines population health levels directly by influencing the immediate surroundings of people, and their health behaviour and their access to health services (Niessen *et al.*, 1997). Health standards can be considerably improved in the early stages of the health transition by food availability and good drinking water supply. In the last stage of the transition, the main health determinants are related to life style, like smoking and hypertension.

Population growth leads to increasing pressure on the environment, due to increases in human activities. Environmental factors, in turn, affect both population density and the quality of life of the population. The use of drugs like antibiotics may cause, via the increase of resistance to external pathogenic micro-organisms, a revival of infectious diseases. Climate change may increase the risks of vector-born diseases like malaria, schistosomiasis and dengue. Air-pollution affects the health by inhalation of toxic products, while depletion of the ozone layer increases the risk of skin cancer and cataracts.

Another important question in relation to the health transition is the increasing proportion of elderly people, which will increase the disability ratio and the demand for health services. The transition also leads to an increase in diseases like cancer, Parkinson's disease, and diabetes.

### Poverty and Inequity

For most of history, a few individuals in many societies had a higher standard of living than their fellow human beings, but the vast majority of people on earth shared a common condition of poverty (Seitz, 1995). The Industrial Revolution created new wealth in the industrialized nations in Europe, which was eventually shared by larger numbers of people. The differences between rich and poor in the world began to increase, where a few nations have achieved their higher living standards by extracting resources from the rest of the world. It is estimated that the difference between the average income of people in rich countries (early industrialized) and poor ('developing') countries was 2 to 1 in 1850, 10 to 1 in 1950, and is expected to be 30 to 1 in 2000 (Miller, 1985). Currently, more than a billion people can be classified as being poor, because they lack a standard of living that includes adequate food, safe and sufficient water, sanitation, a secure shelter, and access to education and health care. It is expected that those poor are more vulnerable to global change than others.

### Resource Use

The increasing use of minerals and fossil fuels will lead to depletion of non-renewable resources. The timing of depletion depends on technological and economic developments. Although fossil fuels are relatively cheap energy supplies to fulfil the energy needs of the growing economies, their use has various side effects. Besides the inequality of acquiring, distributing, and using energy resources, the use of fossil fuels causes serious pressure on the environment. Emissions related to combustion of fossil fuels contribute to the issues of acidification and climate change. In addition to this, land degradation and depletion of resources are important issues. However, suggested alternative energy supplies like biofuels, solar energy, wind, nuclear and hydro-power also have various harmful impacts on the environment. Challenges for the future are to manage the energy demand and balance the energy costs and environmental impact of the various energy supplies.

## Extinction of Cultures

There have been and still are thousands of different cultures on our planet. Each group shares a common history, a common ancestry, and usually a common language and a common religion. They often have common traditions, common ways of doing certain things and of interacting with each other and towards outsiders. Because of these common features that make them different from other peoples, each nation's people see the world and their place in it differently from others, approach problems differently, and have arrived at different solutions to situations human beings face. Extinction of cultures leaves life a little less rich.

## War

Since World War II, there have been about 150 wars, with 90 per cent of those occurring in the less developed nations; these wars have killed about 7.5 million soldiers and 14.5 million civilians. The destructive capacity of weapons increases the number of refugees grows (Figure 2.3) and the ecological damage to the land increases, in a world where people often choose an armed solution to solve territorial disputes, power struggles, ethnic and religious rivalries or other conflicts.

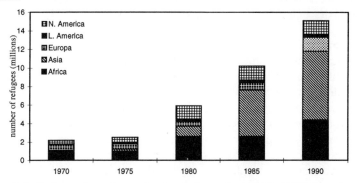

*Figure 2.3: Estimated numbers of refugees by region, 1970-1990. Based on data by UNHCR as depicted in Tolba (1992)*

## 2.4    THE ENVIRONMENTAL SYSTEM

One way of describing the environmental system is to consider a number of spheres: atmosphere, lithosphere, hydrosphere, and ecosphere. Human interventions within the spheres, especially the disturbances of the biogeochemical cycles, cause a number of issues, as will be discussed in Section 2.5

**Global Systems**

**Atmosphere**
The Earth's atmosphere is a complex system of gases and suspended particles. The composition did not have its roots in the origins of the planet. The atmosphere of today has been derived from the Earth itself by chemical and biochemical reactions. This adaptable system forms a gaseous envelope around the Earth and is a composition of mainly five gases: nitrogen, oxygen, argon, carbon dioxide, and water vapour make up 99.9 per cent of the total volume of the atmosphere. Human activities cause emissions of various gases and particles which may cause climate change, stratospheric ozone depletion, air pollution, and acid rain.

**Lithosphere**
The lithosphere is the upper zone of the Earth's mantle. The outer boundary forms a complex interface with the atmosphere and hydrosphere. The inner boundary is adjacent to rock, which is near its melting point and is capable of motion relative to the lithosphere above. The processes in the lithosphere, such as solidification, weathering erosion and rising magma, are relatively slow and they involve considerable residence times in the various compartments. Disturbance of the lithosphere consists of changes in element cycles (see below) and the extractions of mineral resources.

**Hydrosphere**
The processes which bring about changes in phase (water vapour, water, and ice) and the transport of water within the atmosphere are commonly represented by a hydrological cycle. Within the hydrological system, water is stored in the atmosphere (0.001 per cent), the land (1.8 per cent), the oceans (96.5 per cent) and the polar ice caps (1.7 per cent). Transfers between stores are effectuated by the processes of evaporation, condensation, precipitation, runoff, and freezing and melting. The greatest exchanges are those between ocean and atmosphere. Human activities cause pollution and disturbances in the availability of fresh water. Furthermore, climate change and groundwater extraction may cause sea levels to rise.

**Ecosphere**

At the top of the lithosphere, throughout the hydrosphere and into the lower atmosphere, lies a transition zone, which contains and is assumed to be created by living organisms. Life far outweighs its relatively small mass in the significance of its effect on the constitution of the lithosphere, hydrosphere, and atmosphere. The biogeochemical cycles are an essential element in the ecosphere:

**Biogeochemical Cycles**

Living organisms extract chemicals from their environment, hold on to them for a period, and lose them again. In its natural biogeochemical cycles a mineral often goes through a reservoir stage, which can be gaseous, liquid, or sedimentary (see Figure 2.4a-d). Below, I discuss four of the basic element cycles: carbon (C), nitrogen (N), phosphorous (P), and sulphur (S). More detailed discussions can be found in, for example, Lovelock (1979), Bolin and Cook (1983), Begon *et al.* (1990), Schlesinger (1991), Butcher *et al.* (1992), White *et al.* (1992), Anderson *et al.* (1993) and Den Elzen *et al.* (1997)

**The carbon cycle**

Carbon is the most important element for life on Earth. Carbon dioxide in the atmosphere is used by green plants in the process of photosynthesis and is returned to the atmosphere through plant and soil respiration. Carbon is also passed along the food chain and is converted into carbon dioxide by decay processes. The carbon cycle is not only part of the terrestrial web of life, but also a part of the aquatic web as carbon dioxide diffuses in and out of both fresh and salt water. In the ocean, photosynthesis is confined to the light zone, where a large proportion of carbon becomes bound in shells and exoskeletons of ocean invertebrates as calcium carbonate. When these organisms die, their body coverings may be buried in the sediment and are, thereby, isolated from biological activity. Through geological time, some of these carbon deposits become part of coral reefs or limestone rock and some are slowly transformed into fossil fuels.

The carbon cycle is currently disturbed by fossil fuel combustion and deforestation, leading to increased atmospheric $CO_2$ concentrations which may contribute to a climate change.

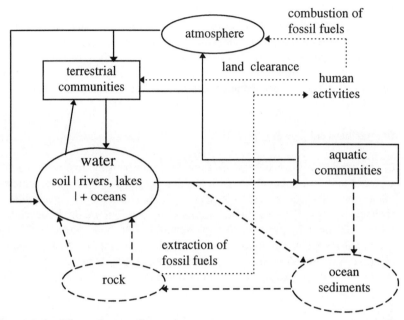

*Figure 2.4a: The carbon cycle*

**The phosphorus cycle**

The phosphorus cycle does not involve an atmospheric phase, since the primary reservoir of this element is rock or sediment. As rocks erode, phosphate is released into the environment. Plants then absorb phosphate through their roots. Organisms acquire this essential element in food and excrete any excess in faeces. When phosphate enters streams and lakes in large amounts, it can act as a stimulant to algae growth and eventually usurp the oxygen that other forms of water life require (eutrophication).

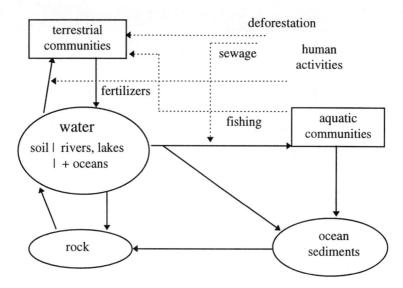

*Figure 2.4b: The phosphorus cycle*

**The nitrogen cycle**
Even though nitrogen makes up approximately 78 per cent of the atmosphere, it is not utilized by most living organisms in its atmospheric form ($N_2$). Life processes generally require nitrate or some other nitrogen compound. Before nitrogen fertilizers were manufactured, the amount of nitrogen removed from the atmosphere by natural processes was closely balanced by denitrifying processes. Today, industrial intervention in the nitrogen cycle appears to fix more nitrogen than can be denitrified. These additional amounts of nitrogen in the soil often disrupt natural balances, resulting in large run-offs of nitrogen compounds into rivers, streams, and lakes.

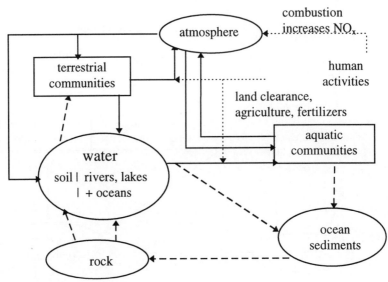

*Figure 2.4c: The nitrogen cycle*

## The sulphur cycle

The sulphur cycle involves both an atmospheric and a sedimentary phase. In nature, sulphur exists in several states. It is used in the manufacture of many products, including chemicals, matches, and fertilizers. As a constituent of coal and petroleum products, sulphur causes atmospheric contamination when its products are burned, which contributes to the acidification and climate change.

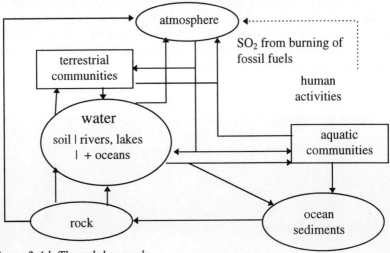

*Figure 2.4d: The sulphur cycle*

## 2.5 THE ISSUES WITHIN THE ENVIRONMENTAL SYSTEM

Human activities cause a lot of changes in the environment, resulting in the pollution of water, land, and air. Reduced availability of clean water, clean and fertile soils, and clean air leads to more harm to human health and wealth and to damage to the well-being of other species. Many species have already become extinct, and some areas have already been ruined by human activities, the Aral Sea being one of them. The expected growth of population, economic activities, land use, resource depletion and pollution may lead to unexpected consequences. Our knowledge of our Earth system is insufficient to project the results of the 'experiment' of humankind. In this book, I will mainly focus on climate change. Therefore, I will restrict the discussion of environmental issues to climate change and the interlinked issues of stratospheric ozone depletion and acid rain.

### Climate Change

Tyndall (1863) had suggested that small changes in atmospheric composition could alter the climate and Arrhenius (1896) estimated that a doubling of carbon dioxide would raise global mean temperature by 4°C to 6°C. However, it was not until the mid-1970s that any attention was paid to this environmental issue. At present, due to the observed changes of the composition of the atmosphere, there is growing concern that increasing atmospheric concentrations of greenhouse gases (like $CO_2$, $CH_4$, $NO_x$ and CFCs) may change the global climate.

The theory of the natural greenhouse effect is scientifically well established (IPCC, 1990). The Earth and its atmosphere receive short-wave solar radiation from the sun. About 30 per cent of the incoming solar radiation is reflected back into space, mainly by clouds. The remainder is absorbed by the atmosphere and the Earth's surface, before it is emitted as long-wave thermal radiation into space (see Figure 2.5). Most of this long-wave radiation is absorbed by a number of radiatively-active trace gases (greenhouse gases), like water vapour ($H_2O$), carbon dioxide ($CO_2$), methane ($CH_4$), nitrous oxide ($N_2O$), chlorofluorocarbons (CFCs), and ozone ($O_3$). Due to the heat trapping of these gases, the Earth's surface temperature is about 15°C instead of -18°C, which is called 'the natural greenhouse effect'.

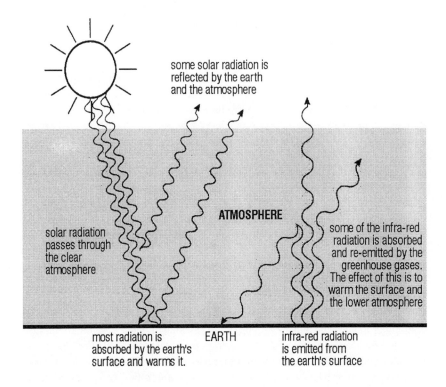

*Figure 2.5: A simplified diagram illustrating the greenhouse effect (IPCC, 1990)*

During the past centuries, the atmospheric concentrations of the greenhouse gases have increased. Carbon dioxide increased steadily from 280 ppmv (around 1800) to 354 ppmv in 1990 (IPCC, 1990). Observation of the isotopic dilution of the atmosphere and surface oceans with respect to radiocarbon and stable carbon isotopes gives strong evidence of the anthropogenic source of the concentration increase. Concentrations of other greenhouse gases have also increased: methane concentration has more than doubled over the last two centuries, nitrous oxide concentration has increased by 8 per cent since 1800, while new greenhouse gases like CFCs have been added to the atmosphere since the 1930s.

Increases in atmospheric concentrations of the radiatively active gases, as observed over the past decades, will lead to a net increase in energy input to the lower stratosphere, and, hence, will be succeeded by elevation of the global mean surface temperature of the Earth. However, many uncertainties exist concerning to what extent, where, and how fast such temperature increases will occur and what the impact will be on the biosphere, including human society.

Scientific evidence of climate change is a complex issue, because of our limited understanding of the global system and since observations are influenced by various natural factors influencing the climate system such as, for example, volcanic activities, fluctuations in solar activity, and anthropogenic factors such as variations in albedo due to land use changes, changes in tropospheric and stratospheric ozone concentration, and sulphur emissions from industry.

Our limited understanding of the global system is illustrated by various issues which are discussed briefly below:

- *Climate forcing by sulphate aerosols*: The radiative effects of sulphate aerosols, derived from emissions of sulphur dioxide and from biomass burning, have only recently been acknowledged to affect the radiation balance, both directly and indirectly. Averaged world-wide, aerosol cooling may partly offset greenhouse warming, although this is a gross oversimplification, since because of their short atmospheric lifetimes the effects exhibit large spatial and temporal differences. First modelling results show regions with a warming and a cooling effect, if forcing by sulphate aerosols and greenhouse gases are combined (Taylor and Penner, 1994; Wigley, 1995; Mitchell *et al.*, 1995; IPCC, 1996a).
- *Indirect climate forcing by CFCs*: Halocarbon-induced stratospheric ozone depletion can, likewise, directly affect climate change via negative radiative forcing due to ozone depletion (Ramaswamy *et al.*, 1992; WMO, 1992). At present, globally and annually averaged ozone forcing is setting off 80 per cent of the total, direct, global-mean radiative forcing caused by the halocarbons under considerations.
- *Geophysical feedbacks*: various physical processes in the atmosphere-ocean-cryosphere system directly modify the response to radiative forcing, such as water vapour formation, cloud feedback, and snow-ice albedo feedbacks.
- *Biogeochemical feedbacks*: influence of uptake of emissions of greenhouse gases, affection of atmospheric chemical condition, by, for example, the $CO_2/N/P$ fertilization effects, eutrophication effect, plankton-related feedbacks, soil acidification, and so on.

If climate change should occur, it might also cause various impacts, such as droughts (desertification), sea level rise, shifts in the growing zones for vegetation (both natural and agricultural), and changes in the availability of fresh water, increased risks of vector-born diseases and heath-stress. Not all changes are harmful. Some countries could eventually benefit from increased rainfall or longer growing periods in the present marginal areas. However, the international community is generally concerned with the impacts of climate change and wants to minimize the risks of damage.

## Ozone Depletion

Molina and Rowland (1974) warned that the use of CFCs might damage the ozone layer, which might lead to increases in UV-B radiation, which might cause a multitude of negative effects, such as augmentations in the incidence of skin cancer and other diseases, reduction of crop yields, and damages to materials. The measurements of the Antarctic ozone gap, and the middle- and high latitude ozone losses suggest the seriousness of this environmental problem (Farman *et al.*, 1985; WMO, 1992).

The main ozone-depleting gases are CFCs and other halocarbons, which are currently in use as refrigerants, aerosol propellants, and solvents. Due to the industrial production of CFCs, the atmospheric chlorine (Cl) levels have increased from about 0.6 ppbv up to about 3.9 ppbv (Fraser *et al.*, 1992). Increased chlorine levels are the major cause of the observed ozone losses over the last decades, although other man-made and natural causes also exist. The concern about the depletion of the stratospheric ozone layer led to the Montreal Protocol in 1987, which was followed by Amendments in London (1990) and Copenhagen (1992), which should finally lead to a phasing-out of a large group of halocarbons by the year 2000.

An important feedback is the decreasing stratospheric temperature (due to climate change) which slows down the rate of ozone destruction. Furthermore, the increased UV-B radiations have a negative feedback impact on biological production (phytoplankton growth). Due to ozone depletion, these gases also have an indirect climate change impact (Ramaswamy *et al.*, 1992; WMO, 1992).

## Acidification

A concern about acidification damage (for example decline in fish populations and ultimate extinction in rivers and lakes) was first voiced by Svante Odén in Sweden (Odén, 1968). Important gases involved in the production of acid deposition are nitrogen dioxide ($NO_2$), nitrous oxide (NO), sulphur dioxide ($SO_2$), and ammonia ($NH_3$), which can be transported by winds for distances of up to 1000 kilometres. The major causes of emissions are the burning of fossil fuels and industrial processes. The forest decline in Europe became a major public issue in the early 1980s, which led to effective measures to reduce the acid emissions, although the deposition levels still exceed the target levels which are necessary to prevent economic and ecological damage in large parts of Europe and North America. Furthermore, due to industrial development, acidification has become a problem in other places of the globe, especially in Southeast Asia.

## 2.6   SETTING THE SCOPE

The many issues related to global change, the scientific uncertainties which surround them, the complex interrelations between the issues and the regional differences in causes and effects leaves the policy makers from the local to the global scale with difficult dilemmas. They would like to know which issues are the biggest threats for which regions, on what time scale, and who and how can we reduce these problems. It is the challenge for the scientific community to help the various stake holders (governments, industry, consumers) with priority setting. The first Global Environmental Outlook (UNEP, 1997) made an assessment of the relative importance of environmental problems in the different regions (Tables 2.1 and 2.2). It shows the relative difference in priorities for the regions and the differences in trends between the regions.

*Table 2.1: Regional concerns: relative importance given to environmental issues by regions (UNEP, 1997)*

| | Africa | Asia Pacific | Europe & former USSR | Latin America | North America | West Asia | Polar Regions |
|---|---|---|---|---|---|---|---|
| Land: degradation | critically important | critically important | important | critically important | important | critically important | lower priority |
| Forest: loss, degradation | critically important | critically important | important | critically important | lower priority | lower priority | negligible |
| Biodiversity: loss, habit fragmentation | important | critically important | critically important | important | important | important | important |
| Fresh water: access, pollution | critically important | critically important | critically important | important | critically important | critically important | lower priority |
| Marine and coastal zones: degradation | important | critically important | critically important | important | important | critically important | lower priority |
| Atmosphere: pollution | important | critically important | critically important | critically important | critically important | important | negligible |
| Urban and industrial: contamination, waste | important | critically important | critically important | critically important | critically important | critically important | important |

■ critically important   ▤ important   ▨ lower priority   ☐ negligible

*Table 2.2: Regional environmental trends (UNEP, 1997)*

| | Africa | Asia Pacific | Europe & former USSR | Latin America | North America | West Asia | Polar Regions |
|---|---|---|---|---|---|---|---|
| Land: degradation | increasing | increasing | stable | increasing | decreasing | increasing | stable |
| Forest: loss, degradation | increasing | increasing | stable | increasing | stable | increasing | not applicable |
| Biodiversity: loss, habit fragmentation | increasing | increasing | increasing | increasing | stable | increasing | stable |
| Fresh water: access, pollution | increasing | increasing | stable | stable | stable | increasing | stable |
| Marine and coastal zones: degradation | stable | increasing | increasing | increasing | stable | increasing | stable |
| Atmosphere: pollution | stable | increasing | stable | increasing | stable | stable | stable |
| Urban and industrial: contamination, waste | stable | increasing | stable | increasing | stable | increasing | not applicable |

■ increasing    ▤ remaining relatively stable    ▦ decreasing    ☐ not applicable

A tool to support priority setting would be a framework which integrates the scientific understanding of the issues of global change with regard to causes, mechanisms, effects and costs. Integrated assessment is such a tool. It helps to improve the communication between science and policy, and between various scientific disciplines. Chapter 3 gives an overview of integrated assessment modelling.

# 3. Integrated Assessment Modelling

## 3.1 INTEGRATED ASSESSMENT

There is a growing demand and interest in an integrated approach to global change. As discussed in Chapter 2 there is a growing awareness of the rapidly increasing complexity of global change, encompassing a diversity of research topics which all seem to be interconnected in one way or another. There is a need for a tool to help the prioritization of policy making and research activities, and to scan the various kinds of uncertainties and missing links of knowledge. Such a tool is integrated assessment which is a process of combining, interpreting and communicating knowledge. This process is an activity of various stake holders such as scientists, policy makers and NGOs. Integrated assessment stimulates the interaction between science and policy, between the various scientific disciplines and between research in different parts of the world.

This complex, intuitive, and value-loaded process cannot be performed by only one, unique approach. Therefore, multiple, diverse approaches to integrated assessment are needed. Among the different kind of tools we may distinguish are integrated assessment models (the topic of this book), policy exercises, dialogues between science and policy, data analysis, scenario-analysis and expert models

An example of integrated assessment for global climate change is the work of the IMAGE 2 group of the RIVM. The model, as described in Section 3.5, is based on a number of expert models. The network of collaborating research institutions and the peer-reviews examine the scientific quality of the model. The model is used in various scientific networks such as IPCC, IGBP and EMF. To bridge the gap between science and policy, a number of workshops were organized with negotiators and policy advisors (Alcamo, *et al.*, 1996). One of the outputs of this process was the safe landing analysis, a simple framework to assess short-term efforts on long-term effects, which was found to be very useful in the negotiations on a 1997 climate protocol (Alcamo and Kreileman, 1996).

The numerous approaches used at this time to address the global change issue from an integrated viewpoint are all incomplete. These efforts vary in their emphasis and in the ensemble of methods employed to achieve integration and assessment. The differences in emphasis are a consequence of the different backgrounds people and institutes have, leading to different problem orientations of these efforts.

In this book, I aim to appropriately reshape existing methods as tools which may support integrated assessment modelling of global change. Therefore, I will discuss integrated assessment modelling in more detail.

## 3.2   INTEGRATED ASSESSMENT MODELS: A GENERAL DESCRIPTION

Among the tools for integrated assessment are integrated assessment models. Current projects in integrated assessment modelling elaborate on a tradition that was founded in the early 1970s by the Club of Rome (Forrester, 1971; Meadows *et al.*, 1972, 1974). Over the past 20 years, numerous global models have been built in the tradition of system dynamics (Brecke, 1993). Those models were useful for their qualitative, rather than quantitative results. But due to the criticisms in scientific circles about the model validation and completeness, this type of model never made it into the scientific mainstream. Risbey *et al.* (1996) wonder if the current generation of integrated assessment modellers ignore the parallels between world systems of the early 1970s and the current stream of integrated assessment because the world systems models were so heavily discredited.

The next generation of integrated assessment models started with focus on the acid rain issue. The RAINS model (Alcamo *et al.*, 1990), which was developed and used to address the contentious issue of acid rain in Europe, was one of the more successful among these earlier studies. More recently, the challenge of global climate change has prompted the development of a new flight of models (see also Section 3.5), such as the IMAGE model (Rotmans, 1990; Alcamo, 1994); the DICE model (Nordhaus, 1992); the PAGE model (Hope *et al.*, 1993); and ICAM (Dowlatabadi and Morgan, 1993b).

Another stream of integrated models focus on the ecological economic developments on a regional scale. Examples of these models are ISLAND (Engelen *et al.*, 1995), QUEST (Biggs *et al.*, 1996), Threshold 21 (Millenium Institute, 1995,1996) and Lakeland (de Greef and de Vries, 1991; Jager *et al.*, 1997).

In general, integrated assessment models try to describe quantitatively as much as possible of the cause-effect relationship of events and of the cross-linkages and interactions between issues. More specifically, integrated assessment models of global change are designed to analyse this phenomenon from a synoptic perspective. Although there are some serious attempts being made to construct an integrated model of the Earth's atmosphere, hydrosphere, and terrestrial biosphere (Fisher, 1988; Krapivin, 1993), it is conceptually and technically not yet possible to link, let alone integrate, a variety of complex, detailed and three-dimensional models. Therefore, it is often more appealing to make use of reduced models for each component of the integrated assessment framework, which are small enough to be comprehensible, flexible, and easily linked to one another. A meta model is a simplified, condensed version of a more complicated and detailed model (expert model), which provides approximately the same behaviour as the expert model from which it is extracted. There are various methods for developing meta models, which vary in complexity, ranging from fully parameterized models to process-oriented models. The parsimony principle applied to meta models within an integrated assessment framework is also justified by the everlasting deficient state of scientific knowledge. However, the prerequisite for these meta models is that they should be tested, verified, calibrated, and validated thoroughly against expert models and observational data. Interlinking a variety of meta models requires the definition of one single conceptual framework, so that harmonization can be obtained with respect to aggregation level, temporal, and spatial scales.

The challenging aspect of building such an integrated assessment model is to find the balance between simplicity and complexity; aggregation and realistic outcomes; stochastic and deterministic elements; qualitative and quantitative linkages; transparency and uncertainty. Furthermore, it is fundamentally important to face the limitations of the model to be built to recognize the type of issues/questions that cannot be addressed by the model and what falls beyond its scope.

## 3.3 LIMITATIONS AND POSSIBILITIES OF INTEGRATED ASSESSMENT MODELS

Integrated assessment models of global change may not pretend to offer a comprehensive picture of all relevant processes of complex reality. In view of the accumulation of uncertainties, which is inherent to integrated assessment modelling, the interpretative and instructive value of an integrated assessment model is far more important than its predictive capability. Therefore, rather than a prediction tool, an integrated assessment model is an interpretative tool, whereby its predictive value is rather low (Wynne and Shackly, 1994).

According to Risbey *et al.* (1996), Janssen (1996), Parson (1996) and Rotmans and Dowlatabadi (1997), general limitations, drawbacks and pitfalls of integrated assessment models are:

1. high level of aggregation level (regions do not correspond to political units; balance between parameterization and inclusion of processes);
2. discipline bias (IA models are largely dominated by the disciplinary background of the model builders);
3. institutional bias (domination of expertise of the institute(s) where the model is designed);
4. lack of transparency (integration of to many components of the real world makes it to complex to communicate);
5. inadequate treatment of uncertainty (balance between 'everything is uncertain' and 'the model says so');
6. limited verification and validation (global models can rather poorly be validated by empirical data);
7. incompleteness of knowledge (there are numerous missing links of knowledge which are hidden in the models);
8. limited, simplistic specification of policies (most climate change analysis are limited to a carbon tax policy);
9. limited, simplistic specification of climate change impacts (damage costs as function of global mean temperature change);
10. methodological controversies (different methodological approaches may lead to conflicting conclusions).

Thus, in view of the above, we must learn from the experiences with the past generation of integrated assessment models. According to Rotmans and Dowlatabadi (1997), the major advantages of integrated assessment models are:

(i) An integrated approach enables the inclusion of systems interactions and feedback mechanisms and can, therefore, yield insights that scatted information cannot offer. Such a model can provide useful indications of the potential range and magnitude of global phenomena and of the scale of the interventions which are necessary to prevent or mitigate symptoms of global change.
(ii) The simplified nature of modules in integrated assessment models permit rapid prototyping of new concepts and exploration of its implications. If the interactions between various systems are well characterized, this rapid prototyping may indicate means of validation for the new concept. Furthermore, if the model is being used as a decision-analysis tool, the rapid prototyping will permit exploration of the implication of the new finding or concept on policy choice, and the value of pursuing this new concept (from purely applied policy science implications). In this way, these models are instruments which can help us keep track of and manage our knowledge and insights into the present and future driving forces behind our complex, social, economic, and ecological structures.

(iii) Uncertainties, crucial lacunae in current scientific knowledge and weaknesses in discipline-oriented expert models can be identified and revealed. Furthermore, accumulation of uncertainties can be analysed and interpreted.

(iv) These models are outstanding means of communication between scientists and exponents of all kinds of disciplines; they also foster communication between scientists and decision makers.

## 3.4 INTEGRATED ASSESSMENT MODELLING: METHODS AND TOOLS

### Aggregation

One of the critical issues in integrated assessment modelling is that of aggregation versus disaggregation. The level of aggregation within a modelling framework refers to the formulation of the dynamics in the model in terms of complexity and level of detail, which is often closely related to the spatial and temporal resolution chosen within the framework. The problem with integrated assessment models is that they consist of a variety of submodels, which have different aggregation levels, in other words, which differ in complexity, spatial, and temporal resolution, and so on. A typical integrated assessment model may consists of the following ingredients: the economic-energy models operate in multi-year time steps on large-nation or regional political boundaries. Atmospheric chemistry models operate in small time steps on a small scale, while climate models have a relatively coarse spatial resolution, grid-cells of a few degrees, but run at a fine temporal resolution. Finally, ecological impact models require data at fine spatial resolutions of about half a degree, but their time resolutions vary greatly from one day to a season or a year.

Often, the climate system is modelled on a global scale, without spatial resolution. These kind of models have a so-called 'hourglass' structure, using the spatial information of expert models to map the regional climate changes for the impact assessment.

### Calibration and Validation

There are many definitions and interpretations of the terms calibration and validation. Moreover, complete calibration of Earth system models is impossible because the underlying systems are never closed (Oreskes *et al.*, 1994). Within the integrated assessment modelling community, calibration is usually defined as the procedure for comparing model results with measurements of the real system (historical output, for instance observational data). The question to answer is how close the model approximates the observational data.

Validation is defined here as the procedure for testing the adequacy of a mathematical model. Validation can be subdivided into two different types. The first is practical validation, which concerns the validity of the outcomes of the model. In fact, this implies that the outcomes of the model are compared with observational data. The major difference with calibration is that the comparison should be based on a new set of data, which lies outside the calibration pathway. However, all the scarce and scattered available data are already needed for calibration of the models, such that this kind of validation is of rather limited use for integrated assessment models.

The second type of validation is conceptual validation, which concerns the test of whether the model represents the real system. This implies the internal structure of the model is tested, by testing whether the concepts and theoretical laws of the system under consideration are interpreted and represented in a sound way.

**Uncertainty**

Because integrated assessment models are intended as a means of capturing the main elements of the co-evolution of the human society and its environment, such models are prone to an accumulation of uncertainties. The issue of uncertainty is, therefore, of crucial importance. Doing uncertainty analysis for integrated frameworks is rather difficult, because of the accumulation of uncertainties, but also because of the different types and sources of uncertainty.

Several approaches to analyse and present uncertainties are possible: (i) specifying a set of future scenarios; (ii) sampling method, assuming probability distributions for numbers of inputs.

A crucial issue in the communication of uncertainty to decision-makers is to make the uncertainties explicit, visible and tangible. Therefore, we need a classification of different sources of uncertainty. Morgan and Henrion (1990) distinguish uncertainty about empirical quantities, uncertainty about the functional form of models, and disagreement among experts, whereas Funtowitcz and Ravetz (1989) distinguish technical, methodological, and epistemological uncertainties.

**Interactive Use of Models**

Too often models are used in a passive way; only results of experiments within the research are presented. Although graphs and diagrams give insights on the model and the related problems, this passive use of models is not very useful for all kind of models. The predictive value of integrated assessment models is rather limited. To exchange the knowledge of the researchers on the processes which they put into the model, next to a passive way an active way of using models might be helpful, such as, for example, gaming and policy exercises.

An example of such exercises is the use of microworlds. Microworlds are used to study how people achieve control over some aspects of a complex system (Brehmer, 1992; Brehmer and Dörner, 1993; Dörner and Schaub, 1994). The computer simulations are interactive and dynamic scenarios of complex problems that allow for repeated and detailed observations. These simulations compress time such that the participants are confronted with the long-term effects of their decisions, and have to cope with the emotional strains of failure, and have to change their strategies. These kind of studies performed by applied psychologists may help to discover systematic mistakes of human behaviour in complex, dynamic and uncertain domains of reality. Within the field of global climate change there is only a little attention to these kind of direct interactions. Some exceptions are the policy exercises of Toth (1988), Parson (1996), de Vries (1995) and Berk and Janssen (1997).

## 3.5    INTEGRATED ASSESSMENT MODELS OF GLOBAL CLIMATE CHANGE

A number of approaches to integrated assessment modelling of climate changes exist. Each approach has strengths and weaknesses relative to the others. Moreover, each modelling team has chosen to focus on different aspects of the climate change issue. A classification of the approaches often used is the distinction in policy evaluation models or process-oriented models, and policy optimization models (Rotmans and Dowlatabadi, 1997; Weyant *et al.*, 1996). The first approach emphasizes the physical, ecological, economic, and social consequences of policies, where the latter optimizes over key policy control variables given formulated policy goals.

Although the models are mixtures of various modelling paradigms, I have clustered them by the dominating paradigm (Table 3.1). I distinguish: the optimization approach, the system dynamics approach, and the deterministic and stochastic simulation approach (the approaches will be discussed in Chapter 4).

*Table 3.1: Summary characterization of integrated assessment models (based on Rotmans and Dowlatabadi, 1997)*

| Model | A | B | C | D | E | F | G |
|---|---|---|---|---|---|---|---|
| **Optimization** | | | | | | | |
| DICE | 0,1 | 0 | 1 | 1 | 0 | 1 | 0 |
| RICE | 0,1 | 0,1 | 1 | 1 | 0 | 1 | 0 |
| CETA | 0 | 0,1 | 1,2 | 1 | 0 | 1 | 0 |
| MERGE 2 | 0,1 | 1 | 1,2 | 1 | 0 | 1 | 0 |
| | | | | | | | |
| **System-dynamics** | | | | | | | |
| IMAGE 1.0 | 0,1,3 | 0 | 0,2,3 | 1 | 1 | 1 | 1 |
| TARGETS 1.0 | 0,1,2,3,4 | 0 | 1,2,3,4 | 1 | 1,2,3,4 | 2 | 1,2 |
| | | | | | | | |
| Deterministic | 0,1,2,3 | 3 | 0,2,3 | 3 | 1,2,3 | 1 | 1 |
| IMAGE 2 | 0,1,2,3 | 2,3 | 1,2,3 | 3 | 0 | 1 | 1 |
| MiniCAM GCAM | 0,1,2,3 | 2,3 | 1,2,3,4 | 3 | 0,2 | 1 | 1 |
| | | | | | | | |
| Stochastic | 0,1,2,3 | 1,2 | 1,3,4 | 2,3 | 0,1,3 | 2 | 1,2 |
| ICAM-2 PAGE | 0,1 | 1,2 | 1 | 1 | 0,1,2,3,4 | 2 | 1 |

*Notes*

A:  Forcings: $0 = CO_2$; 1 = other GHG; 2 = aerosols; 3 = land use;  4 = other
B:  Geographic Specificity:0 = global; 1 = continental; 2 = countries; 3 = grids/basins
C:  Socio-economic dynamics:0 = exogenous; 1 = economics; 2 = tech choice; 3 = land use; 4 = demographic
D:  Geophysical simulation: $0 = \Delta F$; 1 = Global $\Delta T$; 2 = 1-D $\Delta T$, $\Delta P$; 3 = 2-D $\Delta T$, $\Delta P$
E:  Impact Assessment:0 = $\Delta T$ indexed; 1 = sea level rise; 2 = agriculture; 3 = ecosystems; 4 = health
F:  Treatment of uncertainty:  0 = none; 1 = basic; 2 = advanced
G:  Treatment of decision-making: 0 = optimization; 1 = simulation;  2 = simulation with adaptive decisions

## The Optimization Approach

### DICE (Dynamic Integrated model of Climate and the Economy)

DICE is an extended version of a traditional optimal growth model by including a climate sector (Nordhaus, 1992, 1993, 1994). The objective is to maximize the discounted value of utility from consumption. In DICE, population growth and technological change yield productivity growth. Both of these factors of population are exogenously specified and assumed to decline asymptotically to zero.

The single consumer maximizes discounted present value of utility of consumption subject to a Cobb-Douglas production function that includes a climate-damage factor. Emissions per unit output are assumed to decline exogenously at a fixed rate and can be further reduced by costly emission-control measures.

An increasing convex emission-control cost function is estimated from prior studies (Nordhaus, 1991a, 1991b). Current carbon emissions add to atmospheric concentrations via a fixed retention ratio, and realized temperature is modelled by a two-box model representing the atmosphere/mixed-layer upper ocean and deep ocean. Damage from climate change is a quadratic function of realized temperature change with a 3-degree change calibrated to cause a 1.3 per cent world GNP loss.

### RICE (a Regional Integrated Model of Climate and the Economy)

RICE is a regionalized version of the DICE model (Nordhaus and Yang, 1995). In the RICE model, the world is divided into a number of regions. Each is endowed with an initial capital stock, population, and technology. The capital market clears through equalization of the real interest rate across regions, where the real interest rate is determined as the weighted average of the marginal products of capital in different regions.

RICE is able to cope with the possibility of different strategies undertaken by nations, and three distinct approaches are worked out: market (or uncontrolled), global co-operative, nationalistic policies.

### CETA (Climate Emissions Trajectory Assessment)

The CETA suite of models is being developed by Peck and Teisberg (1992, 1993a, 1993b). These models are based on the Global 2100 model of Manne and Richels (1991). Global 2100 combined a macro-economic module of overall economic activity with an energy-technology module. CETA considers only one aggregated region, the world as a whole, instead of several regions as in Global 2100. The focus of the framework is to map out optimal paths of energy investments in the future. Fuel and technology choices are influenced by resource and technology availability as well as policies which (through taxes) manipulate relative prices of different fuels. In CETA, reduced form carbon cycles, climate change, and impact modules are included.

### MERGE (Model for Evaluating Regional and Global Effects of GHG reduction policies)

MERGE is the integrated assessment model which Manne and Richels have developed with additional input from Mendelson (Manne *et al.*, 1994). At the core of this model resides a revised version of the Global 2100, now being exercised to the end of the 22nd century. It embodies a general equilibrium model with 5 world regions, in which each region's consumer makes both savings and consumption decisions. A simple climate model represents atmospheric lifetimes of $CO_2$, $CH_4$ and $N_2O$, which yield global changes in radiative forcing, and equilibrium and realized global-average temperature change. Illustrative impact functions are defined separately for market and non-market components. The former is modelled as a quadratic function of realized temperature change fitted to a single judgement point estimate. The latter estimate is a willingness to pay in each region to avoid a specified temperature change that is a logistic function of regional income, in effect modelled as a world-wide public good.

## The System Dynamics Approach

### IMAGE 1.0 (Integrated Model to Assess the Greenhouse Effect)
IMAGE 1.0 is a model which links models from various scientific areas with policies for controlling global climate change (Rotmans, 1990). The model is meant for developing and evaluating long-term climate strategies; it calculates, on the basis of historical and future emissions of greenhouse gases, the global temperature and sea level rise. In IMAGE 1.0, the climate change problem is modelled as a dynamic system with discrete steps of half a year and a simulation period of 200 years, from 1900 to 2100. IMAGE 1.0 itself is a concatenation of autonomously functioning models (modules): a world energy/economy model, atmospheric chemistry model, carbon cycles model, climate model, sea level rise model, a UVB-impact model and a socio-economic impact model for the Netherlands.

### TARGETS (Tool to Assess Regional and Global Environmental and Health Targets for Sustainability).
Besides the IMAGE model, a second shoot of RIVM's integrated assessment program is the integrated assessment framework TARGETS (Rotmans and de Vries 1997), which aims at the analysis of global change and sustainable development from a synoptic perspective. The model works at exploring the long-term dynamics of the human and the environmental system which may shape the Earth system over the next hundred years. The TARGETS framework basically consists of a population and health model, a resource/economy model, a biophysics model, a land model, and a water model.

All types of model compromise a linkage of pressure, state-descriptive, impact and response modules, in this way representing the (vertically) integrated cause-effect chain. On the other hand, by coupling the various pressures, states, impacts and responses for the various subsystems underlying the models, the horizontal integration comes into play. A first version of the TARGETS model has been made operational on a global level. The time horizon of the TARGETS model spans 200 years, starting at the end of the pre-industrial era, supposed to be in 1900, until the end of the next century, the year 2100, with time steps varying from one month to one year.

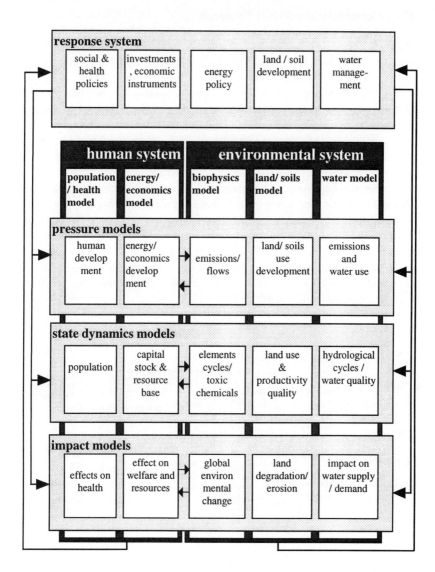

*Figure 3.1: Modular perspective of TARGETS, version 1.0*

## The Deterministic Simulation Approach

### IMAGE 2 (Integrated Model to Assess the Greenhouse Effects)

The IMAGE 2 model (Alcamo, 1994) evolves from the earlier, global-average model version, IMAGE 1.0 (Rotmans, 1990). The model presents a geographically-detailed, global and dynamic overview of the linked society-biosphere-climate system, and consists of three fully linked subsystems: the energy-industry system; the terrestrial environment system; and the atmosphere-ocean system. The energy-industry models compute the emissions of greenhouse gases in 13 world regions, as a function of energy consumption and industrial production. End use energy consumption is computed from various economic driving forces. The terrestrial environment models simulate the changes in global land cover on a grid-scale, based on climatic and economic factors. The role of land cover and other factors are then taken into account to compute the flux of $CO_2$ and other greenhouse gases from the biosphere to the atmosphere. The atmosphere-ocean models compute the build-up of greenhouse gases in the atmosphere and the resulting zonal-average temperature and precipitation patterns. The model includes many important feedbacks and linkages between models in these subsystems.

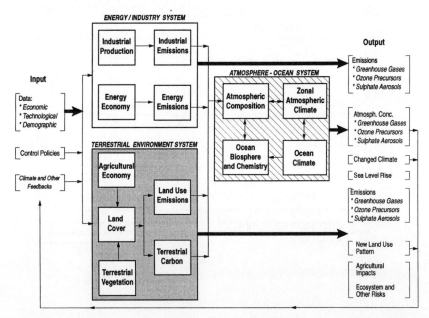

*Figure 3.2: IMAGE 2: framework of models and linkages*

In order to provide a long-term perspective about the consequences of climate change, the model's time horizon extends to the year 2100. The time steps of the various submodels vary considerably, from one day to five years. In general, the submodels of IMAGE 2 are more process-oriented and contain fewer global parameterizations than previous models.

## MiniCAM/GCAM

The Batelle Pacific Northwest Laboratory runs a program which involves a multi-disciplinary team with a long and sustained track record in climate related research. There are two integrated assessment models being developed within the program: MiniCAM and GCAM. The two models are differentiated by their complexity and specificity.

MiniCAM makes extensive use of reduced form modules, characterizing fewer world regions, and fewer economic activities. MiniCAM is specifically designed to be suitable for uncertainty analysis. This framework is composed of the Edmonds-Reilly-Barns model for projection of economic activity and emissions of greenhouse gases and sulphate aerosols. The MAGICC model (Wigley, 1994) is then used to generate a global temperature response commensurate with the emissions. A model called SCENGEN is then used to arrive at regional climate patterns based on the global climate change. The market and non-market impacts are expressed in economic terms and follow the formulation proposed by Manne *et al.* (1994).

GCAM is a much more complex framework, making use of detailed models of human activities. The human activities within this framework are simulated using the Second Generation Model (SGM) which is a Calculable General Equilibrium model. Twenty regionally specific models are being developed through collaboration with regional experts. The suite of SGMs are used explicitly to allocate land-use and other resources and estimates anthropogenic emissions. Again, the MAGICC model is used to convert the emissions data to globally averaged temperature and precipitation change, and the SCENGEN model is used to map this change into regional patterns of changed climate according to the output of one or a combination of GCMs. The regional temperature and precipitation fields are employed in detailed regional agriculture, ecology, and hydrology models, in order to assess regional impacts of projected climate change.

### The Stochastic Simulation Approach

### ICAM (Integrated Climate Assessment Model)

The Integrated Climate Assessment Models (ICAM versions 0, 1 and 2) were developed by the Carnegie Mellon University, at the Department of Engineering and Public Policy (Dowlatabadi and Morgan, 1993a, 1993b). The ICAM model versions have brought increasingly sophisticated and detailed descriptions of the climate change problem, at each stage quantifying the uncertainties in the model components and asking where additional research would most contribute to resolution of the climate change policy dilemma. This information is then used in the next iteration of the research program defining the disciplinary research needs and the direction of refinements of ICAM.

The ICAM model versions are designed to capture the uncertainties in knowledge about the precursors, processes, and consequences of climate change. The models can be used to simulate abatement activities, adaptation to a changed climate, and geo-engineering activities. The development of ICAM 2 has involved updating all previous modules, development of demographics, fuel market, aerosols, terrestrial ecology and coastal impact modules. The spatial and temporal scales have also been refined to 5 years and 7 geo-political regions. The differentiation between high and low latitudes makes it possible to examine the gross differences in the magnitude of climate change, as well as different economic circumstances and availability of resources needed to adapt to changing climate.

ICAM models have been used to show: the wide range of possible emissions, climate conditions, and impacts, and the dangers of deterministic modelling with narrow sensitivity studies; the importance of aerosol forcing in regional policy decision making; the relative importance of decision rules in policy decision making; and the relative contribution of the various parts of the problem in making decision making so difficult. Moreover, illustrative runs of ICAM highlight how uncertainties confound the choice of GHG abatement policy, and how key factors in determining the character of the problem and key uncertainties in making informed judgements can be identified.

**PAGE (Policy Analysis of the Greenhouse Effect)**
The PAGE model is a probabilistic model with an emphasis on decision analysis (Hope *et al.*, 1993). The model is designed to be simple to use and allows extensive specification and propagation of uncertainty. PAGE generates abatement and damage costs estimates for four world regions for the period 1990 to 2100, and projects concentrations, radiative forcing and global mean temperature. The added value of the PAGE model lies in its treatment of uncertainty. All major parameters on the emissions, atmospheric climate and impacts side are represented by triangular probability distributions whose parameters can be set by the user. These parameter uncertainties are then propagated throughout the model.

## 3.6 RETROSPECTIVE

Global change is a difficult issue to grasp in a transparent and univocal way and the integrated assessment modelling activities have only partly got a grip on this complexity. There is no unique modelling approach successful in assessing all relevant aspects of global change. But there are crucial characteristics of global change which are not addressed adequately in the current generation of integrated assessment modelling. In fact, there are a lot of emperors walking without clothes in the world of integrated assessment modelling. Due to the ad hoc policy-oriented focus of the model makers there is less attention for methodological issues. In the next chapter, I will discuss some methodological ingredients which may improve integrated assessment modelling of global change; these ingredients are applied in case studies in the chapters thereafter.

# 4. Methodological Issues

## 4.1 INTRODUCTION

According to the majority of modellers, the source of understanding is the rational process of observation and reflection, not intuition or meditating (Meadows and Robinson, 1985). Furthermore, the world is not only knowable, but also in a certain degree controllable, a view generally shared in Western culture. From this biased modellers starting point, various modelling schools can be distinguished which have, among a number of common concepts, their own set of theories, mathematical techniques, and accepted procedures for constructing and testing models. The implicit assumptions underlying the various modelling efforts seem to fit the concept of a paradigm (Kuhn, 1970). A discussion on modelling paradigms can be found in Meadows and Robinson (1985) and Faucheux *et al.* (1996).

Within the integrated assessment community, various modelling paradigms can be considered as was shown in Chapter 3. In the following list, I will briefly discuss the main paradigms which can be commonly found in integrated assessment modelling: system dynamics, econometrics, optimization, and deterministic and stochastic simulation, and I will add a new approach to those: complex adaptive systems.

- *System Dynamics* According to the system dynamic paradigm, the world can be described by a combinations of interacting feedback loops. By using non-linear equations and time delays, the material stored in stocks and material and information flows through the system. The main efforts are spent on the model structure, while little effort is spent on parameter estimation, which is a difficult activity because of the inclusion of highly aggregated parameters and variables, about which there is not enough data. The purpose of most system dynamic models is to study the dynamic long-term behaviour of systems.

- *Econometrics* Econometricians tend to think in terms of simultaneous equations, linear relations, many exogenous driving variables, and observable statistics. Historical data are rigorously used to determine model parameters, while less time is spent on specifying the model structure. This model structure is limited by the mathematical requirements of its estimation procedures. The model validity is evaluated by a summary of statistics. The purpose of most econometric models is the precise forecasting of economic variables into the short-term future.

- *Optimization* Optimization techniques are mainly used to select the best decision from a set of clearly-defined alternatives. Any policy problem can be separated into three conceptual components: the objective of the policy, the activities available to achieve it, and the constraints within which those activities must take place. Optimization models are normative, usually linear, static or dynamic.

- *Deterministic Simulation* Deterministic simulation models of physical processes consist mainly of sets of differential equations. In such models, the outcome of the operation of the system is fully predicted by the model, so that the precision of the model is only constrained by its realism.

- *Stochastic Simulation* Stochastic simulation models try to include explicit uncertainty into the models, using probability distributions for events and/or parameters values. These distributions are based on historical data or educated guesses from scientists. The results are generally presented by depicting the mean together with the reliability intervals.

- *Complex Adaptive Systems* Complex adaptive systems include a set of agents and take into account that systems change and organize their component parts to adapt themselves to the problems posed by their surroundings. Because the approach aims at describing changes in structure and dynamics, it is not the main purpose to make predictions using such models. It may provide us with insights into the behaviour of complex non-linear systems.

Integrated assessment modelling is current being worked out using various modelling paradigms. In Chapter 3, the integrated assessment models for climate change have been categorized using the modelling approaches. However, it is likely that the relatively new aspects of global change may not taken fully into account by the current modelling paradigms. I will discuss some problems in integrated assessment models and outline approaches which may contribute to improvements. The methodological issues are discussed in more detail in this chapter, while the proposed approaches are applied in a number of case studies in the remainder of this book.

- *Paradigm conflict: econometrics/optimization versus system dynamics (Section 4.2)* The optimization approach adapted by the economists aims at deriving strategies to solve the climate change problem in a cost-efficient manner. In order to apply available tools in a sound way, reduced and strongly parameterized models are used which only include the most important state variables. The process-oriented system dynamics approach aims at describing the global climate system, in order to analyse the consequences of human activities. By trying to capture the main dynamic interactions within this system, those models become rather complex. The models are meant to have an interpretative and instructive value, rather than being predictive.

Although both approaches are potentially able to support policy-making in a useful way, both approaches have limitations in capturing the whole range of scientific knowledge to support policy-making. My aim is to integrate the strengths of both approaches to derive a framework in which optimization experiments are performed with advanced process-based simulation models.

- *'Subjective' uncertainty (Section 4.3)* Global change is characterized by strong uncertainty and great irreversibility on the level of consequences, as well of probabilities of occurrence (Faucheux and Froger, 1995). The use of expected values is of limited value for these kind of problems, because such an approach ignores the notion that values, motivations, world views, and insights differ among the various agents. Furthermore, the use of expected values ignores the fact that uncertainty about the functioning of the earth system and human society lies not only in statistical aspects and measurement errors, but also in fundamental uncertainties which can be made explicit by using the notion of different world views. Therefore, to include the notion of plurality of views on reality, a perspective-based uncertainty analysis is introduced.

- *Structural change (Section 4.4)* The present integrated assessment models are developed from a mechanistic perspective, where prediction and control are appropriate approaches. However, economic, social, technological, and biological systems cannot be adequately described by mechanistic modelling tools, nor can their structure and behaviour be described only in terms of non-linear systems. For such systems, which show evolution and adaptation, we need new tools. These tools should include the learning, evolving and adapting processes which can be found in the new scientific stream of complex adaptive systems. An aim of this book is to incorporate some elements of complex adaptive systems into integrated assessment modelling.

In the next sections, I will go into some more detail about the three methodological issues of integrated assessment modelling which are central to this book.


## 4.2 OPTIMIZATION

### 4.2.1 Introduction

Optimization refers to the act of achieving the optimum, the 'best' solution. The output of an optimization model is a statement of the best way to accomplish a specific goal. Optimization models do not tell what will happen in a certain situation. They are normative models. Although many aspects of optimization theory have been known to mathematicians for centuries, the development of computer science made these methods attractive for practical application. Optimization and the more general Operations Research are widely used as input to operational decision making, especially in industry. The optimization method requires that problems are formulated in a simple and unvarying format: maximize or minimize an *objective function* by controlling *decision variables* subjected to *constraints*.

When the problem has been stated in the proper format, it is solved by finding the right point(s) in the feasible area defined by the constraints and the objective function. The search process is mathematically extremely difficult and, therefore, the process is often simplified by *linearization* of the objective function and constraints. Also the *lack of feedbacks and dynamics* are often necessary simplifications to use suitable optimization tools.

Another limitation of optimization is the difficulty in specifying the objective functions in real life problems. The objective function embodies values and preferences, but which values and whose preferences? How can intangibles be incorporated into the objective function?

Thus, the normative approach creates problems in specifying the problem formulation, whereas the constraints of mathematics results in simplification of the problem. However, the normative view of the world imposed by the optimization paradigm encourages discussion of concrete (policy) goals, which in itself might be a worthwhile exercise. In the next section, I will discuss the use of optimization within integrated assessment modelling of global change. As an organizing framework, I will discuss the concept for the three steps ideally taken in controlling a system.

Deciding how to control a system ideally involves three steps (Beightler *et al.*, 1979).

i.　*An accurate and quantitative description of the system.*

There is little point in optimizing a model that does not describe what is happening in the system; therefore, most efforts in practical optimization studies are directed to understanding the system and describing it in quantitative ways.

ii.　*A single measure of the system effectiveness expressible in terms of the decision variables.*

It is usually either trivially simple or practically impossible to accomplish a measure of the system effectiveness.

iii.　*Find values of the decision variables so that the effectiveness of the system is optimized.*

Given steps one and two, this step is 'just' a mathematical exercise.

### 4.2.2 Optimization Applied to Global (Climate) Change

To date, various optimization oriented models for climate change exist, such as DICE, MERGE and CETA (see Chapter 3). The general aim of these models is to calculate under a range of assumptions optimal carbon tax levels (and eventually other decision variables), so that the discounted value of utility of consumption is maximized, with or without additional environmental constraints. I will discuss the three steps in optimization of Beightler *et al.* (1979) and analyse in which way these steps are taken, and discuss if some steps need to be reconsidered.

### 1) Description of the system
A typical limitation compared with the system dynamics approach is the limited description of the complex dynamics involved in the global system. Nordhaus (1993) argues that 'existing [physical] models are, unfortunately, much too complex to be included in an economic model'. However, the simplified climate system does not likely deliver an adequate representation of the underlying systems' processes and dynamics. As a consequence, such an optimization model is too unrepresentative of what is known of the climate system (Price, 1995; Kaufmann, 1997).

Of course, while a model is never a perfect representation of a problem related to global change, the optimal solution of a model is not an optimal solution of a problem. Two approaches are possible to this difficulty: simplifying the problem or relaxing the optimality constraints. Most of the current approaches follow the first, while I will analyse the prospects of the latter. My starting point is a description of the system, an integrated assessment model, which is within the limits of my approach an accepted representation of the state-of-the-art knowledge and should include a description of the main processes. Unfortunately, these kind of models are often large, complex non-linear systems to which traditional optimization tools can not be applied. As an alternative, however, heuristic search algorithms are able to find suitable (sub) optimal solutions (see step 3).

### 2) Objective function
If goals for future development can be formulated explicitly, they are not likely to be a single number. The concept of sustainable development, which is embraced by the majority of researchers and policy makers involved in global change, is not formulated in an explicit univocal way (Krause *et al.*, 1995; Rothen, 1995). Optimization can, therefore, be seen as one of the many possible tools to analyse a problem, with a specific normative starting point, aimed at concrete policy questions.

### 3) Solving the optimization problem

Steps 1 and 2 are partly restricted by the mathematical tools available. Current optimization models for climate change use traditional optimization tools like the GAMS package (Brooke *et al.*, 1988). The increasing use of non-linear dynamics leads to a world which is fraught with discontinuities and noisy search spaces. Obviously, the traditional optimization techniques depending upon the restrictive requirements of continuity and derivative existence are unsuitable for all but a very limited problem domain. However, new (heuristic) optimization methods have been developed over the last decades, such as simulated annealing and genetic algorithms, which have successfully been applied to various problem domains (for example Kirkpatrick *et al.*, 1983; Davis, 1987; Goldberg, 1989; Forest, 1993). Therefore, it might be recommended to reconsider steps 1 and 2. In this book I will apply an optimization approach on more sophisticated descriptions of the system.

### 4.2.3 Applications in this Book

In this book, I try to make some modest, but firm steps in the process of solving the problems surrounding the optimization approach of integrated assessment modelling. The aim is to investigate whether or not I can use more acceptable descriptions of the system in an optimization framework. This means using simulation models which include important processes, feedbacks and interactions describing expected changes in the system, given an increased pressure of human activities. Applying heuristic search tools on complex simulation models leads to the dilemma of abandoning the nice mathematical conditions for optimality of simpler models. However, I try to explore the benefits without ignoring the mathematical consequences.

In Chapter 5, I will use the model OMEGA, which is a combination of DICE and IMAGE 1.0, to analyse in what strength optimal response strategies are dependent of the modelling approach used for the climate system.

OMEGA was a nicely formulated mathematical system; however, the simulation model TARGETS does not meet the strict requirements for traditional optimization tools like continuous derivatives. Therefore, robust genetic algorithms are applied in Chapter 6 in the search for suitable energy policies by using the TARGETS model.

## 4.3  PERSPECTIVES

### 4.3.1  Uncertainty in Perspective

Scanning for suitable images of the future involves an explicit treatment of uncertainty. Vercelli (1994) distinguishes various modalities of uncertainty: situations of certainty exist when a unique, wholly reliable probability distribution reduces to just one value. Weak uncertainty is defined by a unique probability distribution, additive and fully reliable. Strong uncertainty is described by a distribution of non-additive probabilities and/or by a plurality of probability distributions which are not fully reliable. Near ignorance exists when none of the conceivable probability distributions is reliable.

Global change is characterized by strong uncertainty and large irreversibility on the level of consequences, as well as that of probabilities of occurrence (Faucheux and Froger, 1995). Next to incomplete information and understanding of the system, subjective judgement and disagreement originating from different interpretations of the blind spots can explain uncertainties in images of the future. I propose to capture uncertainties arising from subjective judgement and disagreement by the inclusion of various perspectives.

The attitudes towards society and the environment evolved during history are, to an important extent, determined by perspectives which have been classified in various ways. In recent years, there has been increasing recognition of the usefulness of various socio-cultural perspectives within the context of sustainable development, albeit mainly in qualitative terms (Zweers, 1984; de Vries, 1989; Riebsame, 1990; Jastrow *et al.*, 1990; Schwartz and Thompson, 1990; Thompson *et al.*, 1990; Rayner, 1991; Colby, 1991; de Greef and de Vries, 1991; Coward and Hurka, 1993; Rörsch and de Hart, 1993; Dotto, 1994; WRR, 1994; Bossel, 1996; Rotmans and de Vries, 1997).

A contribution which gives a general description of perspectives on natural and human systems and social relations has been made by Thompson *et al.* (1990) in their Cultural Theory. I will use this theory in applying the notion of various perspectives. This theory is not chosen as being the 'best' available concept, but for practical reasons. I tried to apply a theory which is thought to be suitable for my purposes, that is using it within (mathematical) models. I acknowledge that the theory has its limitations, as any theory has, but this makes it possible to make a first step in applying the plurality of norms and values within models.

### 4.3.2  Cultural Theory

Thompson *et al.* (1990) elaborate the concept of perspectives by introducing the notions of cultural bias (shared values and beliefs) and social relations (pattern of interpersonal relations). By reference to these notions, a cultural perspective is defined as a more or less viable combination of social relations and cultural bias. The degree of viability of a perspective depends upon a mutually supportive relationship between a particular cultural bias and a particular pattern of social relations. Thompson *et al.* (1990) claim that only five perspectives - the hierarchist, egalitarian, fatalist, individualist, and the hermit - are sufficiently viable. The adoption of perspectives is a dynamic process. Change occurs because of 'surprise', that is the discrepancy between the expected and the actual, which is of central importance in dislodging individuals from a previously adopted perspective. Adherents to each of the five perspectives are, as it were, in competition for new adherents to their particular perspective, but are dependent on one another at the same time. In other words, all of the perspectives are needed to ensure each one's viability (Thompson *et al.*, 1990). For example, fatalists are necessary to hierarchists since they constitute elements which can be managed, the existence of fatalists as consuming participants in markets is essential to individualists, while the existence of both hierarchists and individualists is essential to the egalitarians to provide the institutions which act as yardsticks for egalitarianism. Following Rayner (1991) the 'active perspectives', that is the hierarchist, the egalitarian, and the individualist, are taken into account, so that the autonomous and the fatalist perspectives are disregarded. The hermit, as exponent of the autonomous perspective, is not interested in what happens in the world, but prefers to distance himself from it. The fatalist, for whom everything is a lottery (both humans and nature being unpredictable) is likewise not examined as such. Nevertheless, the fatalist plays a significant role in the overall system. Note that I look at decision makers within (international) organizations, assuming that such agents want to be players in the game. If I model personal decisions, the 'powerless' agents are involved, representing also the fatalistic world view.

Rayner (1991) and van Asselt and Rotmans (1996) argue that the active perspectives are the extremes of a continuum which is used to describe all the possible points of the view (Figure 4.1). I will now briefly characterize the active perspectives so that it enables me to operationalize aspects of Cultural Theory within the integrated assessment modelling activities.

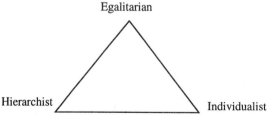

*Figure 4.1: Spectrum expanded by the active perspectives*

**Grid-group typology**

Douglas and Wildavsky (1982) proposed a grid-group typology so that societies can be characterized along two axes, labelled *group* and *grid*. The term group refers to the extent to which an individual is incorporated into bounded units. The greater the degree of incorporation, the greater the extent to which individual choice is subject to group determination. The term grid denotes the degree to which an individual's life is circumscribed by externally-imposed prescriptions. The more binding the prescriptions are, and the more extensive their scope, the fewer the facts of social life that are open to individual negotiations.

Along the grid dimension, it is the element of social control that sets the various perspectives apart from each other. Strong group boundaries coupled with minimal prescriptions produce strong relations that are egalitarian. Because such groups lack internal role differentiation, no individual is granted the authority to exercise control over another. When an individual's social environment is characterized by strong group boundaries and binding prescriptions, the resulting social relations are hierarchical. Individuals in this social context are subject to the control exerted by other members in the group, as well as to the demands of socially-imposed roles. The exercise of control (and more generally the very existence of inequality) is justified on the grounds that different roles for different people enable people to live together more harmoniously than alternative arrangements would. Individuals who are neither bound by group incorporation nor by prescribed roles inhabit an individualistic social context. In such an environment, all boundaries are provisional and subject to negotiation. Although the individualist is relatively free from control of others, this does not imply abstention from exerting control over others; the individualists' success is often measured in terms of the size of the following the person can command. The fatalist belongs to the category weak group boundaries coupled with binding prescriptions, but will not be discussed here (see Thompson *et al.*, 1990).

**Views of physical nature**

Thompson *et al.* (1990) claim that ideas of human and physical nature are socially constructed and adopted by individuals according to their perspective. The concept of 'myths of nature', derived from the work of ecologists (such as Holling, 1977; Timmerman, 1986), may enable the cultural perspectives to be represented graphically by reference to the metaphor of a sphere rolling in a curved landscape (see Figure 4.2). Nature, for egalitarians, is strictly accountable, and their ideas of the world can be represented by the concept of 'Nature Ephemeral' (Holling, 1977; Timmerman, 1986). For them, the world is a terrifying, unforgiving place and the least jolt may trigger complete collapse. The managing institution must therefore take good care of the ecosystem; the egalitarians advocate a preventive management style (Rayner, 1991). For individualists, nature is a 'skill-controlled cornucopia' (Thompson *et al.*, 1990), that is thanks to human skill, nature provides resources in plenty. The individualists' idea of the world is represented by the concept 'Nature Benign' (Holling, 1977; Timmerman, 1986). According to this myth, the world is wonderfully forgiving. The management institution can, therefore, adopt a laissez-faire attitude, that is, the individualists advocate an adaptive management style (Rayner, 1991). The hierarchists see nature as being in an 'isomorphic' relation with the social realm (Thompson *et al.*, 1990); that is its rich differentiation ensuring that it is forthcoming when approached in the right way by the right people, but retributive when pushed beyond these carefully-learned bounds. This idea is represented by the myth of Nature as 'Perverse/Tolerant' (Holling, 1977; Timmerman, 1986); Nature is forgiving in most circumstances, but is vulnerable to the ball flying over the rim on occasion. The managing institution must, therefore, take steps to prevent such unusual occurrences. The hierarchists, therefore, advocate the exercise of control as a management style.

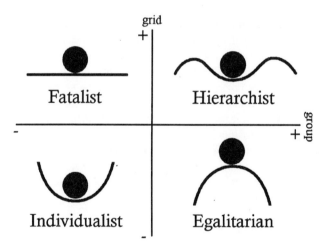

*Figure 4.2: Cultural perspectives (Source: Schwartz and Thompson, 1990)*

### Views of human nature

According to Thompson *et al.* (1990), views of human nature are inextricably bound up with social relations. Egalitarians believe that human beings are born good, but are corrupted by evil institutions. From an egalitarian perspective, human nature is not only good, but also highly malleable. Just as human nature can be corrupted by evil institutions (for example markets and hierarchies), so can it be rendered virtuous by constructing a noncoercive, egalitarian society. The optimistic view of human nature is essential to the viability of egalitarian social relations. For individualists, human nature, like physical nature, is extraordinarily stable. No matter what the institutional setting, human beings remain essentially the same, that is self-seeking. By regarding man as self-seeking and unmalleable, individualists can justify attempts to channel existing human nature, and their refusal to attempt to change it. Hierarchists believe that human beings are born sinful, but can nevertheless be redeemed by virtuous institutions. This conception of human nature helps sustain a perspective rich in institutional restraints.

**Strategies**
The manner in which people make a living is central to their lives. Thompson *et al.* (1990) argue that needs and resources are socially constructed, so that the constraints on behaviour are located in the perspectives, rather than in the needs and resources themselves. This leads to the conclusion that behaviour is never rational or irrational in itself; a particular strategy can only be evaluated in relation to a person's perspective. Strategies do what is most important; that is they uphold a person's perspective. Because the egalitarians perceive resources as being fixed and believe that people can do nothing about them, the only available strategy is to decrease their needs so as to ensure a non-negative overlap. To be effective, such a need-reducing strategy would have to be followed by everyone. In perceiving nature as cornucopian, the individualists clearly have the scope to manage both needs and resources. Therefore, they choose to manage both needs and resources upward to the very limits of their skills. The hierarchists cannot do anything about their needs, so the only available strategy is to increase their resources so as to make sure that the overlap does not become negative. This approach is legitimized by a view of nature as bountiful, but within accountable limits. For each of the perspectives, preferences regarding topics such as economic growth or risks can be derived in a similar manner.

### 4.3.3 Applications in this Book

During the last few years, aspects of the Cultural Theory are used as a heuristic framework, to apply the notion of perspectives in integrated assessment models. A perspective-based uncertainty analysis is introduced as an approach to include plurality of world views of policy agents (Janssen and Rotmans, 1995). We used cultural perspectives determined distributions of parameters and future scenarios in order to allocate emission rights of $CO_2$. A detailed discussion of this study can be found in Chapter 7.

After the introduction by Janssen and Rotmans (1995) of a quantitative approach to take into account subjective judgements and plurality of views on reality in integrated assessment modelling, a more general approach for perspective-based uncertainty analysis is applied in the TARGETS project of the RIVM. van Asselt and Rotmans (1996) worked out alternative model routes for the fertility issue and the climate change issue. Alternative, perspective-based model routes are developed for the whole TARGETS model as described in Rotmans and de Vries (1997).

The idea of 'perspectives' is used to involve the different perceptual screens through which people interpret or make sense of the world and the social dimensions within it, whereby particular visions of reality seem more or less plausible. Trisoglio *et al.* (1994) characterize the cultural perspectives by two dimensions following Thompson *et al.* (1990) (Table 4.1): 1) how the world is seen (the totality of views of physical and human nature); 2) management style (the totality of preferred strategies).

*Table 4.1:    Characteristics of cultural perspectives*

| | **individualist** | **hierarchist** | **egalitarian** |
|---|---|---|---|
| **world view** | | | |
| idea of nature | skill-controlled cornucopia | isomorphic nature | accountable |
| myth of nature | natural benign | nature perverse/tolerant | nature ephemeral |
| concept of human nature | self-seeking | sinful | born good, malleable |
| **management style** | | | |
| driving force | growth | stability | equity and equality |
| type of management | adaptive | control | preventive |
| attitude to nature | laissez-faire | regulatory | attentive |
| attitude towards humans | channel rather than change | restrict behaviour | change social environment |
| attitude to needs/resources | expand resource base | rational allocation of resources | need-reducing strategy |
| economic growth | preferred: aim to create personal wealth | preferred: aim to avoid social collapse | not preferred |
| risk | risk-seeking | risk-accepting | risk-aversive |

The combination of each perspective's world view with its respective favoured strategy is used to assess the utopias (Trisoglio *et al.*, 1994). Agents' utopia are used to describe the management style which corresponds with the agents' view of the world. The dystopias describe what would happen to the world if the agents' favoured strategy were to be applied while reality seems to follow another world view.

The utopia/dystopia approach as applied by Trisoglio *et al.* (1994), van Asselt and Rotmans (1996) and Rotmans and De Vries (1997) is a static approach. Their approach can be seen as an agents' perspective of the future today, which determines their present policy which might consist of a set of decision rules. In their static approach, the agents do not react to observed dystopias. A first exercise to develop a dynamic version in which agents may adapt their behaviour in case of a dystopia will be discussed in Chapter 8.

## 4.4  THE EVOLUTIONARY MODELLING APPROACH

### 4.4.1  The Evolution of Modelling

Newton's publication of his *Principia* in 1687 is generally seen as marking the birth of classical science, and this mechanistic, reversible, reductionistic, and equilibrium-based explanation of the world was to prove successful in stimulating physical science. During the so-called Machine Age, research was dominated by selecting what was to be understood, studying the working of the parts, and assembling the understanding of the parts into an understanding of the whole. This came naturally to men whose view of the universe inspired them to create machines to do their (physical) work, and a product of such efforts was the Industrial Revolution itself. Moreover, the success of the mechanistic paradigm led to the application of the mathematic tools of physical science to life sciences such as economics, social science, and biology. Although the success of classical science was challenged in the first half of this century by new theories in physical science (quantum mechanics and relativity theory), the reductionistic and deterministic view, nevertheless, remained the core of science.

By the second quarter of this century, formulation of a new world view was brought about, in part, by the growing preoccupation with systems, with their growing complexity and the increasing difficulty of managing them effectively. This focus on systems led to the realization that they constitute wholes which lose their essential properties when taken apart. In metaphoric terms, the systems approach follows a holistic view, instead of the reductionistic view of classical (Newtonian) science.

Nevertheless, the dominant world view was still ruled by deductive logic and mathematics: the rationalistic world view. A reversible world in which initial conditions determine a reversible trajectory is postulated so that once the initial state of the system has been determined, deductive logic can chart the past and predict the future trajectories. Whatever has changed can be exactly undone by another change, and using exact prediction, the behaviour of Nature can be precisely controlled. A widely used metaphor of systems remains that of the engineer who is controlling a machine (cf. Kwa, 1984, 1994).

In the last two centuries new scientific insights challenged the machine metaphor. The Second Law of Thermodynamics states that the entropy of a closed system is increasing. This means that heat flows from hot to cold, so that less useful energy remains. One of the consequences of this Law is the irreversibility of system behaviour and the direction of time. Changes within systems cannot reverse back just like that. Charles Darwin's book on the origin of species (1859) fundamentally changed the view of nature. The static concept of unchanging species was placed by a dynamic concept of an evolution by natural selection and adaptation of species. The systems are in continuous disequilibrium and the system parts are interrelated to each other. The theories of quantum mechanics showed us the inherent uncertainty of systems, in particular on the atomic level. The Uncertainty Principle of Heisenberg states that the position in space and the momentum (mass times velocity) of a particle cannot be measured simultaneously. The statement of Laplace that if every position of every atom is known the future will be predictable, becomes therefore a lost illusion.

Von Bertalanffy (1968) noted that while dynamic systems can be used for describing the maintenance of a system, they cannot explain change, diversity, and evolution. Weaver (1948) has been stressing the need for an approach which deals with a *sizeable number of factors which are interrelated into an organic whole*, pointing to biological, medical, economic, and social issues. And already in 1898 there was an advocacy of an evolutionary approach for economics (Veblen, 1898).

There has thus been a growing realization that if long-term processes in social and biological systems are to be studied effectively, the previous approaches are of limited use, since societies, humans and other organisms live in continuous and changing interactions with their environment, leading to structural changes. Furthermore, since each biological or social agent has specific characteristics, the survival of the fittest means that individuals are not equally successful. In metaphoric terms: there is a shift from viewing the system as a machine to the system as an organism.

### 4.4.2 Complex Adaptive Systems

The rapid development of the computer has provided scientists with a new scientific tool, so that during recent decades, various mathematicians, computer scientists, ecologists, and so on. have been developing new tools and novel approaches to facilitate their efforts to investigate complexity in life sciences. Despite the disparities and the difficulties, with these new approaches we are entering a new era in our ability to understand and foster biological and social systems (Holland, 1992b). Scientists have begun to detect a common kernel from these systems, each of which involves a similar 'evolving structure' whereby they change and organize their components to adapt themselves to the problems posed by their surroundings. Such systems can be grouped under a common name: *complex adaptive systems*. In recent decades, new computation-based modelling tools have been developed which enable these systems to be studied, including: genetic algorithms, cellular automata, and artificial life forms. Such evolutionary modelling techniques have been applied in various disciplines which study, for example, economies, ecologies, immune and nervous systems (for example Anderson *et al.*, 1988; Goldberg, 1989; Langton, 1989, 1995; Arthur, 1990; Kauffman, 1991; Holland and Miller, 1991; Holland, 1992a; Waldrop, 1992; Ruthen, 1993; Trisoglio, 1995; Epstein and Axtell, 1996). Although this new modelling paradigm is likely to derive new insights from various complex systems, it still has to prove itself (Horgan, 1995).

In order to highlight differences between the 'Newtonian' approach, the systems approach, and the complex adaptive systems approach, I propose to discuss some of their respective characteristics (Table 4.2). The Newtonian approach offered us universal laws, the systems approach a holistic general cause-effect diagram of the system, while complex adaptive systems deal with the diversity of individual characteristics of the agents.

If the Newtonian approach could describe how systems move to an equilibrium, and complex systems the pathways between multi-equilibria, complex adaptive systems, in contrast, can be seen as evolving over time, thereby adapting to the continuous changes within the system.

The mechanistic perspective of Newtonian science and the systems approach allow us to construct models in order to optimally control the system and to predict future developments. According to the complex adaptive systems approach, however, changes in structure and behaviour can neither be predicted nor fully controlled.

The information exchange between the various elements in the system differ between the approaches. The Newtonian approach assumes perfect knowledge leading to an equilibrium state of the system. In the (complex) systems approach, the information about the state of various parts of the system is modelled through feedback mechanisms. In the complex adaptive systems approach, the agents have preferences and expectations leading to anticipations of their behaviour. Differences in expectations and realized behaviour of the system lead to adaptive behaviour or physical adaptation of the agents.

*Table 4.2 Characteristics of three modelling paradigms*

| Newtonian Science | (Complex) Systems | Complex Adaptive Systems |
|---|---|---|
| reductionist | holistic | holistic |
| answers | insights | insights |
| equilibrium | multi-equilibria | no equilibrium |
| top-down | top-down | bottom-up |
| homogeneity | homogeneity | heterogeneity |
| mechanistic | mechanistic | organic |
| prediction and control | control | unpredictability and (un)controllability |
| perfect knowledge | feedback-control | adaptation/anticipation |
| reversibility | reversibility | irreversibility |
| structural constancy | structural constancy | evolution/structural change |

### 4.4.3 An Evolutionary Integrated Modelling Approach

The present generation of integrated assessment models is mainly based on the mechanical paradigm. The system is thought of as a machine. Mechanical causality, expressing overarching natural laws explains all things. The increasing pressure of human activities causes the environmental system to be forced out of the pre-industrial 'natural' equilibrium. This disequilibrium is thought to be a threat which needs to be solved by reducing the pressure to a level such that the system finds a new equilibrium again. According to Allen (1990), equilibrium models are a most unlikely basis for anticipating the future, particularly with respect to change. Instead of discussing idealized equilibrium systems and focusing on stability, we must try to understand instability and change. Mechanical systems are only capable of 'functioning', not of evolving.

They are unable to restructure themselves or to insert new relationships, while in reality this can happen.

Scanning the future of the global system for the next century, without considering the ability of systems to adapt to changes, may generate a misleading picture of the impact of changes. Ecosystems may adapt to a changing climate, human behaviour to changing economies and insects to the use of insecticides. From an anthropocentric view, risks occur when changes are so fast that systems are not able to adapt. A reduction of the diversity within the system makes it more fragile and less capable of adaptation. From a mechanistic perspective, risks may increase if the system changes (= out of equilibrium), while from an evolutionary perspective, risks may increase if the system is less able to adapt to a change.

The inclusion of evolutionary aspects within integrated assessment models may be important to assess the impacts of present and future human activities on the global system. As noted before, integrated assessment modelling is a relatively young discipline, where various approaches are currently applied. The future will tell us which species of modelling is the fittest in the policy-making process. It is my expectation that an evolutionary modelling approach will be a powerful alternative to the existing ones.

**Change**
An interesting framework to explain the transitions in behaviour of the system is the approach of Holling (1986), who proposes four basic functions common to all complex systems and a spiralling evolutionary path through them (Figure 4.3). This evolutionary cycle can be used to explain transitions in social systems, as well as in ecosystems, which is done by Holling *et al.* (1995). The central idea is that the four phase adaptive cycle emphasizes a loop from conservation to two phases of destruction and reorganization where innovation and chance assume a dominant role. The reorganization phase occurs when a rare and unexpected intervention or event can shape a new future. Holling *et al.* (1995) argue that in this stage, when the system is in a state most likely to be transformed by innovation, agents have the greatest potential to influence the future of the system. Note that the system can also exit the cycles and flip into a new kind of system.

The patterns produced by these four phases are discontinuous and dependent on the interaction of processes that trigger and organize the release and reorganization functions. These interactions create multiple stable states. An illustrative example is the budworm outbreak (Holling, 1978). Successful suppression of spruce budworm populations in eastern Canada using insecticides certainly preserved the pulp and paper industry and employment in the short term by partially protecting the forest. However, this policy has left the forest and the economy more vulnerable to an outbreak over a larger area and of an intensity not experienced before. Examples from more recent data are the problems with cattle in Western Europe, 'mad cow disease' and the pig plague. These examples illustrate that problems could be caused by local human influences that slowly accumulate to trigger sudden abrupt changes that may effect the vitality of societies. There are counteractive forces that give ecological systems the resilience and adaptability to deal with considerable change and that provide people with the capacity to innovate and create (Holling, 1994). However, nature, people, and economies are suddenly now co-evolving on a planetary scale, each affecting the others in such novel ways and on such a large scale that large surprises may overwhelm the adaptive and innovative capabilities of people (Holling, 1994). The question of sustainable development is, therefore, how to stimulate a sustainable co-evolution of human activities and environmental change.

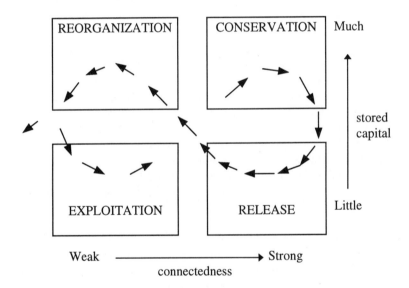

*Figure 4.3: The four general system functions and the flow of events between them (from Holling, 1986). The arrows show the speed of that flow in the ecosystem cycle; arrows close to each other indicate a rapidly changing situation and arrows far from each other indicate a slowly changing situation. The cycle reflects changes in two attributes: on the Y axis, the amount of accumulated capital (nutrients and carbon) stored in variables that are dominant keystone variables at the moment; and on the X axis, the degree of connectedness among variables. The exit from the cycle indicated at the left of the figure indicates the stage where a flip is most likely into a less- or more-productive and organized system, that is, devolution or evolution as revolution.*

**Evolution**

Early-nineteenth-century biology was faced with the concept of unchanging species. Just like Newton's laws were taken as signs of God's law immanent on earth, the diversity of species and similarities between them, were taken to be God's work. Publication of Darwin's *On the Origin of Species* (1859) changed the insights of biological science. Darwin's theory of evolution by natural selection - the survival of the fittest - fundamentally changed the view on the place of Man within the evolution of life. Without further discussing the impact of Darwin's theory, the scientific understanding of the evolutionary process has grown enormously. Darwin's theory was controversial one century ago, nowadays evolutionary principles are widely accepted due to, for example, Mendel's discovery of the basic laws of transmission genetics, Weismann's concept of the continuous germ plasm from which each organism grows, and the advent of population genetics in the effort to account for Darwinian evolution by selection acting on single genes (Kauffman, 1993).

Regarding global change, we are interested in changes on Earth in the coming century. Is a theory which explains the evolution of life during the past several billion years, of use for only a snapshot of evolutionary time? For this very short time horizon evolutionary principles are only of use for species whose genetic evolution is rather fast. The resistance development of insects to various pesticides during this century is an example of genetic evolution within the considered time-horizon. Next to genetic evolution, changes in behaviour can also be explained in evolutionary terms. With respect to human beings, this could be called a cultural evolution. Because changes of behaviour are not likely to depend on the exchange of genetic information, its time-horizon is much shorter than genetic evolution. In the next paragraphs, I will discuss briefly the two types of evolution.

*Genetic evolution*   Most higher organisms evolve by means of two primary processes: natural selection and sexual reproduction. The first process determines which members of a population survive to reproduce, and the second process ensures mixing and recombination among the genes of their offspring. An obvious biological consequence of sexual reproduction is the generation of new combinations by mixing genetic information from different individuals. Without this mixing generated by sex, adaptive evolution would simply consists of the sequential selection of mutations in the genetic information. Selection takes place on the basis of the fitness of the organisms, which is related to the probability of getting descendants (Hofbauer and Sigmund, 1988).

*Cultural evolution*   The diverse individual experimentations which, when successful, can be imitated by others, where the storage medium for passing on behavioural norms consist of, for example, oral tradition, books and films. The fitness functions measuring the 'success' is in the 'mind' of each individual concerned, and here selection will depend on diverse systems of norms and values, leading to cultural evolution (Allen, 1990). Such an evolution is faster than genetic evolution, which requires the physical elimination of the 'unfit'. But the discovery of better strategies, at least in the shorter term, and the concealment or diffusion of this information to other individuals, become the key elements in cultural evolution.

The insights derived from the evolutionary paradigm are used to construct a conceptual framework which is aimed at serving as an integrated modelling paradigm for global change.

### 4.4.4 An Integrated Modelling Paradigm

Research with respect to sustainable development often integrates disciplines from social science, economics, and ecology. Although many attempts are made to come to an integrated approach, it is my opinion that they all fail by considering only one disciplinary modelling paradigm. When modelling the global system, various levels of modelling may be distinguished. De Vries (1994), for example, distinguishes three levels. At the first level, he assumes the physical stocks and flows which constitute the observable reality. The next level maps the behavioural and informational structures which govern human interference in the underlying physical environment. The third level is the values, beliefs, and ideas which here are shared under the term perspectives, and those reflect and motivate people's behaviour.

Based on De Vries (1994), three interwoven levels are distinguished in constructing an integrated modelling paradigm for global change (Figure 4.4). At the first level, the physical laws are assumed to work. The flows of minerals through the various reservoirs can be described satisfactorily by sets of differential equations, as can topics such as atmospheric chemistry, hydrology, and thermodynamics. In the objective to study global change, a time horizon of about one century may be considered. Given this assumption, I believe it is permitted to assume that the mechanisms and structure of the physical system remain unchanged. Of course, the flows between the reservoirs may change due to the living and non-living parts of the Earth system, a deterministic description is likely to be satisfactory for this part.

At the second level, I assume is the living part of the Earth system. In this part of the global system, change in its structure and mechanisms occurs frequently within the considered horizon. Three fields are considered within this part of the system: economy, describing the interactions between agents who maximize their utility by exchanging resources, labour, capital, and the environment; sociology, describing the behaviour of individuals in groups and behaviour between groups; ecology, describing the behaviour of organisms in relation to their environment. The many interacting agents lead to unpredictable behaviour at the macro scale; I assume that agents have no perfect knowledge and act according to their norms and values. Such a system might well be described by the concepts of complex adaptive systems. At the third level, I present the driving forces behind the behaviour of agents: their needs, norms and values. I propose not to describe this level in mathematical formulas, although describing the behavioural 'rules' at the second level might be clarified by conceptual models of the third level. Using the Cultural Theory in describing different management styles and world views is an example of the use of such a conceptual model.

In sum, the integrated modelling paradigm consists of the following elements. At the level of physics, a mechanistic approach is assumed where a set of deterministic differential equations determine the behaviour of the physical elements. The levels ecology, economy, and sociology are dominated by complex adaptive systems, like genetic algorithms and cellular automata. At the level of philosophy, conceptual models like Cultural Theory might be suitable to describe the agents' behavioural rules.

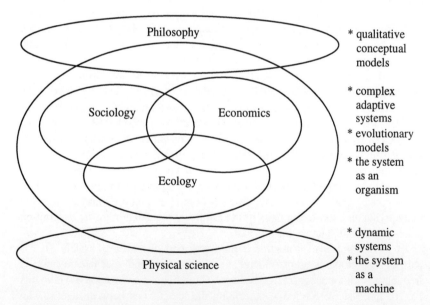

*Figure 4.4: An integrated modelling paradigm*

### 4.4.5 Applications in this Book

Some first sketches are made in the development of an evolutionary modelling approach of integrated assessment modelling. Instead of aiming at a complete integrated assessment model along the lines of evolutionary modelling, I performed two case studies in assessing change and surprise in social and biological systems. The first case study (Chapter 8) deals with the ability of agents to change their behaviour, if their perspectives on the considered problem are changed. A set of agents are modelled having different positions within the perspective triangle (Figure 4.1). Comparison of observations with expectations may lead to a reconsideration of the problem, inducing a possible shift in the world view of the agents. This concept of 'the Battle of Perspectives' is an example of how to integrate the various modelling paradigms for the types of dynamics. The second case study (Chapter 9), which analyses the malaria problem, examines the ecological part of the system, namely the adaptation of mosquitoes and parasites to climate change, insecticides, and antimalarial drugs.

# 5.   Optimizing the Climate Change Problem

## 5.1   INTRODUCTION

An important stream in the integrated assessment modelling of climate change is the optimization approach as used in (neo-classical) economics. As discussed in Chapters 3 and 4, this differs from the simulation approach by the fact that it uses mainly simplified regression-based relations instead of process-oriented system dynamic models, in order to apply traditional optimization techniques.

The economic type of modelling usually optimizes response policies to balance the costs and benefits; one can identify two kinds of limitations to the use of optimization. First, the objective functions are difficult to specify for climate policy (see Chapter 3). The objective function embodies values and preferences, but which values and whose preferences? How can intangibles be incorporated into the objective function? For example, insofar as the cost benefit analysis approach is concerned, there is no consensus about whether it is an adequate aid to policy making because of the arbitrariness in the choice of the discount rate and the inherent uncertainties in monetizing the impacts of climate change (for example Krause *et al.*, 1995; Costanza, 1996).

Second, in order to render large-scale optimization problems tractable, modellers are obliged to simplify their systems, which they achieve by means of *linearization* of the system and exclusion of numerous *feedbacks and dynamics* (Sterman, 1991). Although such simplifications might be preferable from a mathematical point of view, they imply that scientific knowledge of, for example, the non-linear process-oriented dynamics of the climate system, and the existence of many important feedbacks is simply ignored. While such process-oriented dynamics and feedbacks are on top of the agenda in the natural scientific community, they are, nevertheless, neglected for mathematical arguments in optimization studies. Thus, although claiming performing integrated assessment modelling, a lot of economic oriented models do not include state-of-the-art knowledge.

In this chapter, I will discuss the latter limitation of optimization. More specifically, I will investigate the limitations of using very simplified descriptions of the environmental system in optimization studies of climate change. I will address the question about whether or not an optimal response strategy is sensitive to the modelling approach which is used within an integrated assessment model. This is to analyse the need for incorporating more advanced modelling frameworks within optimization studies for global change, in general, and climate change, in particular. In the analysis, I will focus on the climate system part of the model.

In this chapter, I employ a mathematical system for climate change, OMEGA (Optimization Model for Economic and Greenhouse Assessment) (Filar *et al.*, 1996; Janssen, 1997) (Figure 5.1), which combines DICE (Dynamic Integrated model of Climate and the Economy) (Nordhaus, 1992, 1993, 1994) and IMAGE 1.0 (Integrated Model to Assess the Greenhouse Effect) (Rotmans, 1990), from which the dynamic system representation of the environmental system is borrowed (Braddock *et al.*, 1995; Zapert, 1994), allowing me to use a set of non-linear optimization techniques. DICE is primarily an economic model enlarged by the addition of an oversimplified environmental model, while IMAGE 1.0 describes the climate dynamics from a natural scientific perspective. By using the economic component of DICE and the biophysical system component of IMAGE 1.0, a hybrid model is obtained in which the strengths of each model are used to overcome the weaknesses of the other.

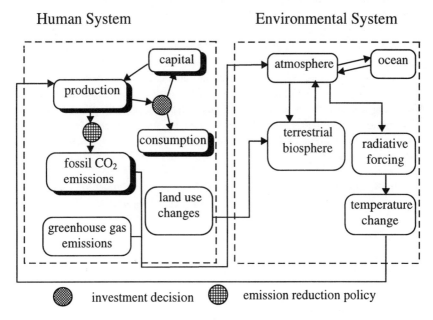

*Figure 5.1:*   *Scheme of the basic relations within the OMEGA model. The shadowed blocks come from DICE, the white blocks from IMAGE 1.0*

In addition, in this chapter, I will use various optimization techniques and compare their performance. Such a comparative analysis is made because the limitations of optimization algorithms are generally used as an argument for using very simple systems, and, furthermore, to get insights into the performance of genetic algorithms, which are used in Chapter 6 in an optimization study of the integrated assessment simulation model for global change, TARGETS.

## 5.2   THE MODEL OMEGA

### 5.2.1  DICE: Dynamic Integrated Model of Climate and the Economy

DICE is an optimization model for the economics of climate change based on aspects of optimal growth theory. It is a transposition of Ramsey's model (Ramsey, 1928) of optimal economic growth to climate change policy. Hence, as well as calculating optimal capital accumulation, DICE calculates greenhouse gas emission reduction by maximizing the discounted value of utility from consumption. DICE envisages the world economy as producing a composite commodity associated with an initial stock of capital, labour, and level of technology. Output is represented by a standard, constant-return-to-scale Cobb-Douglas production function in capital, labour, and technology.

The model contains both a conventional economic component and a novel climate component. Population growth and technological changes are regarded as being exogenous, while the optimized flow of consumption over time determines accumulation of capital. The climate component considers emissions of two important greenhouse gases. Carbon dioxide ($CO_2$) and CFCs are related to gross output, exogenous technological advances and an emission reduction factor.

In the mathematical formulation of DICE, the state variables are represented by $y(t) \in R^9$ which are dependent on the control variables $z(t) \in R^2$.

**Objective function**
The DICE model is designed to model a situation in which the discounted sum of the general level of consumption achieves a maximum. The objective function maximized is:

$$\max_{z_1(t), z_2(t)} \sum_{t=1990}^{2100} l(t) \cdot \ln(y_2(t)) \cdot (1 + \rho)^{(1990-t)} \tag{5.1}$$

which expresses the discounted sum of utilities of consumption summed over the relevant time horizon. The level of utility or social well-being is expressed in

$\ln(y_2(t))$ whereby $y_2(t)$ describes the level of consumption per capita at time t, $l(t)$ is the size of population at time t, and $r$ is the pure rate of social time preference ($r=3$ per cent per annum). The control variables $z_1(t)$ and $z_2(t)$ represent gross investment and the rate of emission reduction, respectively.

## Economics component

Output $y_1(t)$ is given by a standard constant-returns-to-scale Cobb-Douglas production function in the levels of technology $a(t)$, capital $y_3(t)$ and labour which is assumed proportional to $l(t)$, where labour inputs are proportional to population and $\gamma$ represents the elasticity of output with respect to capital taken as 0.25. The impact of emission reductions and global climate change on output is represented by the scale factor $y_9(t)$.

$$y_1(t) = y_9(t) \cdot a(t) \cdot y_3(t)^{\gamma} \cdot l(t)^{1-\gamma} \tag{5.2}$$

Per capita consumption $y_2(t)$ is defined as the ratio of consumption to population, where consumption is equal to economic output minus gross investments,

$$y_2(t) = \frac{y_1(t) - z_1(t)}{l(t)} \tag{5.3}$$

The capital balance equation for the capital stock $y_3(t)$ is,

$$\frac{d\,y_3(t)}{dt} = z_1(t) - \delta_k \cdot y_3(t) \tag{5.4}$$

where $\delta_k$ is the rate of depreciation of the capital stock, 10 per cent per annum, reflecting an average lifetime of capital of ten years on a declining balance method.

The final economic equation represents the fossil and non-fossil emission amount of $CO_2$ and CFCs related to economic output:

$$y_4(t) = [1 - z_2(t)] \cdot \sigma(t) \cdot y_1(t) \tag{5.5}$$

where $z_2(t)$ is the rate of emission reduction and $\sigma(t)$ the trend in $CO_2$ equivalent emissions per unit of gross output in the absence of emission controls.

**Environmental system**

The accumulation and transportation of the greenhouse gases in the atmosphere can be expressed as follows:

$$\frac{dy_5(t)}{dt} = \beta \cdot y_4(t) - \delta_m \cdot [y_5(t) - y_5(1900)] \tag{5.6}$$

where $y_5(t)$ is the concentration of $CO_2$ in the atmosphere, $\beta$ is the marginal atmospheric retention rate (the fraction of an emission that remains in the atmosphere in the short run) which equals 0.64. $\delta_m$ is the rate of transfer from the atmosphere to the oceans and is 0.00833 per cent of the excess of $CO_2$ in the atmosphere per annum.

The relationship between greenhouse gas accumulation and increased radiative forcing, $y_6(t)$ in W/m$^2$ is given as:

$$y_6(t) = 4.1 \cdot \left\{ \frac{\ln(y_5(t) / y_5(1990))}{\ln(2.0)} \right\} + O(t) \tag{5.7}$$

where $O(t)$ represents other greenhouse gases such as methane $CH_4$ and nitrous oxide $N_2O$.

The increase in globally averaged temperature in the atmosphere and the upper level of the ocean is expressed as:

$$\frac{dy_7(t)}{dt} = (1 / R_1) \cdot \{ y_6(t) - y_7(t) / \lambda - (R_2/\tau_{12}) \cdot [y_7(t) - y_8(t)] \} \tag{5.8}$$

where $y_8(t)$ is the temperature increase in the deep oceans, $R_1$ and $R_2$ are the thermal capacities of the upper layer and the deep ocean respectively, $\tau_{12}$ is the transfer rate from the upper layer to the lower layer, and $\lambda$ the climate sensitivity parameter (W/m$^2$°C).

The temperature of the deep ocean is modelled as:

$$\frac{dy_8(t)}{dt} = (1 / \tau_{12}) \cdot [y_7(t) - y_8(t)] \tag{5.9}$$

**Impact on economic growth**

The scaling factor $y_9(t)$ is the ratio of 1 minus the percentage abatement cost and 1 plus the percentage of damage costs:

$$y_9(t) = \frac{1 - b_1 \cdot z_2(t)^{b_2}}{1 + \theta_1 \cdot y_7(t)^{\theta_2}} \tag{5.10}$$

The (market) damage costs are quantified as a relation between global temperature $y_7(t)$ increase and income loss, where $\theta_1$ represents the scale of damage and $\theta_2$ the non-linearity in the damage function. The cost of reducing emissions of greenhouse gases are related to $z_2(t)$, the fractional reduction of greenhouse emissions, while $b_1$ and $b_2$ represent the scale and non-linearity of the cost function.

### 5.2.2 IMAGE 1.0: The Integrated Model to Assess the Greenhouse Effect

A mathematical system extracting the structure of IMAGE 1.0 (see Chapter 3) as a system of 155 differential equations has been developed to investigate the stability of the simulation model (Braddock *et al.*, 1995; Zapert, 1994); it is this system that is used in this study.

The mathematical representation of IMAGE 1.0 is of the form

$$\frac{d}{dt}x(t) = F(x(t)) + u(t) \tag{5.11}$$

$$x(t_0) = x_0$$

where time $t \in [1990, 2100]$, $t_0 = 1990$ is the initial simulation time, $\mathbf{x}(t) \in R^{155}$ is a vector of state variables, $\mathbf{u}(t) \in R^{155}$ is the forcing term and $F(\mathbf{x}(t)):R^{155} \to R^{155}$ describes the biophysical system. The solution $\mathbf{x}(t)$ as a function of time is a trajectory of equation (5.11). For a detailed description of the formulation of the mathematical system of IMAGE 1.0 I refer to Zapert (1994).

$$x = \left[ x^{(1)}, x^{(2)}, x^{(3)}, x^{(4)}, x^{(5)}, x^{(6)}, x^{(7)}, x^{(8)} \right] \tag{5.12}$$

In representing the system components, the state vector $\mathbf{x} = \mathbf{x}(t) \in R^{155}$ at time t, is partitioned into the following variable groups.
where

$x^{(1)}$      $= (x_1,...,x_{12}) \in R^{12}$, the carbon contents of the boxes in an ocean box diffusion model, in giga tons of carbon (GtC).

$x^{(2)}$      $= (x_{13}) \in R$, the concentration of carbon as carbon dioxide ($CO_2$) in the atmosphere, in parts per million by volume (ppmv).

$x^{(3)}$      $= (x_{14},...,x_{62}) \in R^{49}$, the carbon content in seven levels of the seven categorized ecosystems, in GtC.

$x^{(4)}$      $= (x_{63},...,x_{69}) \in R^7$, the area of land in Africa, South America and South East Asia, allocated to each of seven ecosystems, in hectares.

$x^{(5)}$      $= (x_{70},...,x_{91}) \in R^{22}$, land use changes in Africa, South America and South East Asia.

$\mathbf{x}^{(6)}$      $= (x_{92},...,x_{140}) \in R^{49}$, the change in temperature since 1900, in the 49 layers of the ocean under the mixed upper ocean layer, in degrees Celsius.

$\mathbf{x}^{(7)}$      $= (x_{141}) \in R$, the change in temperature since 1900, in the mixed surface layer of the ocean, in degrees Celsius.

$\mathbf{x}^{(8)}$      $= (x_{142},...,x_{155}) \in R^{14}$, the concentration of various CFC gases with $x_{142},...,x_{151}$, in pptv, carbon monoxide, $(x_{152})$ and methane, $(x_{153})$ in ppmv, and nitrous oxide, $(x_{154})$ in ppbv, in the atmosphere and $(x_{155})$ the production of OH.

The forcing term $\mathbf{u}(t)$ is a 155-vector partitioned according to the state vector partitioning and represents the human interference in the system (5.11). The non-zero components of $\mathbf{u}(t)$ are associated with blocks $\mathbf{x}^{(2)}$, $\mathbf{x}^{(5)}$ and $\mathbf{x}^{(8)}$. Therefore

$$\mathbf{u} = \left[ 0, \, \mathbf{u}^{(2)}, 0, 0, \boldsymbol{u}^{(5)}, 0, 0, \boldsymbol{u}^{(8)} \right] \tag{5.13}$$

where

$\mathbf{u}^{(2)}$      $= (u_{13}) \in R$, emission of $CO_2$ from fossil fuel combustion.

$\mathbf{u}^{(5)}$      $= (u_{70},...,u_{91}) \in R^{22}$, ecosystem transfer rates, the amount of land per annum allocated from one ecosystem to another.

$\mathbf{u}^{(8)}$      $= (u_{142},...,u_{155}) \in R^{14}$, other than carbon dioxide greenhouse gas emissions.

Implicitly, the forcing term $\mathbf{u}(t)$ includes the given scenarios estimation of future population growth, fossil fuel combustion, deforestation, and the technology development in the period 1990-2100 (Rotmans, 1990; Braddock *et al.*, 1995; Zapert, 1994).

### 5.2.3 OMEGA (An Optimization Model for Economic and Greenhouse Assessment)

I propose to combine the economic component of DICE (equations 5.1-5.5) and the impact factor (equation 5.10) with the mathematical system formulation of IMAGE 1.0.[1] To be more precise, equations 5.6-5.9 from the DICE model are discarded and replaced by the IMAGE 1.0 framework. This means that the emissions of fossil $CO_2$ ($u_{13}$) are equal to $y_4(t)$. Considering the additional difference I will now only consider fossil $CO_2$ emissions for $y_4(t)$ and, therefore, I adopt a rescaled factor for $b_1$ based on Nordhaus (1991b). Non-fossil $CO_2$ and CFCs emissions are included within the framework of IMAGE 1.0.

Furthermore, because $x_{141}(t)$ represents the temperature of the mixed upper ocean layer and thus not the surface temperature above land, an additional term

$x_{156}(t)$ is included which has the same meaning as expression $y_7(t)$ in the DICE model:

$$x_{156}(t) = \frac{f \cdot x_{157}(t) - k \cdot x_{141}(t)}{f \cdot \lambda + k} \tag{5.14}$$

which represents the atmospheric temperature increase relative to 1900. $x_{157}(t)$ is the total change in radiative forcing which can be derived after estimating the non-$CO_2$ component, $x_{158}(t)$, k represents the heat transfer between land and oceans, f is the fraction of the globe covered by land (=0.3) and $\Delta T_{2xCO2}$ the temperature increase for a doubled $CO_2$ concentration (=2.5°C).

$$x_{157}(t) = \frac{\lambda \cdot \Delta T_{2xCO2}}{\ln(2)} \cdot \ln\left(\frac{x_{13}(t))}{x_{13}(1900)}\right) + x_{158}(t) \tag{5.15}$$

$$
\begin{aligned}
x_{158}(t) = {} & a_{CFC11} \cdot x_{142}(t) + a_{CFC12} \cdot x_{143}(t) + a_{CFC113} \cdot x_{144}(t) \\
& + a_{CFC114} \cdot x_{145}(t) + a_{CFC115} \cdot x_{146}(t) \\
& + a_{H2O} \cdot (\sqrt{x_{153}(t)} - \sqrt{x_{153}(1900)}) \\
& + a_{CH4} \cdot (\sqrt{x_{153}(t)} - \sqrt{x_{153}(1900)}) \\
& - f(x_{153}(t), x_{154}(1900)) + f(x_{153}(1900), x_{154}(1900)) \\
& + a_{N2O} \cdot (\sqrt{x_{154}(t)} - \sqrt{x_{154}(1900)}) \\
& - f(x_{153}(1900), x_{154}(t)) + f(x_{153}(1900), x_{154}(1900))
\end{aligned}
\tag{5.16}
$$

where

$$f(x_{153}(t), x_{154}(t)) =$$
$$0.47 \ln[1 + a_1 \cdot 10^3 \cdot (x_{153}(t) \cdot x_{154}(t))^{0.75}$$
$$+ a_2 \cdot 10^3 \cdot x_{154}(t) \cdot (x_{153}(t) \cdot x_{154}(t))^{1.52}]$$

where $a_i$ are radiative forcing coefficients of the greenhouse gas i, and where the climate sensitivity parameter $\lambda$ is defined as a 4.3 W/m$^2$ increase of radiative forcing for a doubled $CO_2$ concentration divided by the temperature increase for a doubled $CO_2$ concentration is $4.3/\Delta T_{2xCO2}$.

The state space of the combined model can now be written as $(y_1,...,y_5,x_1,...,x_{158},y_{10})$ and is controlled by $z_1$ and $z_2$ (Figure 5.1). OMEGA was developed in the modelling environment and simulation language M (De Bruin *et al.*, 1996), which is ultimately converted into C. The system is solved using 2$^{nd}$ order Runge-Kutta with a fixed time step of 0.05 years (Zapert, 1994).

## 5.3   OPTIMIZATION METHODOLOGY

### 5.3.1  Problem Formulation

The generic optimal control problem which can be associated with the coupled model has the following form:

$$\max_{z(t)} \int_{t_0}^{t_1} f(x(t), y(t), u(t), z(t)) dt$$

$$s.t.$$

$$z(t) \in \mathfrak{S} = \{ z(t) \in R^2 : g(x(t), y(t), u(t), z(t)) \leq 0 \tag{5.17}$$

$$\frac{d(y(t), x(t))}{dt} = F(y(t), x(t)) + (u(t), z(t)) \}$$

where the objective is to maximize f(t), the discounted sum of consumption, in order to satisfy $g(.)$. The input/control can be split into decision variables of the optimization problem $z_1(t)$ and $z_2(t)$ and the remaining input variables $u^{(5)}$ and $u^{(8)}$ which follow prescribed scenarios as given in Rotmans (1990).

The problem described in (5.17) is a continuous dynamic control problem. Due to the dimensionality of the problem it may be practically impossible to find an analytical solution. If the time steps are rendered discrete, the problem can be transformed into an ordinary large scale non-linear problem, which can be solved using various numerical optimization techniques, within the limitation of these methods. The general problem formulation is, therefore, stated as

$$\max_{z \in R^n} f(z)$$

$$\tag{5.18}$$

subject to

$$g_i(z) \leq 0 \quad i = 1, .., m$$

For simplicity, the levels of the decision variables are assumed to change linearly over fixed time intervals during the period under consideration (1990-2100). The following time intervals are used: $[T_0, T_1], \ldots, [T_{10}, T_{11}]$, $T_0 = 1990$, $T_1 = 2000, \ldots, T_{11} = 2100$. The investments and emission control rates are assumed to change in a linear fashion during $[T_k, T_{k+1}]$ where the investments and control rate levels in years $T_k$ and $T_{k+1}$ are denoted by, respectively, $\mu_{1,k}$ and $\mu_{2,k}$. The choice of $\mu_1 = [\mu_{1,k}]_{k=1}^{11}$ and $\mu_2 = [\mu_{2,k}]_{k=1}^{11}$ together with the known value of the initial values $u_{1,1990}$ and $u_{2,1990}$, determine $\mu_{1,k}$ and $\mu_{2,k}$. The $\mu_{1,k}s$ and $\mu_{2,k}s$ can be considered as the decision variables which determine $z$.

In the next Section, I will briefly describe four optimization approaches which are used to solve the problem as defined above: Sequential Reduced-System Programming, Penalty Method, Sequential Quadratic Programming and the Genetic Algorithm.

## 5.4   OPTIMIZATION APPROACHES

### Sequential Reduced-System Programming

This method is specifically designed to enable the optimization of large-scale dynamic systems. Here the system is reduced to a smaller scale representing only the core of the original system (Janssen and Vrieze, 1995; Janssen, 1996). This technique is related to the two-step algorithm designed to solve the problem of combined identification and dynamic optimization as identified by Haimes and Wismer (1972), Ellis and Roberts (1982) and Ferreira and Borges (1994) in that sequentially the dynamic system and a dynamic optimization problem for a reduced version of the system is solved.

The optimal control problem can mathematically be stated as below

$$\max_{z(t)} \int_{t_0}^{t_1} f(x(z(t)), z(t)) dt$$

$$z(t) \in \Im = \{ z(t) \in R^n : g(x(z(t)), z(t)) \leq 0 \tag{5.19}$$

$$\frac{dx(t)}{dt} = A \cdot x(t) + N(x(t)) + F(z(t)) \}$$

where $\Im \in R^n$ is the decision space, where $x(t) \in R^s$ is the state vector of the system which describes all the characteristic quantities, $A$ is a square matrix and $F$ is a vector valued function of $z(t) \in R^n$ , the input vector of the system. $N$ represents the non-linear terms. If $A$, $N$, $x_0$ and $z(t)$ for every t are known then $x(t)$ is assumed to be uniquely determined. Clearly $A$, $N$ and $x_0$ are defined once and for all and $x(t)$ is a function of $z(t)$: $x(z(t))$. All functions are supposed to be continuously differentiable.

The algorithm which can solve (5.19) is based on the idea to reduce the system into a smaller system, fixing certain variables, and which allows the application of optimization methods in order to derive an optimal solution for this smaller system. Next, this solution is used as input for the next iteration of the original system, and so on.

I will now split up the state space into $x^1(t) \in R^m$ and $x^2(t) \in R^{s-m}$, with m<s. The algorithm will treat the variables $x^1(t)$ as normal endogenous and $x^2(t)$ as given exogenous values which are updated every iteration. Observe that, for the small system, $x^1(t)$ is steered by the input variable $z(t)$, and the fixed input $x^2(t)$. The other part of the system, $x^2(t)$, is only influenced indirectly by changes in the input variable $z(t)$ through $x^1(t)$.

The resulting algorithm is therefore:

Choose some start vector $z_0(t)$. Set k=1.

Step 1 (Simulation) Using $z_{k-1}(t)$ solve

$$\frac{dx(t)}{dt} = A \cdot x(t) + N(x(t)) + F(z_{k-1}(t)) \tag{5.20}$$

to derive $x_k(t) = \{x_k^1(t), x_k^2(t)\}$.

Step 2 (Optimization) Fixing the estimates of $x_k^2(t)$ from step 1, obtain $z_k(t)$ by solving

$$\begin{matrix} \max \\ z(t) \end{matrix} \int_{t_0}^{t_1} f(x^1(z(t)), z(t)) dt$$

$$z(t) \in \mathfrak{I}_k = \left\{ \begin{array}{l} z(t) \in R^n : g(x^1(z)(t), z(t)) \le 0 \\ \dfrac{dx^1(t)}{dt} = A_1 \cdot \begin{pmatrix} x^1(t) \\ x_k^2(t) \end{pmatrix} + N_1(x^1(t), x_k^2(t)) + F_1(z(t)) \end{array} \right\} \tag{5.21}$$

Set k=k+1 and go to Step 1.

In step 2 of the algorithm $A_1$ is the appropriate submatrix of $A$, while $N_1$ and $F_1$ refer to the $x^1$-components of $N$ and $F$ respectively. The steps of simulation and optimization are performed sequentially until no further improvement can be observed, or until the convergence criterion is met. In Janssen (1996) and Janssen and Vrieze (1995) convergence of the approach is proved for a large class of problems.

## The Penalty Method (PM)

The penalty method (PM) transforms the constrained problem into an unconstrained problem by substituting a penalty function for the constraints. The idea is to penalize constraint violation by adding a sequence of penalty functions to the objective function in such a manner that the solutions to the resulting sequence of unconstrained problems tend to a constrained minimum (Luenberger, 1984). This straightforward method can be formulated as an unconstrained problem of the form

$$\min f(z) + cP(z) \tag{5.22}$$

where $c$ is a positive constant and $P$ is a continuous function on $R^n$ satisfying $P(z) \geq 0 \ \forall \ z \in R^n$ and where $P(z) = 0$ if and only if $z$ is a feasible solution.

To solve problem (5.22) by the penalty function method is to use a sequence $\{c_k\}$, k=1, 2, ..., tending to infinity such that for each k, $c_k \geq 0$, $c_{k+1} > c_k$. Define the function $q(c,z) = f(z) + cP(z)$ and solve for each k the following problem

$$\min_{z} \ q(c_k, z) \tag{5.23}$$

to obtain a solution point $z_k$ assuming that, for each k problem (5.23) has a solution. In this chapter, the most widely used exact penalty function, the absolute-value penalty function, is applied. The absolute value penalty function may be written as

$$q(\rho, z) = f(z) + \rho \| g(z)^* \|_1 \tag{5.24}$$

This non-differential penalty function has the property that there is a finite threshold value $\rho^+$ such that $z^*$ is an unconstrained minimizer of $P_1$ for any $\rho > \rho^+$.

The direct set algorithm (Press *et al.*, 1988) is used for the experiments to eliminate the need to calculate the derivative of the mathematical system in finding a local optimum.

**The Sequential Quadratic Programming Method (SQP)**

The SQP method solves a sequence of quadratic sub-problems derived using the first and second order terms of the Taylor expansion of f(z) and linear approximations of the constraints g(z) (Nemhauser *et al.*, 1989). SQP is based directly on the optimality conditions of non-linear programming. Necessary conditions for $z^*$ to be a local minimum of (5.18) are the well-known Karush-Kuhn-Tucker (KKT) equations:

$$\nabla f(z^*) + \sum_{i=1}^{m} \lambda_i^* \cdot \nabla g_i(z^*) = 0$$

$$\lambda_i^* \cdot g_i(z^*) = 0 \qquad i = 1,\ldots,m \qquad\qquad (5.25)$$

$$\lambda_i^* \geq 0 \qquad\qquad i = 1,\ldots,m$$

where $\lambda_i^*$ are the Lagrangian multipliers.

The solution of the KKT equations forms the basis for the SQP. At each major iteration an approximation is made of the Hessian of the Lagrangian function using a quasi-Newton updating method, regarding information from the KKT equations. This approximation is then used to form a search direction for a line search procedure.

At each iteration of the method, a Quadratic Programming (QP) problem is solved using the Wolfe algorithm (Wolfe, 1959). The QP sub-problem is a quadratic approximation of the Lagrangian function,

$$L(z, \lambda) = f(z) + \sum_{i=1}^{m} \lambda_i \cdot g_i(z) \qquad\qquad (5.26)$$

The QP sub-problem can then be obtained by linearizing the nonlinear constraints,

$$\text{minimize} \quad \tfrac{1}{2} d^T H_k d \; + \; \nabla f(z_k)^T d$$

$$d \in R^n$$

$$\text{subject to:} \qquad\qquad\qquad\qquad\qquad (5.27)$$

$$\nabla g_i(z_k)^T \cdot d \; + \; g_i(z_k) \leq 0 \quad i = 1,\ldots,m$$

where $d$ is the search direction. The matrix $H_k$ is a positive definite approximation of the Hessian matrix of the Lagrangian function and is updated by a positive-definite quasi-Newton approximation using the BFGS method

(MATLAB, 1992). The solution procedure initially involves the calculation of a feasible point (if one exists), and then the generation of an iterative sequence of feasible points which achieve convergence to the solution.

$$z_{k+1} = z_k + \alpha_k d_k \tag{5.28}$$

The nonnegative steplength parameter $\alpha_k$ is determined by an approximate line search procedure so that a sufficient decrease in a merit function is obtained.

## Genetic Algorithm (GA)

The genetic algorithm is not designed explicitly as an optimization algorithm, as will be seen in Chapters 8 and 9, but has been developed by Holland (1975) by means of trying to abstract and explain the adaptive processes of natural systems. The basic construction is to consider a population of individuals that each represent a potential solution to a problem. The relative success of each individual on this problem is considered as its fitness, and is used to selectively reproduce the most fit individuals to produce similar, but not identical, offspring for the next generation (Figure 5.2). Genetic algorithms are mainly applied in optimization studied because they surpass their more traditional cousins in the quest for robustness (Goldberg, 1989).

Genetic algorithms are different from more normal optimization and search procedures in the following four ways (Goldberg, 1989):
1. GAs work with a coding of the parameter set, not the parameters themselves.
2. GAs search from a population of points, not a single point.
3. GAs use payoff (objective function) information, not derivatives or other auxiliary knowledge.
4. GAs use probabilistic transition rules, not deterministic rules.

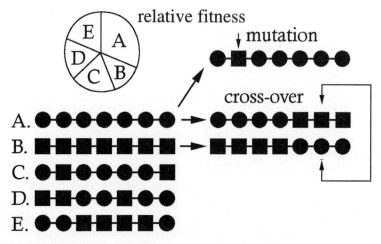

*Figure 5.2: Schematic diagram of a genetic algorithm.*

A formal description of the genetic algorithm is the following:
(1) An individual can be characterized by a binary bit string of fixed length L, which is denoted as $a$, and $a \in B^L$ where $B = \{0,1\}$. The bit string can be separated into n segments of equal length $l_z$, thus implying $L = n * l_z$. Each segment is interpreted as the binary code of the object variable $z_i \in [z^l_i, z^u_i]$ which can be redecoded by applying:

$$\Gamma_i(a_{i1} \ldots a_{il_z}) = z^l_i + \frac{z^u_i - z^l_i}{2^{l_z} - 1} \cdot \left( \sum_{j=0}^{l_z-1} a_{i(l_z-j)} \cdot 2^j \right) \qquad (5.29)$$

where $(a_{i1}, \ldots, a_{il_z})$ denotes the i-th segment of an individual $a \in B^L$. Then $\Gamma = \Gamma_1 x \ldots x \Gamma_n$ yields a vector of real values on the desired range $[z^l_i, z^u_i]$.
Example: $a = 10011$, $z^l = 0$, $z^u = 1$
$$\Gamma = (1*2^4 + 0*2^3 + 0*2^2 + 1*2^1 + 1*2^0)/31 = 0.613$$

(2) Mutation is a bit reversal event that occurs with small probability $p_m$ per bit. This mutation can explore new genetic information and is a powerful operator in finding ways to adapt to a changing environment.
Example: Suppose I have the following bit string:                           11111
At random, roughly one in every 1000 symbols flips from 0 to 1
or vice versa; in the example from 1 to 0:                           11011

(3) The algorithm uses a crossover operator that exchanges substrings arbitrarily between two individuals with probability $p_c$. Length and position of these substrings are chosen at random, but are identical for both individuals.

Example: Suppose I have the following bit strings:     11111 and 00000
A point along the strings is selected at random and the offspring
contain a mixture of the parents:                 11000 and 00111

(4) The probabilistic selection operator forms the next generation by copying
individuals on the basis of fitness-proportionate probabilities

$$p_i = \frac{F(a_i)}{\sum\limits_{j=1}^{N} F(a_j)} \qquad (5.30)$$

where $F:B^L \rightarrow R$ is the fitness function. The less fit individuals are therefore
less likely to reproduce their genetic information.

According to Goldberg (1989) genetic algorithms are successful robust
algorithms in optimization because they are able to select strings with useful
blocks of information, and concentrate their search (selection) on variations
which include those blocks. In complex problems, finding a good solution often
depends upon putting together several of such useful blocks in the right
combination. Genetic algorithms can be a powerful and relatively robust
algorithm for searching in mathematical spaces defined by (non-linear and
nondifferential) functions of multiple variables. Although there is no
convergence criterion and we don't know if the algorithm has found a global
optimum, in many practical applications it is often satisfactory to find a solution
that is better than the solution we started with.

We may start with a set of initial solutions lying in a predetermined range
$[z_{il}^{1}, d_{il}^{u}]$. This approach may be used to incorporate a priori knowledge. The
consequence of this approach is that independent of the degree of optimality,
solutions found are improvements on present or proposed scenarios.

In the following sections, I will discuss some experiments performed with
OMEGA. First I will discuss the problem formulation, thereafter the results and
the performance of the various optimization algorithms. Finally, I will discuss
differences found between OMEGA and DICE experiments.

## 5.5   ANALYSIS

Since climate change policy has numerous objectives, any formulation of an
optimization problem will necessarily neglect some specific aspects, and the
problems which are examined in this study can, therefore, only be seen as
possible illustrative examples in climate policy. The analysis concerns the
investigation of three problems with two starting points. Investments are
assumed to be at an equal level at each starting point, all of which are based on

optimal strategies in the absence of environmental policy. I propose to cover the range of possible policy options based on IPCC scenarios (IPCC, 1991), by referring to two levels of emission reductions:

- *Business-as-Usual (BaU)*:  a continuation of current trends.
- *Accelerated Policies (AP)*:  a shift towards non-fossil fuels is adopted.

Furthermore, I distinguish two scenarios for $\mathbf{u}^{(5)}$ (land use change) and $\mathbf{u}^{(8)}$ (other than fossil $CO_2$ emissions): BaU and AP. This leads to four start scenarios, whereby the resulting temperature increase in 2100 compared to 1900 is given in Table 5.1. If the Business-as-Usual policy is followed for all sources, it is expected that temperature will increase by some 4°C. However, if fossil $CO_2$ as well as other sources are controlled according to the Accelerated Policies scenario the temperature increase will be limited to 1.3°C. Other starting points lead to the following global-mean temperature increases in 2100 compared to 1900 for the various cases:

*Table 5.1: Global-mean temperature increase $x_{156}$ in 2100 as projected by OMEGA (in °C).*

| $z \backslash \mathbf{u}^{(5)}, \mathbf{u}^{(8)}$ | BaU | AP |
|---|---|---|
| BaU | 3.7 | 2.7 |
| AP | 2.3 | 1.3 |

The purpose of the considered optimization problems is to control $\mathbf{z}$, given $\mathbf{u}$, to maximize the discounted sum of utility of future consumption given constraints on environmental impacts. Based on Nordhaus (1992, 1993; 1994), I propose to use the following problem formulations:

*1) Cost-benefit*   This case is a straightforward cost-benefit optimization problem. The impacts of emission reduction cost and damage cost of a temperature increase are included in the objective function. The solution to this problem is an economically-efficient policy designed to slow climate change.

*2) Maximum concentration of $CO_2$*   In order to appraise the effects of anthropogenic emissions, the increase in concentration of greenhouse gases is limited. In several studies, such targets have been used in developing response scenarios (for example Krause *et al.*, 1989; IPCC, 1991). Translated to $CO_2$ concentration an upper limit, $c_{max}$, of 400 ppmv (Krause *et al.*, 1989) will be used: $x_{13}(t) \leq c_{max}$

*3) Maximum temperature increase.* From an environmental perspective, UNEP's Advisory Group on Greenhouse Gases (AGGG, 1990) has identified several climate targets in order to protect the structure and functions of vulnerable ecosystems and to limit risks for society. Such a target might be an absolute temperature limit of 2°C above pre-industrial level. This temperature limit can be viewed as an upper limit, beyond which risks of considerable damage are expected to increase rapidly: $x_{158}(t) \leq \Delta T_{max}$

## 5.6   RESULTS

### 5.6.1   Optimal Responses

**Emissions**

In the case of the optimal cost-benefit formulation, the emissions of fossil $CO_2$ rise to a level of 16 GtC in 2100 which is about 10 GtC above the present level (Figure 5.3). To meet the $CO_2$ concentration target, the emissions stabilize at a level of 5 GtC. The control of non-$CO_2$ gases does not influence the optimal policy of the first two problem formulations. However, including a temperature target in the search for suitable future greenhouse policy leads to large differences in emission reductions, whether emissions of other gases are reduced or not.

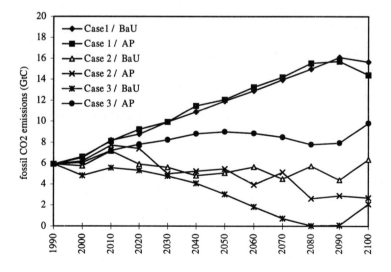

*Figure 5.3: Optimal emission paths of fossil $CO_2$ using OMEGA*

In the event that emissions of greenhouse gases other than fossil $CO_2$ are not reduced, fossil $CO_2$ has to be phased out by the end of the next century in order to meet the 2°C temperature increase target. An additional reduction in emissions of other greenhouse gases results in a modest emission reduction path.

## Concentration of $CO_2$

If environmental constraints are not explicitly taken into account (Case 1), $CO_2$ concentration will reach a level of 630 ppmv by 2100 (Figure 5.4). A phase-out of fossil $CO_2$ emissions (case 3 including BaU scenarios for non-fossil $CO_2$ emissions) is the only strategy which leads to a decrease in the $CO_2$ concentration.

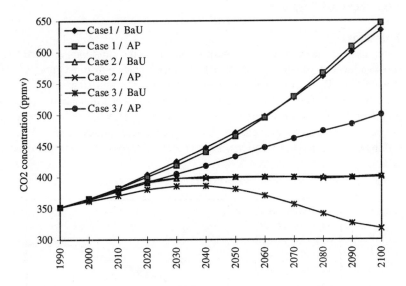

*Figure 5.4: $CO_2$ concentrations pertaining to optimal strategies according to OMEGA*

## Temperature Increase

The extra temperature increase associated with the case in which not all greenhouse gases are controlled leads to an additional 1°C temperature increase (Figure 5.5). Therefore, a cost-benefit policy leads to a temperature increase of between 2.6 and 3.5°C, while meeting the concentration target results in a range of 1.5 to 2.5°C. The reader will note that temperature increases are significant in the next century in all cases, which may lead to serious impacts on economic, agricultural, and social developments.

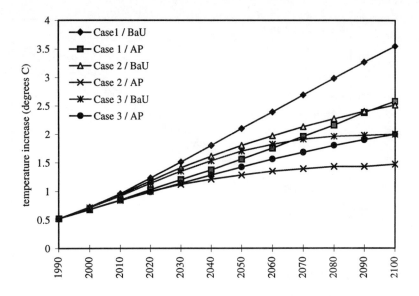

*Figure 5.5: Temperature increases according to OMEGA*

## Output

The differences in economic output among the various cases are relatively small throughout the next century (Figure 5.6). The output will at most, in case of a phase-out of fossil $CO_2$ emissions, lead to a 12 per cent lower output than in the optimal cost-benefit case. Note that the economic output here is 'green' in that it takes account of environmental impacts of economic activities in terms of market damage. However, non-market damage is not taken into account in this study.

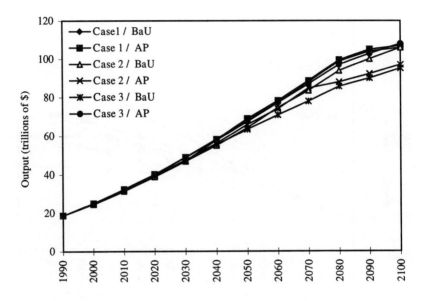

*Figure 5.6: Economic outputs according to OMEGA*

### 5.6.2 Performance Results

The performance of the optimization approaches is illustrated for the solutions of the three test problems, starting the search at three starting points. In order to quantify the performance, criteria are distinguished, based on Hock and Schittkowski (1983):

*Table 5.2: Performance criteria*

| Accuracy | |
|---|---|
| objective: | percentage of difference with the best solution found |
| constraints: | sum of violation of constraints ($\Sigma g(u)$) |
| *Efficiency* | |
| execution time (seconds): | cpu time on Silicon Graphics (Indy) workstation |
| function evaluations: | number of model runs |
| *Reliability* | |
| failures (%): | percentage of runs where no feasible solution was found |

Detailed performance scores can be found in Janssen (1996), while the average scores are shown in Table 5.3.

*Table 5.3: Performance of the four optimization approaches on the test problems. (Only feasible solutions are used to determine the accuracy score.) The function evaluations of the reduced system are given between parentheses (SRSP). The experiments are performed on a Silicon Graphics Indy workstation*

| | *accuracy* | | *efficiency* | | *reliability* |
|---|---|---|---|---|---|
| | objective | constraints | run time | f.e. | % failures |
| SRSP | 10.15% | 0.000000 | 4079 | 5 (41152) | 17 % |
| Penalty Method | 0.01% | 0.000014 | 26807 | 7305 | 0 % |
| SQP | 0.82% | 0.000000 | 8699 | 2097 | 75 % |
| GA | 0.11% | 0.33 | 3408 | 1000 | 0 % |
| | 0.10% | 0.32 | 6818 | 2000 | 0 % |
| | 0.10% | 0.28 | 10227 | 3000 | 0 % |
| | 0.10% | 0.26 | 13635 | 4000 | 0 % |
| | 0.10% | 0.20 | 17044 | 5000 | 0 % |

SRSP performed well on the unconstrained problem, where it found a solution close to the best solution found in a run time which was many times shorter than in the other optimization techniques. However, SRSP failed on the constrained test cases where the efficiency was high (Janssen, 1996), but the derived solutions are of a poor quality. Due to the fact that the dynamics of the constraints might not be taken into full account in the reduced version, SRSP was not able to find good solutions to the problem.

The penalty method which uses the original model, thus being able to cope with all of the dynamics inherent in the problem, was found to be a reliable and accurate, but time-consuming, approach for solving the large scale non-linear optimization problem. Sequential Quadratic Programming is unreliable for the kind of problems as considered in this study as a result of the high degree of non-linearity which is not approximated within a quadratic framework. Therefore, quadratic subproblems do not help the search for the optimal solution, but lead to the rapid exhaustion of the search algorithm. The Genetic Algorithm performs very well on the unconstrained problems but fails on the constrained ones. It is generally noted that genetic algorithms have problems in dealing with constraints (Forest, 1993).

In Chapter 6, I will use a genetic algorithm to perform the optimization experiments. The reason for this is that algorithms such as the penalty method, SRSP and SQP perform relatively well for sound mathematical systems but their approaches have not been designed to handle a large scale simulation model (such as TARGETS, see Chapters 3 and 6), which consists of many discontinuities and non-differentiable points. In such noisy search spaces, the robustness of genetic algorithms outperforms the other algorithms (Goldberg, 1989).

### 5.6.3 Comparing Results of OMEGA with DICE

The optimization problem was rendered a large-scale problem by replacing the small climate model of DICE by the 155 dimensional mathematical system which features in the IMAGE 1.0 model. I recognize that within OMEGA there is an imbalance between the economic part and the environmental part. However, since the aim of the exercise is to show the impact of the choice of the modelling approach for the climate system on the 'optimal' response strategies, I am, nevertheless, able to discuss the differences which occur as a result of using the 'original' DICE model *vis-à-vis* the derived OMEGA model.

In order to compare the results, I propose to start by referring to identical 'business-as-usual' results for both models, to which end I slightly adapt the DICE model. Originally, the temperature increase in 2100 for the DICE model was 3.3 degrees (Nordhaus, 1992,1993,1994). If I use the business-as-usual scenario borrowed from IMAGE 1.0 for the other trace gases ($O(t)$ equation 5.7), and if I only wish to control fossil $CO_2$ emissions, and, furthermore, assume exogenous levels of CFC emissions and $CO_2$ emissions due to land use changes, the temperature increase in 2100 is calculated as 3.8 °C.

The cost-benefit case solution does not significantly differ from the solution produced by OMEGA (Figures 5.7-5.10). OMEGA results support the case for a somewhat enhanced emission reduction strategy compared with DICE results. However, in order to meet the concentration target, emissions have to be stabilized at the level of 1 GtC, which is 80 per cent lower than the level envisaged by OMEGA. The temperature target will be exceeded, unless other greenhouse gases are also controlled.

The differences in emission budgets for the next century can be read off from Table 5.4. The inclusion of environmental constraints leads to larger reductions in emissions according to DICE as opposed to OMEGA. The climate model incorporated in DICE and especially as expressed in equation (5.7) (the atmospheric concentration of $CO_2$) is based on historical trends. Price (1995) argues that 'representing $CO_2$ uptake as instant disappearance, followed by a simple exponential uptake process, is too unrepresentative of what *is* known about oceanic and other sinks to give secure physical predictions'. Furthermore,

Price (1995) concludes that 'gross analysis of historical trends in $CO_2$ emissions and concentrations is likely to be misleading'. According to Kaufmann (1997) the forecast for the airborne fraction generated by the DICE model is in contradiction with forecasts generated by models that represent the physical and chemical processes which determine the movement of carbon from the atmosphere to the ocean. He states that 'when these unsupported assumptions, simple extrapolations, and misspecifications are remedied with simple fixes, the economic impact of global climate change increases several fold'.

*Table 5.4: Emission budgets of fossil $CO_2$ for the period 1990 to 2100 in GtC, for BaU as well as for AP policy for other greenhouse gas emissions.*

| Case\Model | DICE | | OMEGA | |
|---|---|---|---|---|
| | AP | BaU | AP | BaU |
| Cost benefit | 1300 | 1285 | 1280 | 1245 |
| Concentration target | 239 | 239 | 598 | 612 |
| Temperature target | 529 | - | 888 | 338 |

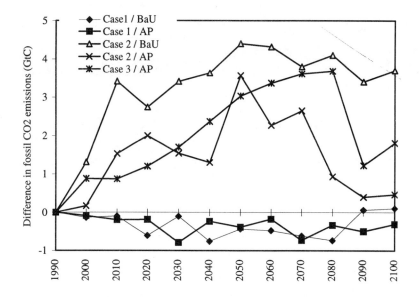

*Figure 5.7: Difference in optimal emission paths between OMEGA and DICE*

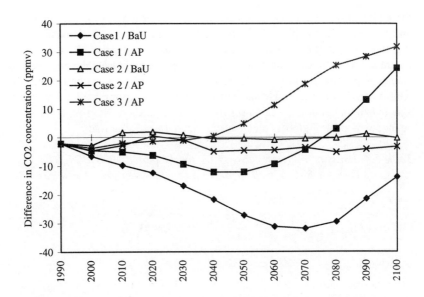

*Figure 5.8: Difference in* $CO_2$ *concentration between OMEGA and DICE*

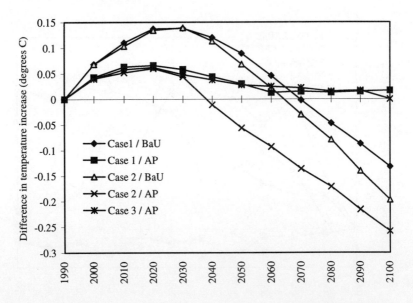

*Figure 5.9: Difference in temperature increase between OMEGA and DICE*

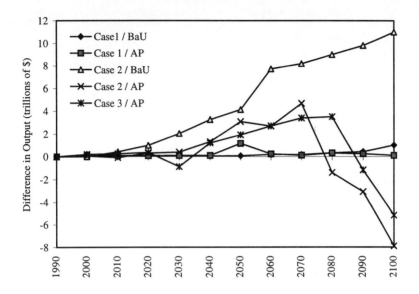

*Figure 5.10: Difference in economic output between OMEGA and DICE*

The DICE model is, therefore, only able to estimate future concentrations by extrapolating historical behaviour. If, however, in the next century, environmental policies were to be implemented which would result in a transformation of economic activities resulting in different patterns of fossil $CO_2$ emissions, the DICE model would no longer be able to capture the consequences of such changes. OMEGA is designed to describe the climate processes insofar as they are understood by natural scientists, and is, therefore, able to capture a wider range of future scenarios. Important aspects which are missing in DICE are the fact that the ocean takes up less, the more $CO_2$ it has absorbed in the past, and the fact that the terrestrial biosphere takes up more $CO_2$ if the $CO_2$ concentration is high (fertilization effect). I have estimated $\beta$ and $\delta_m$ again based on results of OMEGA, where $\beta$ is kept constant on the original values if $\delta_m$ is estimated, and the other way round. Figures 5.11 and 5.12 show the re-estimated parameter values $\beta$ and $\delta_m$ in time for the cost-benefit scenario and the 400 ppmv scenario. The figures illustrate that the parameters which are constant in DICE, but modelled in OMEGA, are not constant in time and differ between scenarios according to experiments with OMEGA. This is caused by the complex dynamics of the carbon cycles, exchanging carbon between oceans, atmosphere and terrestrial biosphere.

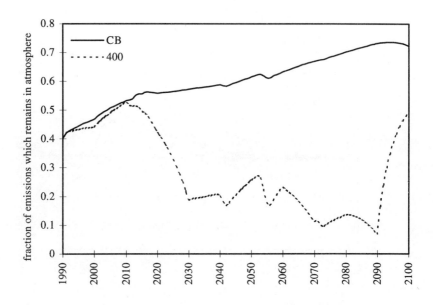

*Figure 5.11: Estimated values of β given a constant δ and concentration*
*estimates from OMEGA for cost-benefit and 400 ppmv case*

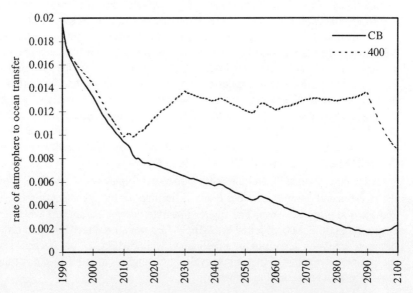

*Figure 5.12: Estimated values of δ given a constant β and concentration*
*estimated from OMEGA for cost-benefit and 400 ppmv case.*

The results show that within the OMEGA framework, limiting temperature change is relatively less expensive than within the DICE model, which results in a lower emission path in the case of a cost-benefit analysis. Consequently, meeting environmental constraints is far more expensive if I use DICE, compared with the results of OMEGA. To estimate the impact of different approaches in cost, the present value of future consumption is calculated. The loss of future consumption is assumed to be the difference between the optimal policy without additional environmental constraints (assuming BaU scenario emissions for non-fossil $CO_2$ emissions) and considered policy (Table 5.5). The loss of the value of consumption goes up from 1 to 6 per cent in case additional environmental constraints are included. This exercise shows that the results are highly dependent on the way the climate system is modelled and underlines the importance of using models which rely on the best available scientific knowledge. Compared to Nordhaus (1992, 1993, 1994), the loss of consumption is in all cases significantly higher because in OMEGA only fossil $CO_2$ is controlled, neglecting the relatively cost-efficient reduction in CFCs and $CO_2$ emission due to land use changes.

*Table 5.5: Loss of discounted value of consumption compared to the reference case (cost-benefit assuming AP scenarios for non-fossil $CO_2$ emissions) (in trillions of 1989 US$). The loss of consumption as a percentage of the discounted value of consumption of the reference case is given between parentheses.*

| Case\Model | DICE | | OMEGA | |
|---|---|---|---|---|
| | AP | BaU | AP | BaU |
| Cost benefit | -2.6 | 0.0 | -2.8 | 0.0 |
| | (0.2%) | (0.0%) | (-0.3%) | (0.0%) |
| Concentration target | 41.2 | 66.4 | 19.0 | 20.7 |
| | (3.8%) | (6.2%) | (1.8%) | (1.9%) |
| Temperature target | 12.8 | - | 1.6 | 43.6 |
| | (1.2%) | | (0.1%) | (4.1%) |

**Delayed response**

Suppose a reduction policy according to the cost-benefit case is started. After a number of years, a new target is set, for example, because of new scientific insights on consequences of climate change. Suppose that such a new target is a $CO_2$ concentration stabilization on a level of 400 ppmv. A number of experiments have been constructed in which the starting year of implementing additional mitigation is varied. The starting years as used in this analysis are 1990, 2000, 2010 and 2020.

Using the OMEGA model, the results suggest that a delay until 2010 may lead to drastic reduction in order to avoid exceeding 400 ppmv (Figures 5.13 and 5.15). If policy follows the reference cost-benefit case until 2030, the concentration will exceed the target level for about two decades. However, a delay until 2000 will not have severe effects on future emission reductions. In case DICE is used, the required reductions are more drastic (Figure 5.14), and the $CO_2$ concentration level exceeds the 400 ppmb concentration targets, if the enhanced mitigation policy is not implemented before 2020 (Figure 5.16). The ignorance of changing carbon flows within the carbon cycle due to a human disturbance will lead to more drastic and costly reductions, according to DICE than according to results with OMEGA.

Note that the results are the consequence of differences between modelling the climate system. I did not vary, for example, economic and technical assumptions which may also change the insights into suitable response policies. These results are, therefore, no advocate for a wait-and-see policy. They do illustrate a reason why a model like DICE leads to advice for modest emission reductions: it takes too much emission reduction to slow down the $CO_2$ concentration increase.

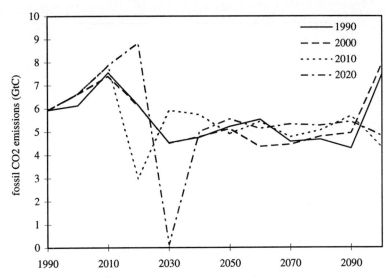

*Figure 5.13: Fossil CO₂ emissions for delayed response strategies starting in 1990, 2000, 2010 and 2020 using the OMEGA model meeting the 400 ppmv target*

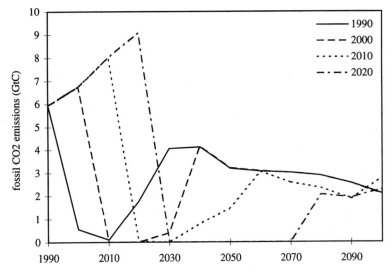

*Figure 5.14: Fossil CO₂ emissions for delayed response strategies starting in 1990, 2000, 2010 and 2020 using the DICE model meeting the 400 ppmv target*

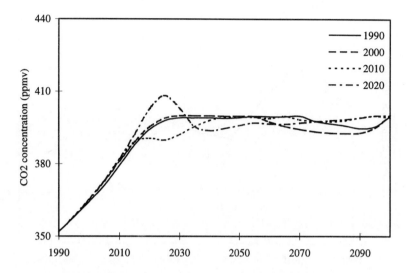

*Figure 5.15: CO$_2$ concentration for delayed response strategies for
experiments with OMEGA*

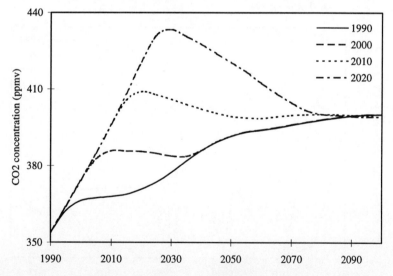

*Figure 5.16: CO$_2$ concentration for delayed response strategies for
experiments with DICE*

## 5.7 CONCLUSIONS

OMEGA combines the strongest component of two widely used integrated assessment models: the economics of DICE and the climate dynamics of IMAGE 1.0. The resulting optimization model makes it possible to scan the range of possible response policies, in order to meet targets for economic development and environmental protection. Cost-benefit analysis leads to an enhanced effort in reducing emission if OMEGA is used compared with DICE. However, in the event of severe constraints on concentration levels or temperature change, far less emission reductions have to be made if I use OMEGA instead of DICE. These differences could be explained by the different descriptions of the dynamics of the climate system.

Rather than simply providing a sensitivity analysis, the insights gained by using a different modelling approach to the climate system are more general. The results underline the conceptual limitation of most optimization studies in the field of climate change by ignoring the dynamics of the climate system as reasonably understood by natural science.

Optimization approaches which use elegant, transparent descriptions of the climate system cannot deliver adequate images of the underlying complex systems' processes and dynamics and, thus, lead to results which may be misleading, given the state-of-the-art knowledge. While I recognize the potential richness of applying optimization techniques to the climate change problem, I argue that such an approach needs to use a description of the climate system as is momentarily understood in the light of current knowledge derived from the natural scientific community. In fact, one may doubt about the degree of integration in the economics of climatic change because the description of the climate system within those models is not valid according to expert knowledge of natural science.

The critical notes made in this chapter are meant to contribute to the development of more sophisticated tools for scanning climate change response strategies. In the following chapter, such an attempt is made by applying optimization to the integrated assessment model for global change, TARGETS.

## APPENDIX: REDUCED VERSION OF OMEGA

Before reducing the model, it is important to consider which variables are essential. It is necessary to know how the global mean temperature will change in response to changes in fossil $CO_2$ emission. This leads to the following variables in the mathematical system of IMAGE 1.0, which represents the reduced IMAGE 1.0 version:

- concentration of $CO_2$, $x_{13}(t)$ from IMAGE 1.0.
- change in temperature in the mixed surface layer of the ocean, $x_{141}$ from IMAGE 1.0.
- change in the global mean surface temperature $x_{158}(t)$.

The rest of the model is discarded. The combined model is, therefore, reduced from 163 equations to a system of 9 equations, which can be solved by Runge-Kutta method 2 with a fixed time step of 0.5.

$$maximize \sum_{t=1990}^{2100} l(t) \cdot \ln(y_2(t)) \cdot (1 + \rho)^{(1990-t)}$$

$$z1(t), z2(t)$$

$$(1) \quad y_1(t) = y_9(t) \cdot a(t) \cdot [y_3(t)]^{\gamma} \cdot l(t)^{1-\gamma}$$

$$(2) \quad y_2(t) = \frac{y_1(t) - z_1(t)}{l(t)}$$

$$(3) \quad \frac{dy_3(t)}{dt} = z_1(t) - \delta_k \cdot y_3(t)$$

$$(4) \quad y_4(t) = [1 - z_2(t)] \cdot \sigma(t) \cdot y_1(t)$$

$$(5) \quad \frac{dx_{13}(t)}{dt} = 0.47 \cdot y_4(t) + \varphi(t) + \tau(t)$$

$$(6) \quad x_{157}(t) = \frac{\lambda^* \cdot \Delta T_{2xCO2}}{\ln(2)} \cdot \ln(\frac{x_{13}(t)}{x_{13}(1900)}) + x_{158}(t)$$

$$(7) \quad \frac{dx_{141}(t)}{dt} = 8/3 \cdot x_{92}(t) - (\lambda / c_m + 8/3) \cdot x_{141}(t) + x_{156}(t)/c_m$$

$$(8) \quad x_{156}(t) = \frac{f \cdot x_{157}(t) + k \cdot x_{141}(t)}{f \cdot \lambda + k}$$

(9)  $y_9(t) = \dfrac{1 - b_1 \cdot z_2(t)^{b_2}}{1 + \theta_1 \cdot [x_{156}(t)]^{\theta_2}}$

where

$$\varphi(t) = 0.47 \cdot \left( \frac{x_1(t)}{\alpha_1} + \frac{x_{12}(t)}{\alpha_{12}} + \sum_{i=35}^{62} x_i(t) \cdot \alpha_i \right) - \alpha \cdot x_{13}(t)$$

$$\tau(t) = N(X)_{13}(t)$$

and where:

$$\frac{d\sigma(t)}{dt} = \exp(\delta_\sigma \cdot t) \cdot \sigma(t) \qquad \frac{dl(t)}{dt} = \exp(\delta_l \cdot t) \cdot l(t) \qquad \frac{da(t)}{dt} = \exp(\delta_a \cdot t) \cdot a(t)$$

$\alpha_i$      are coefficients

$c_m$      in the bulk heat capacity of the ocean mixed layer (10.97 W y/m$^2$ °C)

and where: $x_1$, $x_{12}$, $x_{35}$, $x_{36}$, ..., $x_{61}$, $x_{62}$, $x_{92}$, $x_{158}$ and $N(X)_{13}$ are exogenous input variables.

## NOTE

1. Notice that IMAGE 1.0 as well as DICE do not contain scientific findings of the last years such as the role of CFC and sulphate aerosols. The results presented in this chapter are an academic exercise showing the possibility of including more advanced descriptions of the climate system and its consequences on conclusions of economic cost estimates. In Chapter 6 optimization experiments are discussed using a more up-to-date global integrated assessment model, TARGETS.

# 6.  Global Energy Strategies

## 6.1  INTRODUCTION

The Framework Convention on Climate Change of the United Nations (1992) has as its stated goal to achieve stabilization of greenhouse gas concentrations in the atmosphere at a level that would prevent dangerous anthropogenic interference of the climate system. Concrete goals are not defined, but a widely used exercise is to examine the implications of establishing various ceilings for atmospheric $CO_2$ concentration (for example Wigley *et al.*, 1996; Janssen and de Vries, 1997a+b). A stabilization target of 550 ppmv, a doubling of the pre-industrial level, is a widely used benchmark among climate researchers. Another widely used, but weakly underpinned, climate target is an absolute temperature limit of 2°C above pre-industrial level. This temperature limit can be viewed as an upper limit beyond which risks of considerable damage are expected to increase rapidly (AGGG, 1990).

Despite the many uncertainties surrounding the topic of climate change, there is a need to derive more insight in balancing the risks of a possible climate change and the efforts of reducing greenhouse emissions. From this perspective, this chapter describes a number of illustrative optimization experiments performed with the TARGETS model (Chapter 3). I focus on the energy-cycles part of TARGETS, that is, the energy module which is a system dynamics framework of simulating demand and supply of energy at the global level, and the cycles module which is a global, comprehensive model simulating the consequences of disturbing the element cycles (Den Elzen *et al.*, 1997).

Different sets of assumptions on technological developments are used to explore (global) energy policies which would meet climate change targets. The impact of uncertainties in economic and technological development on possibilities to meet the targets is investigated. Furthermore, the consequences of differences in the timing-pattern of mitigating policies are investigated to illustrate the risks of doing too little or doing too much. This leads to the construction of several hedging strategies which explicitly take account of the possibility of different technology developments in the long run and balance short-term actions, given those long-term uncertainties. Finally, the discussion is broadened by including the acidification problem which is related to climate

94

change by a common cause, $SO_2$ emissions. But first, I briefly consider some methodological questions.

## 6.2    BOTTOM-UP VERSUS TOP-DOWN MODELLING

Top-down and bottom-up modelling techniques have been used to answer the question of how much it would cost to reduce greenhouse gas emissions. Bottom-up modelling requires detailed specification of energy-related and other technologies. In this approach, the present and future probable mix of technologies in each economic sector is described in terms of their costs, inputs and outputs, including emissions. The aggregation level may range from broad economic sectors down to individual plants. The advantage of this approach is that it allows specification of particular technical innovations. On the other hand, it requires huge numbers of technological coefficients and other data, which cannot easily be checked for consistency.

The macro economic top-down approach with embedded input-output coefficients projects future emissions on the basis of neo-classical growth models with production functions, goods and factor markets and utility functions. Usually, optimization of discounted consumption is used to balance the costs and benefits of future activities. The aggregation level may range from simple models of the aggregate economy, through aggregate economic models with a more detailed energy sector, to full dynamic general equilibrium models.

The two types of models were conceived and designed from different disciplines, for different purposes and they lead to quite different conclusions (Wilson and Swisher, 1993). Top-down analysts like Manne and Richels (1992), Nordhaus (1994), Peck and Teisberg (1992), and Burniaux *et al.* (1991) conclude that even moderate steps toward mitigating global warming will be very expensive for society. They support a wait-and-see policy. Bottom-up analysts like Lovins and Lovins (1991) and Williams (1990) conclude that much can be done to mitigate global warming at little or no cost to society and support a take-action-now policy stance. Wilson and Swisher (1993) conclude that the two ways of seeing and describing the world are conceptually incompatible, and the choices between wait-and-see and take-action-now will, therefore, be made on political, rather than scientific grounds.

As the macro economic effects of energy policy are not included in the energy model of TARGETS, it has more components of a bottom-up than a top-down approach. It is, therefore, expected that results will suggest that action-now will be cost-effective. There are various arguments as to why early action is not necessarily costly or why future cost may not be lower (Grubb *et al.*, 1995; Grubb, 1996). First, there are a wide range of options and technologies for limiting emissions, at varying cost levels and with different prospects for cost reductions. Even when 'no-regrets' options, which can be implemented at no net costs, are exhausted, there are a wide range of options, including many cheap ones (Lovins and Lovins, 1991; Grubb, 1996). Second, in macro economic models, technology development occurs usually independent of market conditions. However, this is not a widely accepted hypothesis among economists who work on technology issues. Without early investments, future technology might not be available at lower costs. For example, Arrow (1962) noted that much knowledge is acquired through learning-by-doing and technology development is often induced by market circumstances. Third, technological development tends to be strongly biased towards existing modes, which is called the lock-in effect (Arthur, 1994; Nakicenovic and Grubler, 1991). This causes industries with a large market share to spend large R&D funds along established technological lines to protect their existing positions, thus creating barriers to more advanced and cheaper options. In view of such learning-by-doing dynamics, emission constraints may actually accelerate the development of cost-effective alternatives. Fourth, the inertia of capital stocks in energy-producing sectors makes rapid changes costly. Power generation facilities, petroleum refineries, and so on, have lifetimes of 30-40 years, suggesting that transition to alternatives have to start early. Infrastructural projects may have implications which are even more far-reaching.

## 6.3.  THE MODEL

In this chapter I focus on the energy module of TARGETS which as a stand-alone model is called Targets IMage Energy (TIME) model (de Vries and van den Wijngaart, 1995; de Vries and Janssen, 1996). The starting point for the energy model was to analyse the long-term dynamics of energy conservation and the transition to non-fossil fuels within an integrated modelling framework (de Vries and van den Wijngaart, 1995). The major features of the model are:

(i)    the activity-related demand for heat (in 5 sectors) and electricity, incorporating structural change;
(ii)   autonomous and price-induced change in energy-intensity ('energy conservation');
(iii)  exploration and exploitation dynamics of fossil fuels, including depletion and learning dynamics;
(iv)   price-based substitution of biofuels which are assumed to be subject to learning as well as depletion dynamics;
(v)    electric power generation in thermal power plants, with a non-thermal alternative (nuclear, solar) penetrating the market based on relative costs and learning.

The model builds upon several sectoral system dynamics energy models (Naill, 1977; Sterman, 1981; Davidsen, 1988). The Energy model consists of five submodels: Energy Demand, Electric Power Generation, and the supply of Solid (SF), Liquid (LF) and Gaseous (GF) Fuels (Figure 6.1).

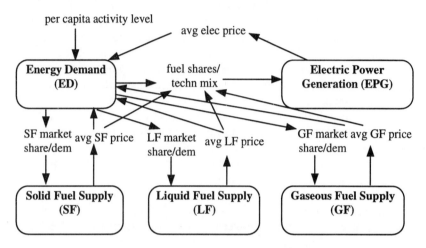

*Figure 6.1: Outline of TIME: the Energy model of TARGETS*

The Energy Demand model (Bollen *et al.*, 1995) calculates the demand of a number of commercial fuels (solid, liquid and gaseous) for five separate economic sectors: residential, commercial/services, industrial, transport and other (including agriculture). The demand for electricity is calculated for the economy as a whole. For each of the sectors, the activities are given exogenously in the form of scenarios. To calculate sectoral energy demand these activities are multiplied by the sectoral energy intensity which is influenced by 1) structural change, 2) autonomous energy efficiency improvement, and 3) price-induced efficiency improvement. The sectoral energy demand is translated into a demand for the different kind of secondary fuels (gaseous, liquid and solid) with a price-based allocation: a type of fuel that becomes relatively expensive will be used less.

The Electric Power Generation model represents the generation of electricity by way of thermal, non-thermal and hydropower generation capital stocks. A distinction is made in base-load and peak load capacity. The thermal generation of electricity uses solid, liquid or gaseous fuel depending on their relative prices. Non-thermal electricity generation is viewed as a competing alternative source, representing nuclear, solar energy or others (not hydropower) which penetrate the market. The costs of non-thermal electricity production depend on learning-by-doing. The expansion of hydropower capacity is based on an exogenous scenario.

The primary energy production models comprise the exploration and exploitation dynamics of fossil fuels (coal, oil and gas). As a substitute for oil and gas alternative fuels, biomass-based fuels are included. Substitution between the various fuels is price-driven. Important features in the Energy Production models are the learning rate and the depletion multiplier. These two factors influence the Capital Output Ratio (COR), which in turn determines production costs. For the alternative (bio)fuels the production costs are determined by learning-by-doing, depletion (of available land) and capital-labour substitution. In the various submodels some more detailed features are present: for example the liquid fuel model contains two types of fuel (heavy and light fuel), and the solid fuel model contains two types of production: underground mined coal and surface mined coal. Important outputs of the primary production models are the actual production of each fuel-type, their prices, investments and reserves remaining.

The global element cycles module of the TARGETS model is used to estimate the impacts of energy policies on the environment and it describes at a highly aggregated level the main element cycles (den Elzen *et al.*, 1997). An essential part of the module is the integration of the element cycles (C, N, S and P) and the interactions between the cycles in the biosphere. Simulated impacts of the perturbed cycles and chemical substances on the global environment are climate change due to changes in concentrations of greenhouse gases and sulphate aerosols, stratospheric ozone depletion due to atmospheric chlorine and bromine concentrations and soil acidification due to deposition of soil-acidifying compounds.

## 6.4   METHODOLOGY

The problem addressed in this chapter is to find out which strategies for $CO_2$ reduction can meet certain targets at the least cost to the economy. As an indicator of costs, the performance of the energy system is measured in energy expenditures, which is defined as the sum of prices for fuels times the production of each fuel, plus the cost of efficiency improvements. Moreover, the energy expenditures are used as a percentage of GWP to compare the levels of expenditures from year to year. This means that the energy expenditures are discounted by the growth rate of GWP. Thus, the objective of the adopted optimization problem is to minimize the energy costs relative to gross world output, aggregated over the period 1995 until 2100. I assume no social discount rate, which means that a fraction of 10% energy expenditures is equal weighted in 2000 as in 2100. However, the investment decisions within the model are based on discounted investment costs with a discount rate of 10%. Given this objective, additional constraints on environmental quality can be investigated, like $CO_2$ concentration and global mean temperature increase constraints.

The decision variables which will be optimized consist of a carbon tax policy and R&D programs in non-thermal electric and biomass fuels. The carbon tax increases prices of fossil fuels and will stimulate energy conservation and penetration of alternative fuels, while the R&D programs stimulate the learning process, so that the production costs decline and the alternative options become more competitive in the energy market.

*Problem Formulation:*

*Minimize energy expenditures as percentage of GWP aggregated for the period 1995-2100.*

*Decision variables:*   *- carbon tax ($/tC),*
                        *- non-thermal electric demonstration program (MWe/yr),*
                        *- bioliquid and biogas demonstration programs (EJ/yr).*
*Constraints:*             *- $CO_2$ Concentration or Temperature Increase.*

Although rule-based investment decisions characterize the system dynamics approach of the model as used, an optimization algorithm is employed to find a carbon tax policy and R&D programs which steer the system to the preferred performance. A genetic algorithm is used to search for (sub)optimal solutions to the previously defined problem. By simulating a competition between scenarios to derive cost-effective ways to meet the policy targets, the algorithm generates new scenarios, leading to a family of scenarios of which the performance increases over time (Goldberg, 1989). Such an algorithm does not lead to better results in sound mathematical search spaces, but outperforms most of its cousins in noisy search spaces (Chapter 5; Goldberg, 1989). While the TARGETS model shows complex non-linear behaviour, such a robust algorithm is desired. Another important aspect is the fact that the genetic algorithm treats the model as a black box, so that it can be used in the original appearance, which is attractive in evolving model versions in integrated assessment modelling. Finally, it is not the primary purpose to find *the* optimal solution, but to find, with the help of an advanced simulation model, a suitable strategy which is as good as can be found in a limited amount of time. The optimization algorithm is, therefore, no more than a tool to search for specific scenarios.

## 6.5   FOUR GLOBAL ENERGY SCENARIOS

In recent years, a number of global long-term energy scenarios have been
published, primarily to support the development of policies with respect to
climate change. In general, these scenarios can be characterized as either
'business-as-usual' (or 'no-intervention', 'reference' or 'Conventional
Wisdom') scenarios or 'policy' scenarios. The scenarios usually capture a wide
range of outcomes with respect to the main reported variables: energy supply
and associated greenhouse gas emissions. The differences between high and low
emission scenarios are either caused by divergent assumptions about economic
and population growth or by assumed changes in energy efficiency and fuel mix
or both. Further differences emanate from the assumptions about new
technologies, fuel prices and policy measures.

In de Vries and Janssen (1996), four scenarios are described which have been
constructed with the energy model of TARGETS. The aim was to investigate
the sets of assumptions underlying published scenarios of the IPCC (1992),
Kassler (1995), and IIASA/WEC (1995) and to see whether the outcomes as
published by the authors of the aforementioned scenarios can be reproduced.
The four scenarios, for which the same population and economic growth
projections are assumed (Figure 6.2), are briefly described here.

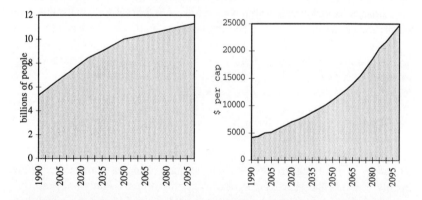

*Figure 6.2: Assumptions about the population and the gross world product
(GWP) per capita for the period 1990-2100.*

The IPCC-IS92a scenario is one of the most widely discussed scenarios in
the context of energy and climate, and is constructed by Pepper *et al.* (1992) for
the IPCC Working Group 3. In many studies, it serves as a reference scenario
against which other options and developments are judged. Its key features are,
from a global long-term perspective (1990-2100), that: (i) GWP grows with an

average of 2.3 per cent a year; (ii) use of secondary fuels and electricity triples; (iii) oil and gas are largely depleted within the next century; (iv) coal is the major substitute; (v) electricity is increasingly generated by non-thermal technologies (NTE), up to 60 per cent by 2100; (vi) biofuels penetrate the market for liquid (BLF) and gaseous (BGF) fuels slowly up to 10 per cent by 2100. Using the characteristics of the IS92a scenario, assumptions within the energy model are constructed in such a way that it simulates the main aspects of IS92a, which I call Conventional Wisdom scenario (CW) (Figure 6.3). The continued use of fossil fuels in the next decades initially leads to a relative decrease in energy expenditures (Figure 6.7), due to efficiency improvements in the use and production of energy. Given the assumption of the IS92a scenario that oil and gas largely deplete during the next century, the CW scenario shows an increase in energy expenditures as a fraction of GWP from 2010 onwards. A difficult transition period follows, in which even more expensive oil and gas are replaced by still costly alternatives (biofuels, NTE). By 2040, this transition is largely over. Energy efficiency improvements lead to a decreasing trend in relative expenditures in the period thereafter. The fossil $CO_2$ emissions in this scenario increase up to about 19 GtC in 2100 (Figure 6.7); the penetration of biofuels leads to a temporary decrease of global $CO_2$ emission in the middle of the next century. According to simulations with the CYCLES module, the global energy scenario leads to a $CO_2$ concentration increasing to about 750 ppmv in 2100 and a global mean temperature increase of about 2.5°C degrees compared to 1900.

The first alternative scenario is based on more optimistic assumptions on technological progress in the supply side of the energy system (Figure 6.4). In this Supply Oriented Technology Change scenario (SOTC), economic growth is the same as in IS92a. Final energy demand closely follows the IS92a scenario, but the supply side differs significantly. New technology will be developed so that non-carbon energy options will become much cheaper and markets will ensure their subsequent introduction. Coal is assumed to be much more expensive, among other things, because subsidies are removed, and coal use is, therefore, much smaller. Because alternatives are introduced in this scenario at lower costs than the CW scenario, energy expenditures as a fraction of GWP will decrease earlier during the transition to alternatives (Figure 6.7). Fossil $CO_2$ emissions steadily decline, leading to a $CO_2$ concentration of 620 ppmv and a temperature increase of 2.3°C in 2100. Due to the reduction of the fossil fuel burning, the cooling effect of sulphate aerosols is lower in the SOTC scenario compared with the CW scenario, leading to a higher increase of the global mean temperature, in the short term.

Using other assumptions on the demand side of the energy system leads to the third scenario: Demand Oriented Technology Change (DOTC) (Figure 6.5). Its key message is that waves of innovative energy efficiency technologies, in combination with shifts in economic activity patterns, make it possible to sustain a 2.3 per cent/yr GDP-growth at much lower energy use and, hence, a lower carbon emission path. Estimated final energy demand is much lower than IS92a, but the supply side assumptions are the same as used for the IS92a scenario. Due to a lower energy demand, the pressure on fossil fuel resources is lower, leading to a lower increase of relative energy expenditures (Figure 6.7). In the DOTC scenario, $CO_2$ emission trajectory is until 2080 lower than in the SOTC scenario. After 2080, the lack of cheap alternatives causes an increase of $CO_2$ emissions, leading to a $CO_2$ concentration of 590 ppmv and a temperature increase of 2.1°C in 2100.

Finally, by combining assumptions of SOTC and DOTC scenarios, the fourth scenario is constructed, which I call Energy System Technological Change (ESTC) (Figure 6.6). Energy production stabilizes at 50 per cent above the present level. Together with the successful introduction of alternatives, fossil fuel use decreases during the next century. Because alternatives can be introduced at low cost and because of large short-term efficiency improvements, relative energy expenditures in this scenario are the lowest of all four scenarios (Figure 6.7). The $CO_2$ concentration stabilizes at 500 ppmv, resulting in a global mean temperature increase of 1.9°C in 2100.

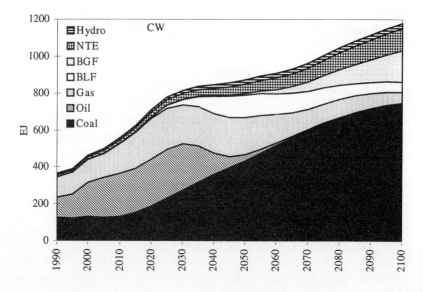

*Figure 6.3: Fuel mix of the energy production for the CW scenario*

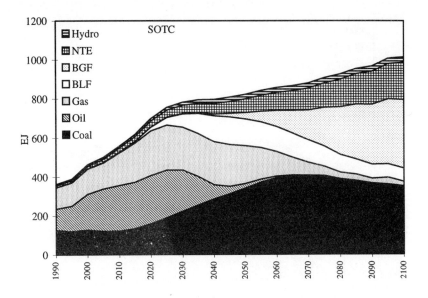

*Figure 6.4: Fuel mix of the energy production for the SOTC*

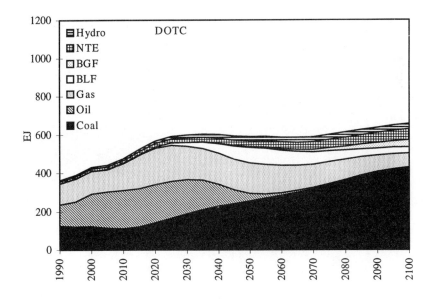

*Figure 6.5: Fuel mix of the energy production for the DOTC*

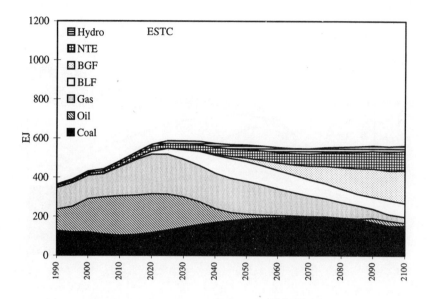

*Figure 6.6: Fuel mix of the energy production for the ESTC*

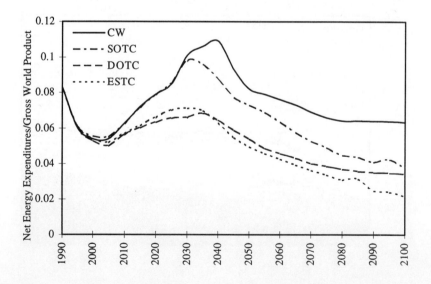

*Figure 6.7a: The net expenditures per GWP projections for the four constructed scenarios*

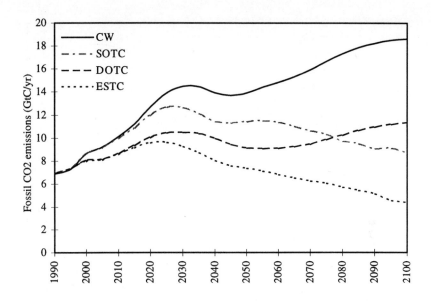

*Figure 6.7b: The fossil $CO_2$ emissions projections for the four constructed scenarios*

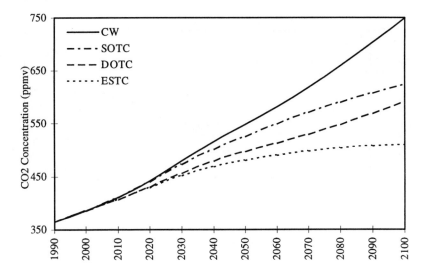

*Figure 6.7c: The $CO_2$ concentration projections for the four constructed scenarios*

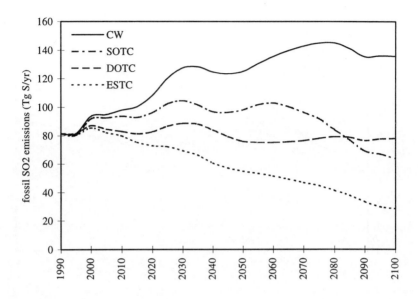

*Figure 6.7d: The fossil SO$_2$ emissions projections for the four constructed scenarios*

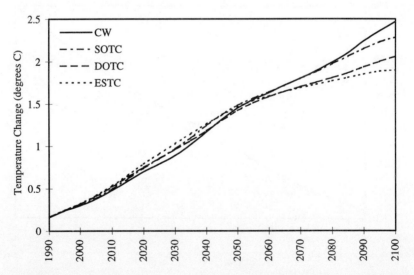

*Figure 6.7e: The global mean temperature projections for the four constructed scenarios*

## 6.6 CLIMATE CHANGE CONSTRAINTS

I used the assumptions for the CW scenario to scan the decision space for $CO_2$ emission reduction strategies which meet a range of possible climate change targets using a genetic algorithm. Thereafter, I will analyse the consequences of the uncertainties in technological and economic developments. An 'optimal' path is defined as a scenario of R&D programs and carbon tax which meets the climate change constraints at the lowest possible costs for the next century, using energy expenditures as a fraction of GWP as a measure for costs.

**$CO_2$ Concentration Target**
A range of $CO_2$ concentration upper levels (not necessary stabilization) is considered from 700 ppmv to 500 ppmv for the next century. A lower $CO_2$ concentration than 500 ppmv by 2100 was not found in the model exercises. Figure 6.8a shows the emission paths of the strategies, which do not look like the traditional macro economic optimal emission paths. The fluctuations of emissions are caused by using a different type of model, where various investment decisions are based on rule-based behaviour of agents with a short time horizon. This may result in strong fluctuations in the 'optimal' decision variables. An optimal result, therefore, represents the utopian case that the 'government' has a perfect knowledge of the system where all private agents (for example oil companies, industry and consumers) make short time decisions. The optimal policy steers the decisions of the private agents in such a way that the long-term objectives of the 'government' will be met.

In all cases, an early reduction of emissions was found to be efficient. An explanation for this is the fact that an early taxation of fossil fuels to stimulate alternative fuels also reduces the energy demand and stimulates price-induced energy efficiency, which has a long-term effect in a lower energy demand. This conclusion conflicts with the conclusions of Wigley *et al.* (1996); I use a kind of bottom-up approach excluding the macro economic feedbacks, while Wigley *et al.* (1996) base their conclusion on macro economic insights, neglecting the insights from bottom-up studies. Note that fossil fuels are not phased out in any scenario because of the assumption of large inexpensive coal resources, and the assumed slow price induced penetration possibilities of alternative fuels.

The resulting $CO_2$ concentration and global mean temperature projections are depicted in Figures 6.8b and c. The reduced warming due to reductions of $CO_2$ emissions is compensated, in global mean terms, by an increased warming due to reductions of $SO_2$ emissions. Therefore, a reduction policy leads to relatively warmer temperatures in the coming 50 years, followed by a reduced temperature increase. The transition to a fossil-low energy supply leads to a reduction of $0.7°C$ in 2100.

The cost-effectiveness of the target strategies is illustrated by plotting the average net energy expenditures as a fraction of GWP as a function of the $CO_2$ concentration in 2100 (Figure 6.9). The results suggest that the first steps in reducing the $CO_2$ concentration can be made with relatively few extra investments in agreement with most bottom-up analyses. Meeting the 550 ppmv concentration targets requires in the CW-scenario an increase of 50 per cent in energy expenditures. In the latter experiment, an immediate carbon tax policy of the fossil energy prices triples in the coming years.

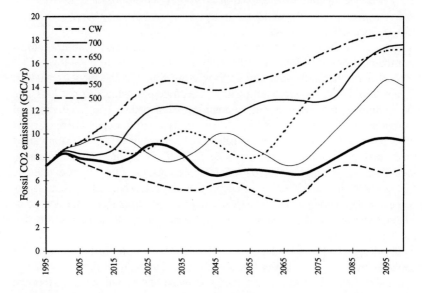

*Figure 6.8a: Emission paths of fossil $CO_2$ for strategies meeting the $CO_2$ concentration targets*

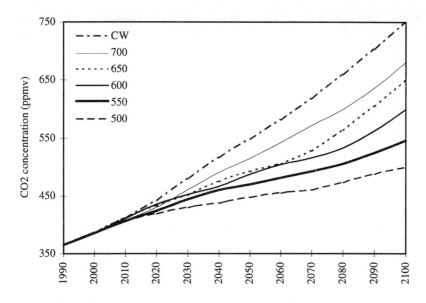

*Figure 6.8b: $CO_2$ concentration projections for strategies meeting the $CO_2$ concentration targets*

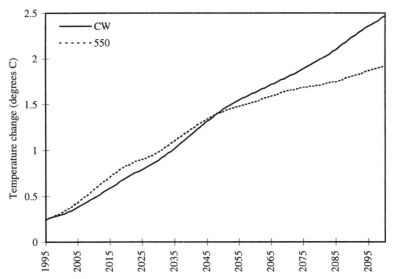

*Figure 6.8c: Global mean temperature change projections for the strategy meeting the 550 ppmv concentration target*

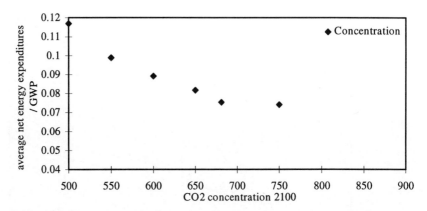

*Figure 6.9: Average net energy expenditures divided by GWP versus the $CO_2$ concentration in 2100 for the strategies meeting the $CO_2$ concentration targets*

**Temperature Target**

I have also explored emission reduction strategies to meet a set of global mean temperature constraints. Due to the reductions of both cooling and warming effects if fossil fuel use decreases, relative costs rise rather strongly for relatively small reductions in the global mean temperature increase (Figure 6.10). Due to the dependence on $SO_2$ reduction policies, which are taken to be exogenous, this result is highly uncertain (see also Section 6.9).

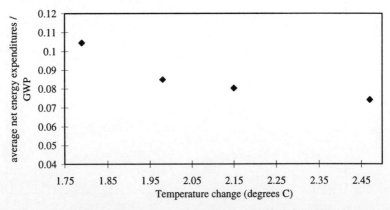

*Figure 6.10: Average net energy expenditures divided by GWP versus the global mean temperature in 2100 for the strategies meeting the global mean temperature targets*

## Technological Transition

The ability to meet environmental constraints in an efficient way greatly depends on the technological development of the energy system, as discussed in the previous paragraphs. Figure 6.11 illustrates this by including the three other scenarios SOTC, DOTC and ESTC within the cost-effectiveness representation. The kind of technological transitions assumed for these scenarios could reduce the $CO_2$ concentrations in 2100 at much lower relative costs. Still, meeting the 550 ppmv $CO_2$ concentration constraint requires additional policy measures except for ESTC. The probability of a technological transition is an important element for energy policy in the short-term, an issue discussed in more detail in the coming paragraphs. First, another highly uncertain and important energy policy issue is discussed: long-term economic growth.

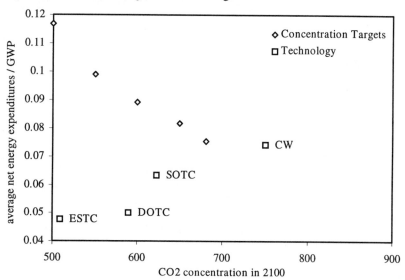

*Figure 6.11: As Figure 6.10 plus three scenarios which include a technological shift*

## Economic Growth

In the four scenarios, an average 2.3 per cent/yr GWP growth between 1990 and 2100 is assumed. An annual growth rate of 3.0 per cent/yr would lead to an average GWP per capita of about 50.000 US90$ in 2100, about twice as high as in the CW scenario. The resulting increase in the use of fossil fuels leads to $CO_2$ emissions of 35 GtC in 2100. Because of high $SO_2$ emissions, the projected global mean temperature increase is only slightly higher. The impact on energy expenditures is shown in Figure 6.12. Higher energy demand leads to higher use of fossil fuels and higher energy prices, which is only partly offset by more energy conservation and greater penetration of renewable energy sources. Hence, higher economic growth reduces the impact of technology improvement on the $CO_2$ emission reduction goals.

Because the interactions between energy policy, economic developments, and technological innovation are not modelled, it is speculative to discuss the consequences for abatement in greater detail.

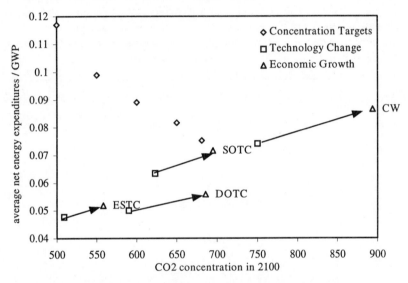

*Figure 6.12: As Figure 6.11 plus four scenarios for which a higher economic growth rate is assumed (=annual average of 3.0 per cent)*

## 6.7   DELAYED RESPONSE

The large uncertainties in economic and technological developments and the large sensitivity of the 'optimal' response in order to meet climate change targets determine the effectiveness and costs of policy options in the short term. What are the risks of implementing abatement policies at a later date? As an illustration, a delayed response strategy is explored in which no active energy policy is assumed to be implemented until 2010. The CW scenario is used to look for an optimal strategy thereafter to meet the 550 ppmv constraint. That is to say that governments initially assume a low impact of emissions on the climate system and/or a rapid technological transition to a non-fossil energy system. After 15 years (1995-2010), a change in insights and facts leads to a new energy policy. In the TARGETS model, such a delayed response leads to higher costs (Figure 6.13 (wait and see); Figure 6.15) because of a rapid and perhaps drastic emission abatement policy just after 2010, in order to meet the $CO_2$ concentration targets. The consequences in terms of global mean temperature change are an accelerated increase from 2010 onwards (Figure 6.14). If the rate of temperature change is viewed rightly as one of the indicators of climate change related risks (Alcamo and Kreileman, 1996), the delayed response strategy of 'wait-and-see' is probably a risky one (Figure 6.16).

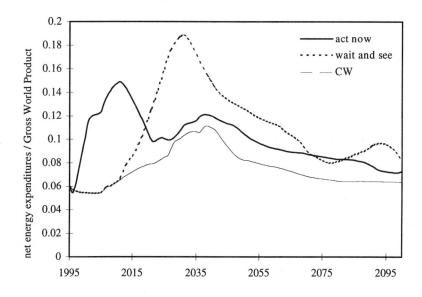

*Figure 6.13: The net energy expenditures per GWP for an optimal path and a delayed response in meeting the 550 ppmv target*

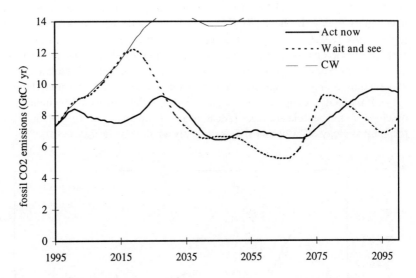

*Figure 6.14: Fossil CO₂ emissions for an optimal path and a delayed response in meeting the 550 ppmv targets*

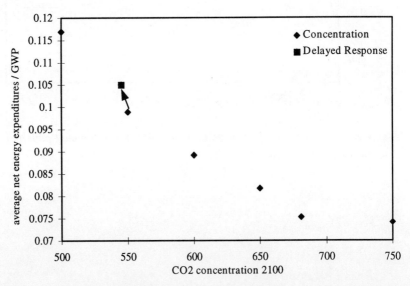

*Figure 6.15: The delayed response leads to a higher level of the average net energy expenditures per GWP*

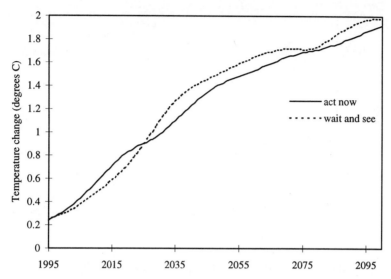

*Figure 6.16: The delayed response leads to a fast increase in the global mean temperature when the policy is implemented*

Next, the reverse situation is examined: implementing strong energy policies which turn out to be unnecessary. Using ESTC scenario assumptions, what are the consequences of an active climate change policy, which is then terminated in 2010?

In the first decades, the relative net energy expenditures increase sharply if the carbon tax and R&D policies are implemented; they fall when they are terminated (Figure 6.17 (act now ESTC)). However, the price-induced efficiency improvements in the first decades induce large energy efficiency improvements, which leads to lower relative expenditures after 2020 than in the ESTC scenario without policy measures. As a result, the aggregated net energy expenditures over the period 1995-2100 are lower in the case of early intervention than without. It is not surprising that the $CO_2$ emissions are lower in case of a short period of active energy policy (Figure 6.18). However, given reference assumptions on the climate system, a no-policy scenario was already sufficient to meet frequently used climate targets (see Figures 6.7). Early emission reduction measures are found to be efficient because early taxation of fossil fuels not only stimulates alternatives, but also stimulates price-induced energy conservation investments.

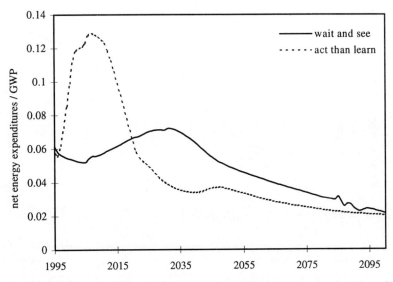

*Figure 6.17: The net energy expenditures per GWP for an optimal path and a delayed response when a technological transition occur*

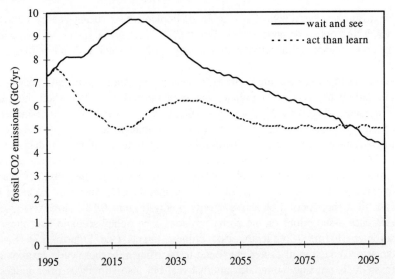

*Figure 6.18: Fossil CO$_2$ emissions for an optimal path and a delayed response when a technological transition occurs*

## 6.8 HEDGING STRATEGIES

The above exercises illustrate the important consequences of first (not) act and then learn. Whether or not technological innovations are accelerated, it makes a difference in determining cost-effective strategies. In this section, I will focus on the short-term policy (until 2010), assuming perfect knowledge of the technological developments in the period thereafter. So, whether a technological progress is accelerated or not, short-term policy is required, given expectations on the likelihood of accelerated technological progress.

Manne and Richels (1992) introduced the concept of hedging as a method to deal with uncertainty in decision making. Instead of assuming perfect knowledge of the system over the coming century, a period of learning is proposed. In the used optimization framework, this means that the objective function $(1-\alpha)f_{CW}+\alpha f_{ESTC}$ is optimized where $\alpha$ is the subjective probability, whether technological developments evolve along ESTC assumption or not (assuming a Conventional Wisdom Scenario). In fact, the decision variables for the two model versions are optimized, given the restriction that the decision variables have the same values until 2010, and may differ thereafter.

The illustrative experiment assumes a 50 per cent chance of accelerated technological development as in the ESTC scenario and a 50 per cent chance of technological development according to the Conventional Wisdom scenario. Carbon tax policy is the dominating factor in reducing emissions. The global level of the model makes me cautious of making explicit statements about carbon tax levels. Nevertheless, in Figure 6.19 the carbon tax levels of the hedging exercise are depicted to illustrate the concept and the different kinds of results compared with top-down models. The carbon tax jumps to high levels at the start of the period. An illustrative nice increasing carbon tax scenario in line with a top-down approach is depicted in the same figure. The difference between the approaches is caused by the fact that the system dynamics approach as adopted in the TARGETS model assumes a current state of the energy system which is not necessary optimal in terms of costs. An additional policy may, therefore, lead to a more efficient energy system and lower costs. In the optimization models adopted by the top-down approach, the current state of the energy system is optimal in terms of cost, and any additional policy (like a carbon tax) will lead to extra costs. Therefore, a smoothly increasing tax level path is found to be optimal in those models.

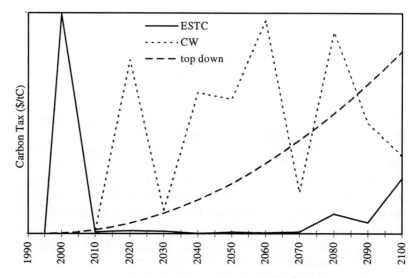

*Figure 6.19: Carbon tax levels for the hedging strategy when after 2010 an optimal level is derived according to the technological developments, and a hypothetical carbon tax path for a traditional top-down approach*

In Figure 6.20, the relative changes, compared with the reference scenario, in the energy mix are shown for both the CW and the ESTC scenario, given a concentration target of 550 ppmv. While the short-term policy for both the CW and the ESTC scenario are the same in the hedging exercise, relative changes do not differ significantly. Due to the fact that carbon intensive energy carriers become more expensive (because of a carbon tax), there will be a reduction of coal, oil and gas. However, because of the inertia of the system, oil will first be substituted for coal, before oil will be replaced by bioliquids. Therefore, the oil use will first increase by 20 EJ, compared to the CW and ESTC scenario (current use about 130 EJ), while the reduction of coal is about 30 EJ compared to the CW and ESTC scenario (current use about 100 EJ). Once the extra production of bioliquids reaches levels of 30 EJ, the use of oil is decreased by about 70 EJ compared to the CW and ESTC scenario. The overall energy use declines relative to the CW and ESTC scenario, due to price induced efficiency improvements.

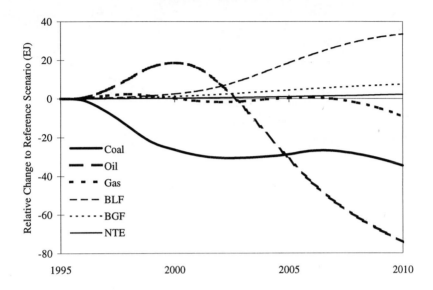

*Figure 6.20: Relative change of the fuel mix compared to the reference scenario in case of hedging uncertainties in technological development*

The emission profiles of the hedging strategy are depicted in Figure 6.21, where the impacts on both CW and ESTC are illustrated. The relative reduction to the 'no-policy' scenario is about the same in both cases of technological development. However, due to a fast technological development, emissions can be reduced compared to the 1995 levels, while in the case of CW assumptions, it is less likely. The relative energy expenditures (Figure 6.22) are only a little bit lower, in case of a fast technological development due to a lower energy use. Not shown in the figures are the pathways after 2010, where an active policy will be required to meet the 550 ppmv concentration target if the technological development follows the CW assumptions, while no active policy is necessary if technological development is fast (ESTC).

The influence of uncertainty on the technological development-paths of the scenarios is analysed by optimizing hedging strategies for a number of different uncertainty estimates on technological transition ($\alpha$). The results show that the uncertainty in technological development does not have a large influence on the active policy. Only when it is certain that a technological transition does not occur ($\alpha = 0$), the energy policy is on an intensified level in 2010, leading to relative high costs. Given the exercises discussed in Section 6.7, these findings are not surprising.

*Modelling Global Change*

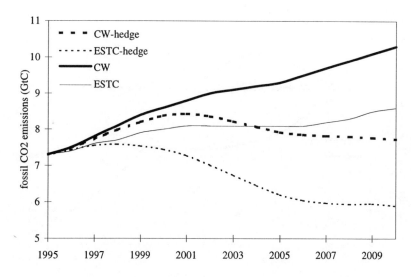

*Figure 6.21: The impact of the hedging strategy on fossil CO₂ emissions for the two considered scenarios*

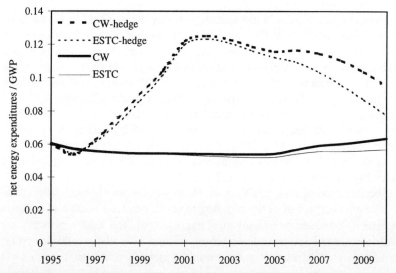

*Figure 6.22: The impact of the hedging strategy on net relative energy expenditures for the two considered scenarios*

To summarize, the hedging exercise tells us that an active policy in the short term has benefits for the long term, irrespective of technological developments. This is caused by the fact that efficiency improvements realized now have their benefits in the decades thereafter, given an unchanged economic development (Janssen and de Vries, 1997). This last remark, however, denotes an important omission of this study, while it does not incorporate impacts of technological development, energy policies and climate change on economic growth levels.

## 6.9   INTEGRATED POLICY FOR CLIMATE CHANGE AND ACIDIFICATION

The recent quantification that sulphate aerosols have, in global mean terms, a cooling effect has complicated the climate change debate. Because $SO_2$ emissions are also an important contributor to acid deposition at the regional level, it is expected that $SO_2$ specific emission reduction measures will be implemented. This reduction may enhance the expected temperature increase, so that an integrated analysis is required for both $CO_2$ and $SO_2$ emission reduction strategies. Ideally, the local impacts of climate change and acidification should be taken into account. Here, I only illustrate likely trade-offs between the two problems. Recent studies of Alcamo *et al.* (1995) and Posch *et al.* (1996) linked the integrated assessment model for climate change IMAGE 2 (Alcamo, 1994) and the integrated assessment model for acid rain RAINS (Alcamo *et al.*, 1990; Foell *et al.*, 1995) to assess the combined impact of sulphate policy on ecosystems in Europe and Asia. In their analysis, they conclude that in Europe the impact of sulphate reduction policies benefits ecosystems more than it harms them, while for Asia there is no clear best policy.

The analysis with TARGETS focuses on the fossil fuel transition and the impact of technological change. Given different futures of the energy system, trade-offs between acid rain and climate change can be identified. The $SO_2$ emissions of the IS92a scenario (IPCC, 1992) are simulated by adjusting the emissions per Joule of fossil fuel (Figure 6.23; reference). Two alternative $SO_2$-specific policies are formulated in relation to acidification policy: an acceleration and a delay of $SO_2$ reduction per Joule of fossil fuels. If no technological transition occurs and no active policy is implemented, both the problems of acidification and climate change intensify (Figure 6.24). All three scenarios lead to higher risks for the world to suffer from the impacts of acidification and climate change, if one consider the risks to be proportional to global projections.

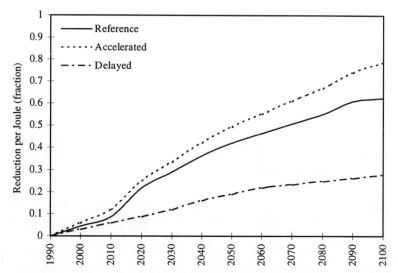

*Figure 6.23: Reduction fractions of SO₂ emissions per Joule of fossil fuel relative to 1990. The reference case meets the IS92a emission scenario, while accelerated and delayed policies represent alternative SO₂ policies*

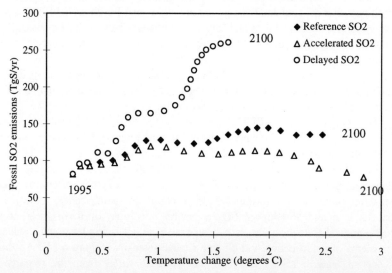

*Figure 6.24: The indicators of global SO₂ emissions and global mean temperature change are used to illustrate trade-offs between acidification and climate change policies in relation to energy use. Given the CW scenario, a delay of SO₂ policy leads to a lower global mean temperature increase*

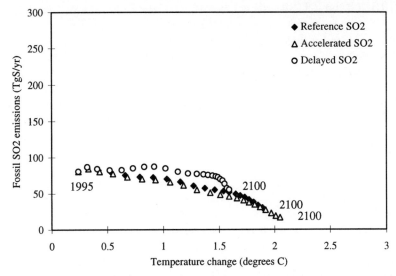

*Figure 6.25: As Figure 6.24 where a technical transition according to the ESTC scenario is assumed*

In the previous paragraphs, the use of fossil fuels may decline in the coming century, due to environmental policies, accelerated technological innovations or delayed economic growth. In Figure 6.25, the technological transition scenario (ESTC) gives an illustration of the integrated impact of reduced fossil fuel use. The $SO_2$ emissions decline for the three $SO_2$ policies, due to an overall reduction in fossil fuel use. However, the projected global mean temperature change is not significantly lower (Figure 6.25). Thus, climate change impacts remain close to the higher risk area, while the impacts of acidification drop to a lower risk area.

## 6.10  CONCLUSIONS

The experiments with the Energy-Cycles part of the TARGETS model as presented in this chapter explore ways to meet climate changes targets and the role of technological change in the energy system. Given conventional wisdom assumptions on technological developments within the energy system, early action is cost-effective to meet long-term climate change policy targets. Even with an accelerated technological change in the energy system, early action is found to be cost-effective in the long run, while an optimal functioning energy system was not assumed for the present situation. Such early action may accelerate the energy savings options, reducing the long-term energy demand, and stimulating alternative fuels as a competitor for fossil fuels.

Important omissions in the current version of the model are the lack of feedback from the energy system to economic growth projections, the highly uncertain relation between economic growth and technological development, the damage costs of climate change impacts and their effect on the economy, absence of regional disaggregation, exclusion of a number of potentially important technical options (among them electric cars, and coal liquefaction and gasification), and the impact of required land for biomass on food production. The performed experiments are, therefore, a first step towards a more comprehensive integrated analysis of the global energy system and its (long-term) consequences on the global system.

Some of these shortcomings will diminish because of a follow-up of this study; the energy model will be disaggregated in the 13 IMAGE 2 regions to improve the IMAGE 2 energy (demand) model (Bollen *et al.*, 1996), including fuel trade and technology transfers.

The experiments show that an optimization-oriented analysis with a complex simulation model such as TARGETS can be performed. Such an approach may help to fill the gap between the process-oriented simulation models and the trend-based optimization models which are both found in the integrated assessment modelling community. I hope that such an approach may help to find insights in the complex problem of global change and yield possible long-term policy strategies.

# 7. The Initial Allocation of Emission Rights

## 7.1 INTRODUCTION

The possibility that increasing atmospheric concentrations of radiatively active gases may lead to significant changes to the global climate confronts society with a problem of unusual complexity. International response to reduce the expected risks of climate change is now considered appropriate by the majority of developed and developing countries. How strong a response is implemented depends on the evaluation of the risks of ecological and economic damage and costs of reducing emissions. As a tool for developing policies which limit the risks and effects of climate change, the Advisory Group of Greenhouse Gases (1990) identified several targets for climate change response strategies to protect the structure and functions of vulnerable ecosystems: for example, limiting the rate and magnitude of the change of temperature or of sea level. Achieving these international targets requires the implementation of policies that will involve reduction of greenhouse gas emissions. Therefore, significant changes in industrial technology are necessary, which may have profound economic impacts on modern societies.

This brings us to another important issue of such an international climate policy: how will the responsibility for future reductions in greenhouse gases be allocated among countries? Regardless of ethical and political considerations, allocation of responsibility will have to take into account differences in economic development, technical know-how and demographic development, which largely characterize the different parts of the world both in the present state, as well as changes in history. In the early development stages, agriculture dominated the economy and emissions have been largely due to deforestation. In the next stages of industrialization and rapid growth of per capita income levels, emissions from the combustion of fossil fuels rapidly surpassed these biotic emissions.

This chapter focuses on the greenhouse gas $CO_2$ which is the most important anthropogenic greenhouse gas which contributes to an enhanced greenhouse effect. Furthermore, I mainly focus on emissions caused by fossil fuel combustion because of its relatively small uncertainties in measurements, its large share of total $CO_2$ emissions (about 70 per cent) (IPCC, 1991), and because several other greenhouse gases are related to the combustion of fossil fuels ($CH_4$, CO, $NO_x$). In this way, I reduce the question of the responsibility of reducing greenhouse gas emissions to the question of the responsibility of reducing fossil $CO_2$ emissions. In the analysis of the historical regional contributions of $CO_2$ emissions, however, I will also indicate the contribution of $CO_2$ emissions due to land use changes.

An important factor supporting the $CO_2$ debate is the uniform mixing property of $CO_2$ in the atmosphere. A ton of carbon emitted in Europe, for example, influences the climate in the same manner as the same ton of carbon emitted in Africa, for example. Recent findings on the local radiative forcing effects of sulphate aerosols (see Chapter 2), however, disturb the uniform mixing argument of trace gases. In the utopian case of sharing the responsibility of greenhouse gases, local climate change impacts, acidification impacts of $SO_2$ emissions and carbon storage of the regional ecosystems should be taken into account. However, in developing a practical and simple tool to support decision making and given the large uncertainties of local impacts, I hold on to the $CO_2$ allocation issue.

A tool designed to stimulate co-operation and to facilitate the implementation of cost efficient measures is the concept of tradable emission permits. Given an initial allocation of emission rights, actors will buy an amount of emission rights, if the costs of buying rights is less than investments to reduce the same amount of emissions in their own country.

One of the main problems in developing an effective international market for emission rights is the initial allocation of greenhouse gas emissions with respect to a constraint free anticipated or desired future. In theory, the optimal allocation of emission reductions depends on the marginal cost levels of the regions which cooperate and will not be influenced by an initial allocation of emission rights. However, the initial allocation will determine the flows of emission rights and, thus, also the assets between regions. Acceptance of an initial emission rights allocation will, therefore, largely depend on the resulting flows of emission permits.

Especially striking is the large 'North-South' disparity in energy-related carbon emissions. Current per capita carbon emissions differ by nearly a factor of 9. The burden of the developing countries is two-fold. The developing countries need to increase their per capita energy consumption in order to improve the quality of life and are also more vulnerable to adverse consequences of climate change. While industrialized countries are in a better position to achieve emissions reductions, they are also in a better situation to respond and adapt to climate change.

I begin this chapter by estimating the historical regional carbon dioxide emissions due to fossil fuel combustion and land use changes and the regional contributions to the past rise in atmospheric $CO_2$ concentration.

An egalitarian way to quantify the historical inequalities between world regions is introduced through the concept of 'emission debt', based on an equal emission quotum per capita per year, irrespective of both the country a person lives in and the generation to which that person belongs. The emission debt is the amount of $CO_2$ which some world regions have emitted over and above what they were allowed to, using an equal emission quotum per capita. The budgets left over can be considered as an egalitarian allocation of regional emission rights.

Finally, an extension of the emission right allocation model is presented which involves the weighting of various criteria (for example size of population, gross national product [GNP], and energy consumption). A perspective-based uncertainty analysis is introduced to evaluate the influence of perspectives on the allocation of emission rights. On one hand, differences in perspectives lead to differences in preferred future developments, while on the other hand, the method for weighting indicators depends, among other things, on those perspectives.

## 7.2 HISTORICAL REGIONAL $CO_2$ EMISSIONS

### 7.2.1 Introduction

In this section, I will examine the regional $CO_2$ emissions over the time period 1800-1990 from fossil fuel combustion (plus minor industrial sources like cement production) and changes in land use, which have been the primary cause of the observed increase in atmospheric $CO_2$. I distinguish the following eleven regions:

- OECD: European Community (EC), Rest of Western Europe (RW.Eur.), OECD East (OECD E.), North America (N.Am.)
- Former centrally planned countries: Eastern Europe (E.Eur.), CIS (former Soviet Union)
- Centrally planned Asia (CPA)
- Other developing regions: Latin America (Lat.Am.), Africa, Middle East (M.East), and South/Southeast Asia (SSEA).

I will first discuss the $CO_2$ emissions caused by fossil fuel combustion, followed by those caused by changes in land use.

### 7.2.2 Fossil Fuel Combustion

The global annual emissions of $CO_2$ from fossil fuel burning and cement manufacturing (although the latter contributes less than 2 per cent) have shown an exponential increase since 1800 (about 3 per cent yearly). There have been major interruptions during the two World Wars, the economic crisis in the 1930s and the oil crisis in the 1970s (see Figure 7.1). The cumulative release of $CO_2$ from fossil fuel use from 1850 to 1987 is estimated at 201 GtC, which is within the uncertainty range of 200 GtC $\pm$ 10 per cent (Marland *et al.*, 1989). In 1989, the global emission was about 6.0 GtC (Marland *et al.*, 1989). There is a main difference, however, between the contribution of the industrialized countries and the developing countries: about 85 per cent of the fossil $CO_2$ emissions in the past has been emitted by industrialized countries, where annual releases reach up to 5 tC per capita (Rotty and Marland, 1986). In most developing countries, $CO_2$ emissions are between 0.3 and 0.6 tC per capita per year, although the relative rate of increase in the developing countries has been much larger during the last few decades (about 5 per cent per year in developing regions in contrast to 1 per cent per year in the industrialized regions during the last decade). The historical $CO_2$ emissions by fossil fuel combustion before 1800 were expected to be small, while the fossil fuel consumption in 1800 was already very low (Mitchell, 1981) and, thus, has a negligible contribution to the observed present atmospheric $CO_2$ increase.

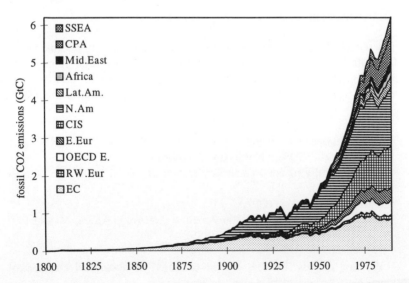

*Figure 7.1: Regional $CO_2$ emissions due to fossil fuel combustion and cement production over the period 1800-1990*

In Table 7.1, the sources are summarized which are used to estimate the fossil $CO_2$ fluxes for the period 1800-1990 (see also Janssen, 1992). The differences between total $CO_2$ emissions calculated from the different sources and global emission data from Watts (1982), Marland and Rotty (1984), Rotty (1987), and Marland *et al.* (1989) are within the uncertainty ranges of about 5 per cent.

*Table 7.1: Sources used in estimating fossil $CO_2$ fluxes*

| Source | Time period | Data | Type of data and period used |
|--------|-------------|------|------------------------------|
| Mitchell (1981, 1982 ,1983) | 1800-1975 | Production and im- and export | Only almost complete source of national data for Europe, Russia, North/Latin America *before 1925* |
| Darmstadter (1971) | 1925-1965 | Consumption | National data for the whole world *1925-1950* |
| Marland et al. (1989) | 1950-1989 | $CO_2$ emissions | National data for the whole world *after 1950* |

### 7.2.3 Land Use Changes

Changes in land use over the past two centuries have caused a significant release of $CO_2$ from terrestrial biota and soils to the atmosphere. About one-third of past $CO_2$ emissions is supposed to have come from land use changes (Siegenthaler and Oeschger, 1987; Houghton and Skole, 1990). During the 19th century, the emissions induced by land use changes were even larger than those from fossil fuels. Europe, North America, and the CIS have caused the largest contributions to emissions through expansion of croplands. In this century, land use changes in temperate and boreal zones have declined, while in tropical regions, they have accelerated. The major cause of this accelerating change in land use is the tremendous pressure from increasing demands of growing populations. Other damaging effects of large-scale changes in land use are the extinction of species, increased erosion, threats to indigenous people, and the destruction of a wide variety of possible important assets.

Estimates of $CO_2$ emissions from land use changes depend on the rates of these changes, the amount of carbon in soil and biomass, rates of oxidation of wood products (through burning or decay) and rates of decay of organic matter in soil. In this study, the *net* release of regional $CO_2$ emissions due to land use changes has been estimated for the period between 1800 and 1990 (see also

Janssen, 1992). The changes in carbon storage are mainly caused by forest clearing, which converts forest to permanent agriculture and pasture. The contributions of selective logging and shifting cultivation are much smaller (Detwiler and Hall, 1988). Rates of land use changes for the period 1800 - 1980 are derived from Houghton *et al.* (1983). The conversion rates are extrapolated for the period between 1980 and 1990. For other than tropical regions, the extrapolated rates are assumed to be the same as in 1980. For the tropical regions, the extrapolated rates of conversion of ecosystems are based on FAO data (FAO, 1988, 1991). As in Houghton *et al.* (1983) I have used a simple bookkeeping model, to calculate the yearly net changes of carbon in ecosystems (Figure 7.2), by using estimates of carbon in soil and vegetation before and after changes in land use (Houghton *et al.*, 1983; 1987).

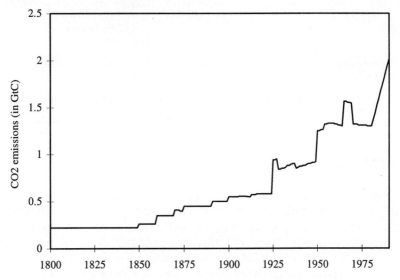

*Figure 7.2: Global CO$_2$ emissions due to land use changes*

Houghton (1991) gives four factors which cause uncertainties in estimating CO$_2$ fluxes from land use changes. First, the rates of deforestation differ, depending on the study, even if they have used satellite imagery. This is largely because of differences in purpose and definitions. Second, large differences in estimates of carbon stocks cause uncertainties. Estimates vary by almost 100 per cent, which may be caused by possible errors in emission factors and differences in surveys (Houghton, 1991). Third, differences are caused by the fate of deforested land or land use. Is deforestation permanent or temporary? Finally, uncertainties are caused by exchanges of biotic CO$_2$ which are not associated with deforestation.

Comparisons of different studies show the large uncertainties in estimating $CO_2$ emissions by land use changes (Table 7.2). The fluxes derived in this study for 1980 are within the uncertainty ranges of other studies, which is also the case in 1990 with fluxes in tropical regions. IPCC (1990) gives an 1850-1986 estimate of $117 \pm 35$ GtC, while the estimate over this period amounts to 107 GtC.

*Table 7.2. Ranges of $CO_2$ emissions (in GtC) from land use changes according to different studies*

| Sources | 1980 World | 1980 Tropical regions | 1980 Temperate and boreal regions | 1990 Tropical regions |
|---|---|---|---|---|
| Moore *et al.* (1981) | 2.2 - 4.7 | 1.8 - 3.8 | 0.4 - 0.9 | |
| Houghton *et al.* (1983) | 1.8 - 4.7 | 1.3 - 4.2 | 0.5 | |
| Houghton *et al.* (1987) | 1.0 - 2.6 | 0.9 - 2.5 | 0.1 | |
| Molofsky *et al.* (1984) | | 0.6 - 1.1 | | |
| Detwiler *et al.* (1985) | | 1.0 - 1.5 | | |
| Detwiler and Hall (1988) | | 0.4 - 1.6 | | |
| Hao *et al.* (1990) | | 0.9 - 2.5 | | |
| Armentano and Ralston (1980) | | | -1.0 - -1.2 | |
| Johnson and Sharpe (1983) | | | -1.6 - -1.9 | |
| Houghton (1991) | | | | 1.1 - 3.6 |
| IPCC (1992) | | | | 1.1 - 2.3 |
| IMAGE 1.0 (1990) | | 1.2 | | 1.3 |
| IMAGE 2.0 (1994) | 0.7 | | | 1.1 |
| TARGETS 1.0 (1996) | 1.9 | | | 2.0 |
| This study | 1.2 | 1.3 | -0.1 | 2.1 |

## 7.3 EMISSION DEBTS

### 7.3.1 Historical Contribution to $CO_2$ Concentration Rise

Until now, industrialized countries have contributed much more to $CO_2$ emissions than the developing world. Using the IMAGE 1.0 model, I have estimated the regional contribution both from fossil fuel use and land use changes, to the increase in the $CO_2$ concentration since 1800. This has been done by calculating the difference in $CO_2$ concentration increase in 1990 with and without the emissions of the region under concern. For these calculations, IMAGE 1.0 had to be adapted in order to start in 1800. For the ocean model, the initial values of the amount of carbon in the surface layers were taken from Goudriaan and Ketner (1984). The deforestation and terrestrial modules are set off in this version for practical reasons. This implies that the $CO_2$ uptake by the terrestrial biosphere through negative feedbacks is not simulated, resulting in an unbalanced carbon budget over the period in the past, and a simulated $CO_2$ concentration of 371 ppmv in 1990 (while the observed value is 354 ppmv). Also the fact that the $CO_2$ fluxes from land use changes in this study are higher than those of IMAGE 1.0 causes a higher concentration level, but this does not affect the relative contributions of the regions.

Figure 7.3 shows the relative contributions of the world regions to the rise in atmospheric $CO_2$ concentration. The contribution from Western Europe and North America amounts to about 40 per cent, for Eastern Europe (including the CIS) about 20 per cent, and OECD East about 5 per cent; the combustion of fossil fuels being the major cause. On the other hand, the relative contributions from Africa, Latin America and South/Southeast Asia (exceeding 30 per cent) are for about 75 per cent due to land use changes.

When the relative part of emissions in the past is used to estimate the regional contribution (for example Krause *et al.*, 1989) to climate change, regions with relatively large emissions in the last century will be overestimated, in contrast to those from which emissions have accelerated in the last few decades. This overestimation is caused by the atmospheric lifetime of $CO_2$, which is about 50 to 200 years (IPCC, 1990).

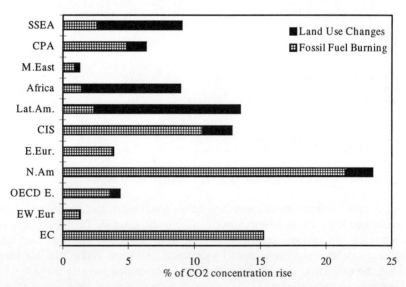

*Figure 7.3: Relative regional contributions to the $CO_2$ concentration rise caused by fossil fuel combustion and land use changes*

## 7.3.2 The Concept

The natural carbon cycle involves exchanges of carbon dioxide between the atmosphere, the oceans, and the terrestrial biosphere which amount to hundreds of billions of tons of carbon per year. The extra anthropogenic emissions associated with land-use changes and fossil fuel combustion appear to be relatively small in comparison with such enormous quantities, but are, nevertheless, believed to account for an imbalance in the carbon cycle, which has caused an increase in the atmospheric $CO_2$ concentration during the past century. Because oceans and terrestrial ecosystems act as sinks for large amount of $CO_2$, only about 40 per cent of the anthropogenic emissions remain in the atmosphere.

If international policy targets based on maximum $CO_2$ concentrations are to be met, anthropogenic emission levels will have to remain below a target level during a specified period. Such policy targets, thus, imply that only a limited amount of anthropogenic $CO_2$ emission may be permitted during a fixed period, an amount referred to as 'the global $CO_2$ emission budget'. This budget takes account of historical, as well as projected future contributions.

The global fossil $CO_2$ budget (GB) over the period $T_B$ (base year) to $T_E$ (expiry year) is defined as the total of regional fossil $CO_2$ emissions ($e(t,r)$) emitted, or considered to be permissible during that period. This amount is equivalent to the cumulative historical $CO_2$ emissions (from $T_B$ to $T_R$, where the latter denotes the reference year) and future, scenario-dependent $CO_2$ emissions (from $T_R+1$ to $T_E$):

$$GB = \sum_r [ \sum_{t=T_B}^{T_R} e_{his}(t,r) + \sum_{t=T_R+1}^{T_E} e_{scen}(t,r)] \tag{7.1}$$

where r = region and t = time; his = historical, scen = scenario.

If the world community is to accept constraints on $CO_2$ emissions, how can future $CO_2$ emission rights be allocated to the world regions? In the last section, it was shown that the $CO_2$-concentration increase in the past is largely caused by industrialized regions, while Figure 7.4 shows that historical $CO_2$ emissions per capita are unevenly divided among the world regions. In this section, I will try to quantify the fact that some regions have emitted more $CO_2$ in the past than they were allowed to by equity rules. This so-called emission debt is defined here in terms of population levels.

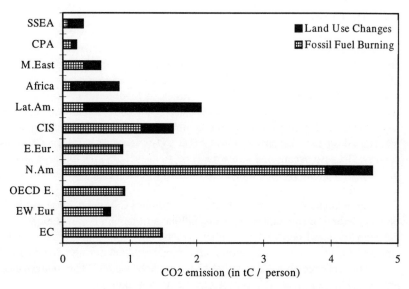

*Figure 7.4: Average emission per capita for the period 1800-1990. Regional differences exist in sources and levels of emissions*

Although the results in this section are based on population levels, several other indicators for allocating future emissions to regions can be considered. Actually, the process of finding acceptable indicators as a base for allocation of payments or permits is now gaining momentum, as part of the attempts to set up a global climate agreement. Indicators for such an allocation could be based on present and past emissions, area, population levels (equal allocation per capita carbon budget), state of the economy (equal allocation per unit GNP budget), energy intensity or a combination of these factors (Krause *et al.*, 1989; Grubb, 1989; Grübler and Fujii, 1991; Grubb and Sebenius, 1992; Den Elzen *et al.*, 1992).

Because the per capita quotum approach[1] is conceptually attractive and computationally simple, it is used here for quantifying the egalitarian thesis that some regions have emitted more in the past than they were allowed to. The per capita approach can be translated into the following equity ideal for the allocation of the emissions: *Every human being has an equal emission quotum per year irrespective of both the region one lives in and the generation one belongs to* (Grübler and Fujii, 1991). This quotum is denoted by $Q_{cap}$ (in tC per capita per year).

The equal emission quotum is dependent on the target imposed. The global budget approach considers the atmosphere as a 'sink' which can absorb only a limited amount of carbon dioxide. Then $Q_{cap}$ can be calculated by dividing the total carbon budget by the total number of person years in this period:

$$Q_{cap} = \frac{GB}{\sum\limits_{r}\left(\sum\limits_{t=T_B}^{T_R} pop_{his}(t,r) + \sum\limits_{t=T_R+1}^{T_E} pop_{scen}(t,r)\right)} \qquad (7.2)$$

where $pop_{his}(t,r)$ and $pop_{scen}(t,r)$ are the historical and future regional population size, respectively, in year t for region r.

I will now define the regional emission debt as the difference between the amount of $CO_2$ allowed to be emitted by the regional population [pop(t,r) in $10^9$ persons], based on the equal quotum per capita [$Q_{cap}$ in tC per (cap * year)] and the actually cumulated regional emissions in the past [em(t,r) in GtC per year]. The emission debt in $T_R$ [ED(r) in GtC] is described in mathematical terms:

$$ED(r) = \sum_{t=T_B}^{T_R} em(t,r) - Q_{cap} \cdot \sum_{t=T_B}^{T_R} pop(t,r) \qquad (7.3)$$

Note that I have assumed that the emission data is gained by measurements of regional emissions and not by regional end-use of production. Ignoring the transactions between regions may bias the results. However, for lack of sufficiently reliable data, especially those related with land use changes, I am forced to use the regional emissions.

How should the remaining global carbon budget be distributed over the different regions, taking into account past and present emissions of $CO_2$? Here I focus on a simple allocation rule for the remaining carbon budget based on population size. The future $CO_2$ emission rights [ER(r)] consist of the $CO_2$ emissions allowed to be emitted in the period $T_R+1$ to $T_E$, based on the equal emission quotum minus the emission debt built up in the past:

$$ER(r) = Q_{cap} \cdot \sum_{t=T_R+1}^{T_E} pop_{scen}(t,r) - ED(r) \qquad (7.4a)$$

This can also be written as the regional carbon budget minus the historical emissions:

$$ER(r) = Q_{cap} \cdot \left(\sum_{t=T_B}^{T_R} pop_{his}(t,r) + \sum_{t=T_R+1}^{T_E} pop_{scen}(t,r)\right) - \sum_{T_B}^{T_E} e_{his}(t,r) \qquad (7.4b)$$

### 7.3.3 The Results

Three scenarios of the IPCC (1992) (see also Table 7.4) are used to define a range of global carbon budgets. Remaining budgets for the scenarios are listed in Table 7.3 for both total $CO_2$ emissions and for fossil $CO_2$ emissions only. These budgets are between 710 GtC and 2226 GtC. Krause *et al.* (1989) derived a global remaining budget of about 300 GtC for fossil $CO_2$ emissions based on a 400 ppmv $CO_2$ concentration target, including fossil fuel $CO_2$ emissions between 1985 and 2100.

The budgets are significantly higher than various studies propose as sustainable futures (for example Krause *et al.*, 1989; Den Elzen *et al.*, 1992), although IS92C leads to a stabilization of projected temperature change of 2°C above 1990 (Den Elzen, 1993).

*Table 7.3: Carbon budgets for the used IPCC 92 scenarios and $Q_{cap}$ values [in tC per(cap \* year)].*

| Scenario | Remaining budget (GtC) | | $Q_{cap}$ [tC per (cap • year)] Tot. | $Q_{cap}$ (tC per (cap • year)] Ind. |
|---|---|---|---|---|
| | Tot.[a] | Ind.[b] | | |
| IS92 A | 1543 | 1458 | 1.36 | 1.21 |
| IS92 C | 788 | 710 | 0.97 | 0.80 |
| IS92 E | 2226 | 2141 | 1.86 | 1.70 |

[a] Tot.: $CO_2$ emissions from fossil fuel use and land use changes.
[b] Ind.: $CO_2$ emissions from fossil fuel use.

Based on this per capita quotum, the global carbon budget for the period 1800 to 2100 under the IS92C scenario of about 1130 GtC corresponds with a permitted emission per capita of 0.97 tC. Under the high emission IS92 E scenario, $Q_{cap}$ amounts to 1.86 tC.

There is no global emission debt from past to future generations using the per capita quotum of the IPCC scenarios. In Den Elzen *et al.* (1992), smaller carbon budgets are used, based on more severe climate targets, so that a global emission debt would exist so that we and our ancestors have reduced emission quota for our descendants.

The resulting regional emission debts in the different scenarios are presented in Figure 7.5. The industrialized regions are, in most cases, highly indebted, in contrast to Asian regions. Excluding land use changes leads to a large decline of emission debts in most developing regions, which in all cases have an emission credit (Figure 7.6). The industrialized regions, however, have an emission debt for almost all the budgets.

*Table 7.4: Summary of assumptions in the IPCC 1992 alternative scenarios*

| Scenario | Population | Economic Growth | Energy Supply | Other | CFCs |
|---|---|---|---|---|---|
| IS92a | World Bank 1991 11.3 B by 2100 | 1990-2025: 2.9 % <br> 1990-2100: 2.3 % | 12,000 EJ Conventional Oil 13,000 EJ Natural Gas Solar costs fall to $0.075/kWh 191 EJ of biofuels available at $70/barrel | Legally enacted and internationally agreed controls on SOx, NOx and NMVOC emissions | Partial compliance with Montreal Protocol. Technological transfer results in gradual phase out of CFCs also in non-signatory countries by 2075 |
| IS92b | World Bank 1991 11.3 B by 2100 | Same as 'a' | Same as 'a' | Same as 'a' plus commitments by many OECD countries to stabilize or reduce $CO_2$ emissions | Global compliance with scheduled phase out of Montreal Protocol |
| IS92c | UN Medium Low Case 6.4 B by 2100 | 1990-2025: 2.0 % <br> 1990-2100: 1.2 % | 8,000 EJ Conventional Oil 7,300 EJ Natural Gas Nuclear costs decline by 0.4% annually | Same as 'a' | Same as 'a' |
| IS92d | UN Medium Low Case 6.4 B by 2100 | 1990-2025: 2.7 % <br> 1990-2100: 2.0 % | Oil and gas as 'c' Solar costs fall to $0.065/kWh 272 EJ of biofuels available at $50/barrel | Emission controls extended worldwide for CO, NOx, NMVOC and SOx. Halt deforestation. Capture and use of emissions from coal mining and gas production and use | CFC production phase out by 1997 for industrialized countries. Phase out for HCFCs |
| IS92e | World Bank 1991 11.3 B by 2100 | 1990-2025: 3.5 % <br> 1990-2100: 3.0 % | 18,400 EJ Conventional Oil Gas same as 'a' Phase out nuclear by 2075 | Emission controls (30% pollution surcharge on fossil energy) | Same as 'd' |
| IS92f | UN Medium High Case 17.6 B by 2100 | Same as 'a' | Oil and gas same as 'e' Solar costs fall to $0.083/kWh Nuclear costs increase to $0.09/kWh | Same as 'a' | Same as 'a' |

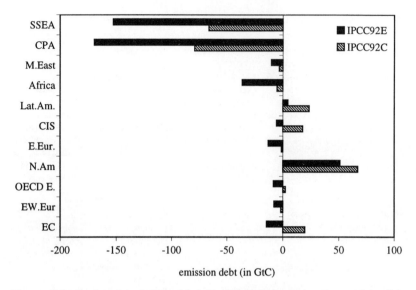

*Figure 7.5: Regional emission debts for fossil fuel combustion and land use changes 1800-1990, using different carbon budgets*

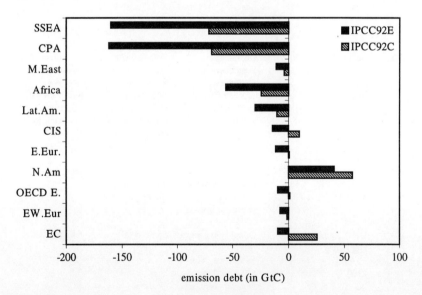

*Figure 7.6: As Figure 7.5 without land use changes*

After having estimated the regional emission debts, the emission rights left for the different world regions can now be calculated. Figure 7.7 summarizes the emission rights per capita per year based on different carbon budgets. Almost all industrialized regions and Latin America have emission rights per capita, which are all lower than present emission levels. North America has emitted more $CO_2$ in the past 191 years than was allowed for the whole period of 301 years and ends up with negative emission permitted for all scenarios. Most of the developing regions, however, have emissions permitted per capita which are higher than the emission rights of industrialized regions, but in some cases lower than their present emission levels. This means that in a world striving towards sustainable development and equity, emission levels per capita are not allowed to increase, not even in developing regions.

When considering only fossil $CO_2$ emissions, the emissions permitted per capita in developing regions are somewhat higher than for land use changes, but they will never reach the present emission levels of the industrialized regions (Figure 7.8). If developing regions are empowered and supported to continue their development towards higher standards of living, large technological improvements will have to be realized.

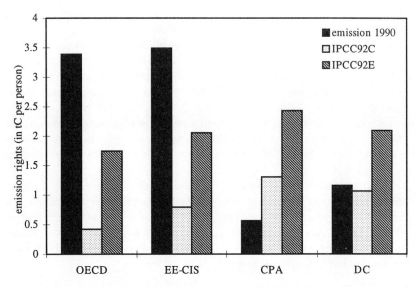

*Figure 7.7: Regional emission rights per capita for fossil fuel combustion and land use changes for the period 1991-2100, using different carbon budgets*

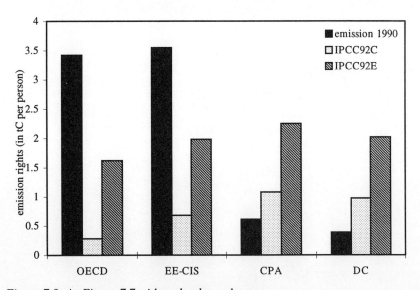

*Figure 7.8: As Figure 7.7 without land use changes*

## 7.4 EMISSION RIGHTS

### 7.4.1 The Allocation Model

The distributions in the last section are based on a rather egalitarian criteria: population size. A more sophisticated allocation model including various allocation criteria will be presented in this Section. Furthermore, I will introduce a perspective-based analysis to quantify subjective judgements in order to scan the range of possible allocations.

Since fossil $CO_2$ (that is $CO_2$ from fossil fuel combustion) is the main contributor to anthropogenic $CO_2$ emissions (about 70-90 per cent) I will consider only fossil $CO_2$ emissions. Target scenarios adopted as policy by the world community imply that only a restricted amount of $CO_2$ may be emitted in the future. I define regional emission rights (ERs) for the future as the fractions per region (FRs) of the global $CO_2$ budget, that is permitted emissions in region r during the entire period under consideration minus the historical $CO_2$ emissions:

$$ER(r) = FR(r) \cdot GB - \sum_{t=T_B}^{T_R} e_{his}(t, r) \qquad (7.5)$$

The regional fraction (FR) depends on a combination of various criteria. For simplicity's sake, I will first present the case in which fossil $CO_2$ emission rights are allocated according to the single criterion of population size. Thereafter, the approach is extended to enable a weighted cluster of criteria to be incorporated in the model.

If every person living in the period between $T_B$ and $T_E$ is credited with equal annual fossil $CO_2$ emissions, the annual regional fraction can be expressed as follows:

$$fr(t, r)_{pop} = \frac{pop_{his}(t, r)}{\sum_r [\sum_{t=T_B}^{T_R} pop_{his}(t, r) + \sum_{t=T_R+1}^{T_E} pop_{scen}(t, r)]} \quad \text{for } t \leq T_R \qquad (7.6a)$$

$$fr(t, r)_{pop} = \frac{pop_{scen}(t, r)}{\sum_r [\sum_{t=T_B}^{T_R} pop_{his}(t, r) + \sum_{t=T_R+1}^{T_E} pop_{scen}(t, r)]} \quad \text{for } t > T_R \qquad (7.6b)$$

where:

$pop_{his}$ = population during the historical period;
$pop_{scen}$ = scenario-dependent population projections for a future period.

The total regional fraction $FR_{pop}(r)$ is the sum of the annual regional fractions, $fr_{pop}(t,r)$:

$$FR_{pop}(r) = \sum_{t=T_B}^{T_E} fr_{pop}(t,r) \qquad (7.7)$$

To incorporate time preference, the population size in the past and future will be discounted by introducing the discount parameter, $\delta$, where it goes without saying that discounting past responsibility differs from discounting future projections. However, for simplicity's sake I assume that both past and future developments can be discounted by the same discount parameter $\delta$.

$$fr(t,r)_{pop} = \frac{pop_{his}(t,r) \cdot \delta^{T_R-t}}{\sum_r \left( \sum_{t=T_B}^{T_R} pop_{his}(t,r) \cdot \delta^{T_R-t} + \sum_{t=T_R+1}^{T_E} pop_{scen}(t,r) \cdot \delta^{t-T_R} \right)} \quad \text{if } t \leq T_R$$

$$(7.8a)$$

$$fr(t,r)_{pop} = \frac{pop_{his}(t,r) \cdot \delta^{t-T_R}}{\sum_r \left( \sum_{t=T_B}^{T_R} pop_{his}(t,r) \cdot \delta^{T_R-t} + \sum_{t=T_R+1}^{T_E} pop_{scen}(t,r) \cdot \delta^{t-T_R} \right)} \quad \text{if } t > T_R$$

$$(7.8b)$$

In order to incorporate a cluster of criteria rather than considering the 'egalitarian' criterion of population size alone, the regional fraction will be extended to a weighted value of allocation indicators. Among such indicators are criteria such as: present and past emissions, population levels, state of the economy, energy use, and land area, or a combination of these (Krause *et al.*, 1989; Grubb, 1989; Grübler and Fujii, 1991; Grubb and Sebenius, 1992; Rose, 1992). In this section, the regions have been allocated a restricted fossil $CO_2$ emission budget based on a weighted combination of the indicators: population size (per capita equity), GNP (economic affluence) and primary energy use (efficiency), because these are the main underlying factors associated with an increase in fossil $CO_2$ emissions.

$$FR(r) = \alpha_1 \cdot FR_{pop}(r) + \alpha_2 \cdot FR_{gnp}(r) + \alpha_3 \cdot FR_{energy}(r) \qquad (7.9)$$

where:
$\alpha_1$ = fractional weight of population
$\alpha_2$ = fractional weight of GNP
$\alpha_3$ = fractional weight of energy use
and where: $\alpha_1 + \alpha_2 + \alpha_3 = 1$.

Thus, the allocation of a $CO_2$ emission budget for the period $T_R$ to $T_E$ to an important degree depends, in modelling terms, on the parameters $\alpha_1$, $\alpha_2$, $\alpha_3$, $\delta$ and $T_B$. The preferred values of the parameters can vary according to the perspective(s) upon which subjective judgements are based.

### 7.4.2 Emission Rights Allocation Based on Uniform Parameter Distributions

In this section, an approach is introduced which is designed to generate statistical distributions for regional fossil $CO_2$ emission rights. For each parameter of the allocation model, an uncertainty interval can be found. The parameters $\alpha_i$ are assumed to vary between 0 and 1. Because the sum of the set of $\alpha_i$ equals one, they form a simplex of possible $\alpha_i$ values. The interval for the discount parameter $\delta$ is assumed to be [0.9, 1.0]. The base year ($T_B$) varies between 1800, which is taken as the beginning of the industrial revolution, and $T_R$.

It is to be expected that, having adopted different perspectives, actors will express dissimilar preferences for parameter values. In order to estimate the influence of these differing preferences, I assume that they can be represented by a distribution plotted in terms of an uncertainty interval. Such distributions represent actors' preferences for parameter values, and are used because I assume that policy makers' preferences are imprecise and distributed around a preferred value. This procedure enables the fuzziness of the preferences to be taken into account. For the purposes of this section, I assume that preferred values for $\delta$ and $T_B$ are uniformly distributed on the uncertainty interval. The $\alpha_i$ values are uniformly distributed on the simplex. If I may assume that all actor preferences are uniformly distributed, allocations which I subsequently derive can be used to estimate the range of preferred allocations.

The reference scenario (IS92A) published by the IPCC (1992) has been used to derive distributions of regional emission rights.[2] The allocated global emission budget addresses emissions in the period 1991 ($T_R$=1990) to $T_E$. An extensive range[3] of regional emission rights was obtained by running the allocation model using different parameter values for each run. The parameter values are derived from a uniform distribution. The cumulative 'probability' of regional emission rights for the period 1991-2000 is depicted in Figure 7.9. The emission rights accruing to the industrialized regions (OECD and Eastern Europe and the Community of Independent States [EE-CIS]) are, in about 90 per cent of the cases, between -30 and 30 GtC and between -5 and 10 GtC, respectively. For Centrally Planned Asia (CPA), the 90 per cent confidence interval lies between 5 and 20 GtC and, in the case of the developing countries (DC), between 25 and 70 GtC. This implies that if perspectives are uniformly distributed, and scenario IS92A is adopted, the emission rights for the period 1991-2000 lie within the above bounds.

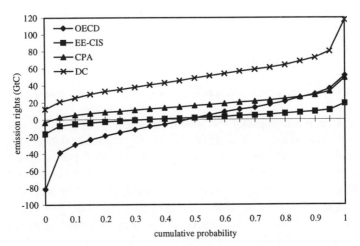

*Figure 7.9: Cumulative probability of regional $CO_2$ emission rights using a uniform distribution for the parameter values (1991-2100)*

Figure 7.10 depicts the relative regional shares of the mean values of the global fossil $CO_2$ emission budget for several values of the time horizon $T_E$. A remarkable result is that the relative distribution is stable after 2050, an effect mainly caused by the impact of historical emissions reducing the emission rights of industrialized regions, where short-term horizons are concerned.

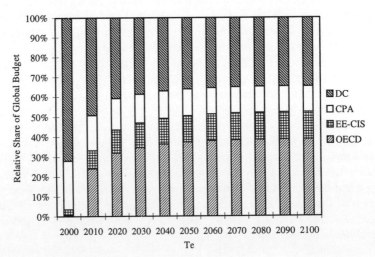

*Figure 7.10: Relative regional share of the global $CO_2$ emission budget for different values of $T_E$*

### 7.4.3 Emission Rights and Perspectives

**Perspective-based parameter distributions**

The aim in this section is to quantify the influence of perspectives on the allocation of fossil $CO_2$ emission rights; therefore, I need a distribution function for the preferences of parameter values (see Section 4.3 for a discussion of perspectives).

As an introduction to the perspective-based parameter distribution functions, I will discuss the choices for the values of $\alpha_1$, $\alpha_2$ and $\alpha_3$. In Section 7.4.2, preferences of a group were assumed to be uniformly distributed across the entire simplex. In this section, however, I will assume that actors with different perspectives prefer certain parameter values to a certain degree of preference. For simplicity's sake, I assume that egalitarians base their allocation on population size (equity per capita), individualists on GNP (economic affluence), and hierarchists on a mixture of criteria (compromise). For the egalitarians (E), the preferred area of parameter values of $\alpha_i$, therefore, tends towards a high value of $\alpha_1$, *vis-à-vis* other perspectives (Figure 7.11).

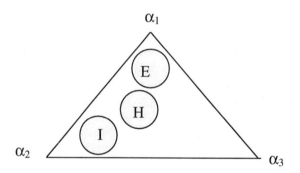

*Figure 7.11: Preferred parameter values of $\alpha_1$, $\alpha_2$ and $\alpha_3$ in the perspective simplex. E=Egalitarian, I = Individualist and H = Hierarchist*

Preferences of a group of actors for a particular value of a parameter are described in terms of a distribution function. The distribution function reflects the preference for certain parameter values and is assumed to be a truncated normal distribution function (Equation 7.10). This function has been selected for its approximate symmetry and the fact that it can be represented by two parameters. Of course, selecting this particular distribution function is somewhat arbitrary and several other functions might have been used. The parameter value for which the density function reached a peak value ($\sigma_1$) is called the preferred value. The variance can be influenced by the parameter $\sigma_2$, which can be interpreted as expressing the degree of preference. Here, a higher value of $\sigma_2$ reduces the variance of the preference and, therefore, represents a more pronounced preference (see Figure 7.12).

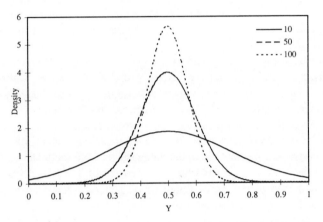

*Figure 7.12: The density of a truncated normal distribution function with $\sigma_1$ =0.5, for the values of $\sigma_2$*

The general density function $f(x)$ of the parameters in the uncertainty range [a,b] can now be written as follows:

$$f(x) = \frac{1}{c} \cdot e^{-\sigma_2 \cdot (\frac{x - \sigma_1}{b - a})^2} \quad \text{for } a \leq x \leq b$$

where :                                   (7.10)

$$c = \sqrt{\frac{\pi}{4 \, \sigma_2} \cdot (1 - e^{-\sigma_2 \cdot (\frac{a - \sigma_1}{b - a})^2})} + \sqrt{\frac{\pi}{4 \, \sigma_2} \cdot (1 - e^{-\sigma_2 \cdot (\frac{b - \sigma_1}{b - a})^2})}$$

Since the values for $\sigma_1$ and $\sigma_2$ are not known for the various perspectives, the results presented here, based on parameter distributions, are informed by my 'heuristic' attribution of values to perspectives. The results should be interpreted as representing an illustration of the model. The chosen approach, thus, results in somewhat stereotypical perspectives which, nevertheless, demonstrate the implications of differences in perspectives. Moreover, the method can be regarded as an uncertainty analysis in which values of parameters are varied according to the characteristics of perspectives. I will now briefly discuss the preferred values of the distribution function for each perspective as given in Table 7.5. Most of this material is based on Schwartz and Thompson (1990) (see Section 4.3).

*Egalitarians:* The emphasis placed on equality by egalitarian actors implies that each individual is allowed to emit an equal amount of fossil $CO_2$ emissions annually and will, therefore, presumably allocate rights according to population sizes (high value of $\alpha_1$). This preference for equality strongly reduces the preference for allocation on the basis of GNP and energy consumption. Egalitarians prefer a long-term horizon for policy making, as well as being keen to take account of historical inequality. Therefore, high values of $T_R$-$T_B$ and $T_E$-$T_R$ are preferred. Because all past and future human beings are considered equal, discounting is not regarded as appropriate.

*Hierarchists:* Hierarchists are assumed to be concerned with maintaining institutions and are, therefore, deemed to prefer a balanced mixture of the allocation criteria regarding energy use, GNP and population. The main concern of hierarchists is to maintain the currently functioning system, which influences their attitude towards the distinction between the shorter and longer term. Climate change discussions are assumed to focus on a long-term period of 40 years for both past and future horizons. Finally, I assume a 2 per cent discount rate ($\delta$) for the past and future; this being a moderate pure rate of 'social time preference'.

*Individualists:* Individualists may prefer an allocation based on skills, as measured here by economic output (GNP), and will, therefore, prefer a higher value of $\alpha_2$. Furthermore, $\alpha_1$ and $\alpha_3$ are assumed to be equally weighted, because they are both important inputs for the economic system. The time horizon adopted by individualists tends to be rather short, because they assume that future generations will take care of themselves. Furthermore, they tend to prefer a higher discount rate than the hierarchists, because of their shorter time horizon.

The indicative estimated values of $\sigma_1$ for each of the various perspectives are given below. Because the value of $\sigma_2$ is unknown, it is assumed to be 50 for all parameters, reflecting a medium degree of preference (see also Figure 7.12).

*Table 7.5: Estimated parameter values ($\sigma_1$), best guesses, of the allocation function for various perspectives*

| parameters | individualist | hierarchist | egalitarian |
|---|---|---|---|
| $\alpha_1$ (population) | 0.1 | 0.333 | 0.8 |
| $\alpha_2$ (GNP) | 0.8 | 0.333 | 0.1 |
| $\alpha_3$ (energy use) | 0.1 | 0.333 | 0.1 |
| $\delta$ (discount rate) | 0.95 | 0.98 | 1.0 |
| $T_R$-$T_B$ (past time horizon) | 0 | 40 | 100 |
| $T_E$-$T_R$ (future time horizon) | 10 | 40 | 100 |

**Perspectives-based scenarios**
Scenarios for future development, which determine the size of the overall $CO_2$ emission budget, will depend, among other things, on the degree of dominance of perspectives. In view of their attitude towards nature conservation, egalitarians can be expected to prefer lower emission levels than individualists. I assume that the IPCC scenarios (IPCC, 1992; see also Table 7.4) can be used in a first attempt in representing different perspective scenarios[4] (utopias). Following on Rayner (1991), I distinguish three scenarios characterized by prevention (egalitarian), control (hierarchist), and adaptation (individualist).

*Egalitarians:* From the viewpoint of egalitarians as defined here, it is morally wrong to distort natural processes. Therefore, a preventive response strategy for a human-induced climate change is preferred. In order to relieve anthropogenic pressure on the environment, growth of economic output should be zero, or very modest at least. Furthermore, the rate of population growth will have to decrease. These conditions will result in a low growth of energy use, and especially of fossil fuel consumption. Among the IPCC scenarios, IS92c best meets the above requirements, since it results in a temperature increase of 2°C in 2100 (relative to 1900). This is just the minimum target for a low-risk future (AGGG, 1990).

*Hierarchists:* Hierarchists seek to balance economic growth and environmental quality. Such 'sustainable' development can be achieved by means of careful stewardship aimed at keeping economic growth within the limits of what nature will allow. A modest degree of economic growth is generally preferred in view of the need to feed a growing population. Developments in energy use are determined by technical innovations and the recognition of the exhaustible nature of non-renewable (energy) resources. The IPCC's IS92a scenario, to some extent, shares these assumptions and is, therefore, chosen as the hierarchist scenario.

*Individualists:* Individualists argue that it is morally wrong to restrict economic growth. Nature is assumed to be robust and, even in the event of a human-induced climate change, new opportunities might well be created which could stimulate economic behaviour. Because (energy) resources are regarded as inexhaustible and nature is expected to be robust, no restrictions on population growth and energy use are set. The IPCC's IS92e scenario is, therefore, the one which will here represent the individualist.

**Distribution of emission rights**

Given the perspective-based parameter distribution functions and using perspective-dependent future scenarios as defined above, a utopian distribution of emission rights can be derived for future periods. I now propose to discuss the results by reference to allocations for the period 1991 to 2000. For each perspective, a large sample of 1000 regional emission rights allocations is derived for the period $T_R$ (=1990) up to $T_E$ (fixed and perspective dependent; E = 2090, H = 2030, I = 2000). Thereafter, the resulting relative allocations are used to scale the emission rights distribution for the egalitarians and the hierarchists for the period 1991 to 2000 to compare the results of all three perspectives.

The cumulative probability of these allocations is depicted in Figures 7.13a, b and c. The variances of the regional rights are much smaller than those of a uniform distribution, since the preferences for specific parameter values result in specific allocations. The results set out in Table 7.6 and Figures 7.13a, b and c show that the distributions of emission rights vary remarkably among the perspectives. From the egalitarian point of view, industrialized regions have emitted such large amounts of fossil $CO_2$ in the last decades that, according to equity principles, they should derive fewer emission rights than the projected level (IS92c) allows them. Consequent trading in emission rights may result in transfers of capital, technology and know-how from 'North' to 'South' to compensate the developing countries for the 'inequitable treatment' in the past.

The allocation of emission rights associated with the hierarchist results in a flow of assets from industrial to developing regions. The magnitude of the flow is smaller than that associated with egalitarian preferences, because the economic system may become unstable if drastic measures are implemented. Moreover, hierarchists prefer to allocate emission rights by reference to a balanced valuation of equity and economic power. Since hierarchists take historical emissions into account, a surplus of emission rights allocated to developing countries is created.

Although individualists regard measures to reduce $CO_2$ emissions as redundant, I propose to discuss the allocation as preferred by individualists, if a system of tradable emission rights were, nevertheless, to be introduced. According to the individualist, the high levels of GNP in OECD countries imply that they should be entitled to greater emission rights than emission scenario IS92e allows them. Fossil $CO_2$ intensive economies suffer more than others, if rights are allocated according to an individualist perspective and the result is a lower level of emission rights in EE-CIS and CPA. Although developing countries and EE-CIS are holding about the same share in GNP in the 1990s, emission rights accruing to the 'developing' countries are much greater. This is because of assuming (a small degree of) the historical responsibility. The result will be a significant transfer of emission rights in EE-CIS to developing countries (see also Figure 7.10).

Thus, according to the general allocation model, the trading of emission rights seems, in line with the views of the egalitarians and the hierarchists, to be preferred. This will result in a flow of assets from 'North' to 'South'. Which combination of parameter values of the allocation model may lead to a politically acceptable allocation depends, among other things, on the willingness to pay from the North and the common opinion about the seriousness of reducing emissions.

*Table 7.6: Means of distribution of emission rights (1991-2000). Emissions envisaged by the perspective based scenarios are in parentheses. (In GtC for the 10 year period)*

|                          | OECD   | EE-CIS | CPA   | DC     |
|--------------------------|--------|--------|-------|--------|
| *Egalitarian*            |        |        |       |        |
| Emission rights (mean)   | 7.4    | 4.0    | 13.1  | 37.9   |
| Emission scenario IS92c  | (28.3) | (15.6) | (7.4) | (11.2) |
| *Hierarchist*            |        |        |       |        |
| Emission rights (mean)   | 26.0   | 8.0    | 9.0   | 25.1   |
| Emission scenario IS92a  | (31.1) | (16.7) | (8.0) | (12.4) |
| *Individualist*          |        |        |       |        |
| Emission rights (mean)   | 43.0   | 6.0    | 1.8   | 20.2   |
| Emission scenario IS92e  | (32.2) | (17.3) | (8.5) | (13.0) |

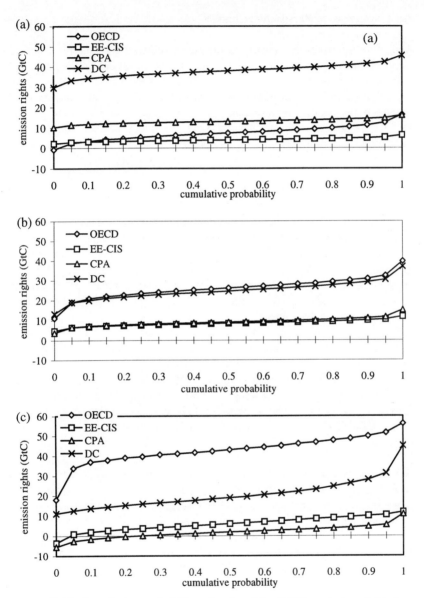

*Figure 7.13: Cumulative probability of regional fossil $CO_2$ emission rights from an egalitarian, hierarchistic and individualistic perspective*

### 7.4.4 Scenarios of Perspective Change

Agents' perspectives may change as they are faced with a persistent pattern of surprises. In Chapter 8, a broad discussion of perspective changes is made and an evolutionary model to simulate such dynamics is introduced. In this section, simple scenario-based exercises are performed to analyse the influence of changes in perspectives by two scenarios in which the dominant attitude towards the climate change problem changes. Since the policy makers considered in these scenarios represent the world community, global scenarios of future developments can reasonably be expected to change in the course of time. The scenarios envisage transitions from egalitarian to individualistic management style and vice versa.

*'Transition from individualistic to egalitarian'.* The individualist scenario is traced for the period 1991-2020, because there is no shared belief in the existence of a real risk. In the years following, the perspective is to become hierarchical in character, since the first effects of climate change become apparent around that date. In about 2050, the new dominant perspective is egalitarian in response to scientific evidence of large-scale anthropogenic influence on the global climate.

*'Transition from egalitarian to individualistic'.* The egalitarian scenario is traced for the period 1991-2020 because decision makers aim at minimizing the risks of human-induced climate change. After 2020, the new perspective is hierarchist because no convincing scientific evidence for a human-induced climate change can be found. Around 2050, the new perspective changes to that of the individualist because the hypothesis of a human-induced climate change is rejected.

Where $T_R$ is equal to 1990, 2000,..., 2100, emission rights are allocated according to the dominant perspective at that particular moment in time. The future scenarios for population size, GNP, energy use and emissions are derived by reference to the growth rates associated with the perspective scenarios which are dominant. Mean values of the emission right distributions are derived using the corresponding $\sigma_1$ values themselves. The relative regional shares are used to allocate the expected emissions for the years $T_R$ (Figures 7.14a, b).

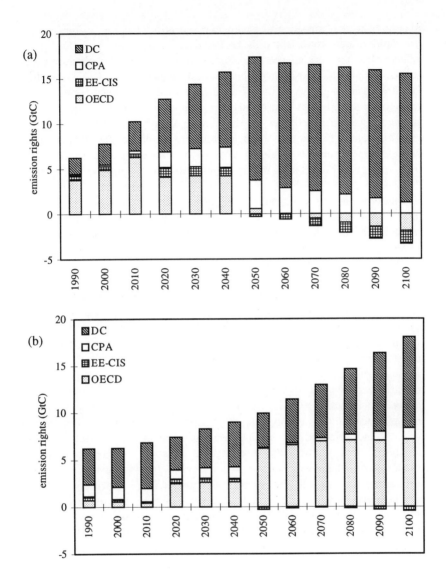

*Figure 7.14: (a) Regional emission rights of a 'transition from individualist to egalitarian' scenario. (b) Regional emission rights of a 'transition from an egalitarian to an individualistic' scenario*

According to the 'transition to egalitarian' scenario, global emissions initially rise rapidly, as is consistent with the individualist scenario. According to the individualist, there is no need to allocate emission rights at all during this period. With the transposition to a hierarchical perspective, the OECD countries forfeit emission rights in favour of (formerly) centrally-planned regions in the years following 2020. In view of high emission levels over several decades, the influence of human activities on the climate system becomes apparent and results in policy changes after 2050, according to the dominant egalitarian view. Because the population continues to grow at a rapid rate up to 2050, the emission rights of developing regions jump sharply as the dominant perspective changes. However, by that stage, the cumulative contemporary and historical contributions in the industrialized regions have reached a level at which emission rights have expired. This scenario thus suggests that playing down the possibility of an anthropogenic climate change becoming a problem creates a hostage to fortune. In the long run, the industrialized countries, and especially the OECD members, will pay dearly in the loss of fossil $CO_2$ emission rights, if they are forced to admit that a problem exists.

According to the 'transition to individualistic' scenario, the increase of global emissions in the coming decades is limited because of preventive policies, according to the egalitarian perspective. The emission rights of developing regions are higher than in the emission scenario, while those allocated to industrialized regions are lower. The egalitarian perspective anticipates the exchange of surplus emission rights through international transfers between industrialized regions and developing regions. However, as soon as the dominant perspective gives way to hierarchist thinking, global emissions start to increase once again. The emission rights of developing regions are curtailed and those of industrialized regions increase. As soon as the hypothesis of the possibility of a human-induced change is rejected, development will be unrestricted and there will be no reason for an allocation mechanism.

Limiting emissions in the absence of human-induced climate change may have negative consequences for global economic development in the short term. However, in the long term the same levels might be reached as in the 'transition to egalitarian' scenario. Moreover, (technological) transactions from 'North' to 'South' may cause economic growth to be enhanced, especially in developing regions.

The scenarios tracing changing perspectives demonstrate that it is difficult for a region to determine its strategy. The failure to do not take measures in the present may, if climate change does occur, in the long run be advantageous to developing countries, in the light of the initial allocation of emission rights. On the other hand, taking measures in case of a rejection of the hypothesis of a human-induced climate change may be advantageous to developing regions in the short term. The position of OECD countries is precisely the opposite, while neither scenario envisages more than modest emission rights being allocated to EE-CIS countries. This state of affairs underlines the delicate international economic position of the EE-CIS region.

## 7.5   CONCLUSIONS

The industrialized countries have so far caused the major part of $CO_2$ emissions. Analysing past carbon emission from fossil fuel use, cement manufacturing and land use change indicates that present wealth in the industrialized countries has been at the cost of large emissions in the past. The relative contribution of Western Europe and North America to the $CO_2$ concentration rise over the period 1800 to 1990 is about 40 per cent, almost completely due to fossil fuel combustion and cement manufacturing. The contribution from Africa, Latin America and South/South-East Asia, exceeding 30 per cent, is for about 75 per cent due to deforestation.

From an egalitarian perspective, the industrialized world should take prime responsibility in responding to and supporting the developing countries in contributing their share to mitigating climatic change without thwarting their development. As a consequence, the international policy discussion understandably adds the economic North-South issues to the search for technical options. A reduction of the risk of adverse climate change according to the 'precautionary principle' approach implies that future global emissions of greenhouse gases are constrained.

Under the premises of a future scenario (for example IS92C), the world would be constrained by the global carbon budget, defined as the cumulated $CO_2$ emission from fossil fuel combustion, cement manufacturing, and land use change over the period 1800 to 2100, of about 1130 GtC. About 30 per cent of this budget has already been used up in the past. If all world citizens living in the period 1800-2100 were allocated an equal emission quotum, this would result in a per capita emission of 0.97 tC/cap yearly. The industrialized regions would have exceeded their allocated budgets for 1800-1990 by about 87 GtC (OECD) and 16 GtC (CIS). The developing countries, however, have an emission credit of about 130 GtC.

A more sophisticated allocation model is presented which takes into account historical and future developments. Criteria used in allocation are population size (equity per capita), GNP (economic affluence), energy use (efficiency), the length of historical responsibility, and time preference.

There are various perspectives pertaining to the allocation of a constrained global fossil $CO_2$ emission budget. In the first place, there might be differences in the scenarios concerning fossil $CO_2$ emissions, energy use, population, technology and economic growth. Second, the preferred value distribution of parameters of the model might be skewed by perspectives. Drawing on Schwartz and Thompson (1990), the perspectives are labelled 'individualist', 'hierarchist' and 'egalitarian', and are represented by distributions of preferred values of parameters in the allocation model and by various preferred future scenarios.

The method can be interpreted as an example of a quantification of subjective judgement which is intended to take account of perspectives affecting the allocation of emission rights. The resulting three perspective-based allocations of emission rights span a much wider range of possible allocations than other studies so far. It demonstrates the importance of the influence of subjectivity on the ranges of the initial allocation of emission rights. Because of the political dimension of the subject and the dynamic shifting of the mixture of perspectives in time, the results show that there is no optimal allocation of emission rights.

A logical follow-up of this study is to use a regionalized energy model[5] to analyse the effectivity of various initial emission right allocations and their trade schemes on the ability to meet global policy targets on climate change. Next to official IPCC scenarios, target scenarios, as will be determined similar to the approach in Chapter 6, may then be used to calculate regional emission debts and rights. I hope that scanning the impact of the various distributions may help the discussion on sharing responsibility to meet emission targets.

## NOTES

1.  The population data between 1800 and 1920 are based on Durand (1967) and the population data covering 1920-1990 have been obtained from the United Nations World Population Prospects (UN, 1966; UN, 1990a). The future population figures are based on IPCC (1992). Global population figures are estimated to increase from 5.3 billion in 1990 to 11.3 billion in 2100, mainly due to the growth in the developing countries.
2.  The scenarios for fossil $CO_2$ emissions, population, GNP and primary energy use are based on the IPCC (1992) scenarios. In the IPCC scenarios the following 4 world regions are distinguished: OECD, Eastern Europe and the Community of Independent States (EE-CIS), Centrally Planned Asia (CPA) and the Developing Countries (DC). The main assumptions in the IPCC scenarios are given in the appendix. The historical estimates for GNP levels are based on growth rates as given in Mitchell (1981, 1982, 1983), IMF (1992), UNCTAD (1985) and 1987 values of regional GNP levels as given in WRI (1990/1991) and UN (1990b). Historical data for primary energy use are derived from Darmstadter (1971), Mitchell (1981, 1982,1983) and OECD (1989, 1991a, 1991b, 1991c, 1992).
3.  Since the distribution function of the regional emission rights, which is based on the distributions of the  parameter values, is not known, I could not formally determine the minimum number of simulation runs. Experiments show that the mean and standard deviation converge after several hundred runs. Therefore the number of runs used in this study was set at 1000.

4. In fact the IPCC scenarios are variations of the hierarchistic perspective. The egalitarian and individualistic scenario chosen seems to include some arguments of egalitarians and individualists.
5. A regionalized version of the energy model as used in Chapter 6 is under way, including a trade model for energy carriers (Targets-IMage Energy model Regional - TIMER).

# 8. The Battle of Perspectives

## 8.1. INTRODUCTION

In this chapter, an approach is presented which includes explicitly the adaptive behaviour of humans in the face of incorrect assumptions about the functioning of the global system. I focus on the problem of human-induced climate change, since several aspects of this problem are controversial and it has an important policy component. Although the majority of climate researchers support the theory of the enhanced greenhouse effect (IPCC, 1990; 1996a, b, c), it is unclear where and how fast temperature increases will occur and what the impact will be on the biosphere, including human society.

Not surprisingly, many attempts to understand and forecast the future development of such complex systems have failed. For instance, Malthus (1798) regarded food production as a land-limited resource that could not possibly be increased quickly enough to keep in pace with a growing population. His expectation did not come true for various reasons, among them the sharp increase in agricultural productivity and the decrease in birth rates. Another example is provided by the 1971 report to the Club of Rome, *Limits to Growth* (Meadows *et al.,* 1972), which concluded from a model-based analysis that the ongoing depletion of resources would result in a collapse of the world economy. However, the oil crises of the 1970s led to intensification of exploration efforts and subsequently additional reserves; they also induced investments in energy efficiency and renewable energy sources (Meadows *et al.,* 1991). The simulations made in 1971 included neither the oil crises nor the responses to it. The complexity of the system is seriously underestimated in such analyses. This is particularly true with respect to the response and adaptation options and the capability of humans to apply and expand such options.

Two of the techniques used in integrated assessment modelling are scenario analysis and optimization. Scenario analyses tend to lose their meaning if scenarios are reduced to simple trend extrapolation without any human response, as is often the case. Optimization is based on the assumption that rationally acting agents have perfect knowledge about the system in question and are able to determine the optimal strategy for some future period. Although this approach may yield valuable insights into efficient strategies, it is seriously limited by the necessary model simplifications. Thus, there is a need to support scenario analyses with model-based simulation experiments without resorting to abstract, oversimplified system descriptions. Inclusion of adaptive agent behaviour can contribute to this.

The recognition that changing behaviour of agents should be an important consideration in global modelling is not new (see for example Bossel and Strobel, 1978, Costanza *et al.*, 1993). During recent years, a number of studies related to climate change have appeared which investigate the concept of adaptive or sequential decision-making (Manne and Richels, 1992; Hammitt *et al.*, 1992; Peck and Teisberg, 1992; Lempert *et al.*, 1996). The first three of these studies employ a sequential-decision model in which the optimal trajectory is derived in two steps, taking account of a learning phase in the initial period. In Lempert *et al.* (1996), a simple adaptive strategy is examined, whereby different assumptions of the costs and damage functions are juxtaposed with optimal policies. Another approach to modelling social behaviour is the 'artificial society'. An interesting example is to be found in the work of Epstein and Axtell (1996), who designed a program which generates artificial societies by modelling simple rules for hundreds of individual agents which evolve over time. The purpose of such an artificial society is to enable the investigation of social processes within a so-called 'CompuTerrarium'.

These models use rather ad-hoc decision rules, and do not base the agent behaviour from insights from social science (Durlauf, 1997). For example, they do not take into account the diversity of world views among the agents. Thompson *et al.* (1990) argue that agents are forced to cast around for alternatives in the event that they are confronted with a persistent pattern of surprises, and that this constitutes an important element of social dynamics. So far, only a few studies have tried to model such changing world views or perspectives. Thompson and Taylor (1986) devised a computer simulation of a 'surprise game' in which a so-called payoff matrix is used to value the 'nice' and 'nasty' consequences of various surprises. The game was implemented for an imaginary industrial enterprise with a considerable number of competitors, and simulates the number of adherents to one of the four perspectives distinguished in the Cultural Theory: egalitarians, hierarchists, individualists, and fatalists.

In a set of exploratory experiments, Janssen and Rotmans (1995) generated various scenarios in which climate policy changes as a result of shifts in the dominant perspective among the agents. The dominant perspective may change if expectations about the functioning of the system fail to correspond with reality. The study assumed that scenarios would involve change of perspectives but did not simulate the underlying dynamics how agents may change their perspectives. This is the aim of this chapter on the 'Battle of Perspectives' (Janssen and de Vries, 1997a).

## 8.2 PERSPECTIVES AND AGENTS

The aim of the 'Battle of Perspectives' is to simulate changing world-views of the agents which are assumed to change the behaviour of those agents. The first element of my approach is a simple economy-energy-climate model which through different relationships and parameter values is used to describe three different views on how the world functions and on how it should be managed. The model is described in the next section. The second element is the inclusion of explicit perspectives on the world system and of agents which base their decisions on such perspectives in relation to real-world observations. This is discussed in this section.

As a framework to classify possible diverging interpretations of the world, the three 'active' *perspectives* from Cultural Theory are used (see Chapter 4): the Hierarchist (H), the Egalitarian (E) and the Individualist (I) (Thompson *et al.*, 1990; Rayner, 1991; Thompson, 1996). The perspectives are interpreted as the corners of a triangle and the agent population can at any moment in time be positioned within this triangle if it is known which proportion adheres to each of the three perspectives. Briefly, the three perspectives can be characterized as follows for the energy climate debate (de Vries and Janssen, 1996).

The *hierarchist* wishes to avoid disruptions to the smooth functioning of the energy system in view of its consequences for economic growth and voter behaviour. To this end the hierarchist institutions of society will anticipate and respond on the basis of scientific expert knowledge. The need for governance structures is emphasized. There is a preference for a risk-reducing control approach and for reliance on and legitimization by the outcomes of cost minimization and cost-benefit analyses. Technologies which can be planned and controlled are favoured and issues like oil dependence and public acceptance rank high. Energy consumers can and should be guided towards 'rational energy use' - which is the justification for regulation, taxes, information campaigns and the like.

The hierarchist will make a prudent assessment of the potential for energy conservation and have an institutional bias towards large-scale supply-side options. Resource estimates will be rather conservative. There will be a cautious approach to the issue of climate change, judging it in terms of 'acceptable risks', including strategic and societal risks such as the OPEC oil oligopoly, nationalism and fundamentalism. Hierarchists will support cost-effective 'no-regrets' measures which reduce the risk of climate change, but they are keenly aware of the fact that fast and stringent cutbacks in $CO_2$ emissions may be socially disruptive and create competitive disadvantages. Hence, a climate policy should be 'realistic' and only be introduced if an internationally negotiated consensus is reached to avoid windfall profits or free riders (see for example Hourcade *et al.*, 1996). Hierarchists prefer unambiguous, scientifically robust indicators on which to found their analyses and policies - for example, global mean temperature change. R&D programs for new energy supply and efficiency options are advocated, also because they stimulate economic growth and (national) status.

The *egalitarian* wishes to reduce inequity and stresses the rights of those without a voice: our children, the poor and nature. High and rising $CO_2$ emissions are seen as one more sign that humans are maltreating the earth and that this may lead to catastrophes. The aspiration for continuing economic growth has to be curbed, which is only fair and feasible if it is accompanied by a narrowing of the gap between the rich and the poor. Mathematical tools and models can play only a minor role because many of the issues at stake cannot be expressed in numbers or money. From an egalitarian perspective, science and technology can certainly solve part of the problem but add as much to it as long as their course is governed by centralized and commercial interests and market ideology. Being risk-aversive, egalitarians consider all uncertain processes and feedbacks to amplify climate change. They also wish to take feedbacks or catastrophic impacts into account, which are strongly disputed within the scientific community; on the other hand, they tend to ignore potential negative feedbacks.

The egalitarian will embrace the 'precautionary principle' as a way to express his/her risk-averse attitude. Energy futures will be judged not only in terms of costs, but also with regard to distributive aspects and ecological impacts. Hence, policies should be based on assessment studies of the possible impacts from anticipated increases in temperature and sea level. No or only a modest economic growth is to be preferred. Energy taxes are promoted as a means to change wasteful production and consumption practices and stimulate the penetration of non-polluting alternatives. It will also conserve high-quality oil and gas reserves for later generations. Energy demand projections are much lower than official ones and have to be met to a large extent with non-fossil sources (Lovins and Lovins, 1991). There will be a preference for decentralized and clean technologies, and therefore a natural tendency to focus on energy end-use needs and efficiency (Johansson et al., 1989). Estimates of fossil fuel resources are on the low side, whereas the prospects of renewable energy sources are usually on the high side if compared with the hierarchist perspective. Development of renewable sources should be strongly supported by government R&D programs.

For the *individualist*, entrepreneurial freedom and unhampered working of market forces gives the best guarantee for increasing material wealth and at the same time solving resource and environment problems. If energy supply companies can operate in a regime of free trade and with a minimum of government regulation and interference, price signals will steer the transition away from fossil fuels before they are depleted. The earth itself is also far more resilient than we tend to think, so climate change impacts are probably exaggerated by those advocating strict measures. Moreover, there are several and relatively cheap options for adaptation (Nordhaus, 1991b). The key resource is human ingenuity: human skills generate science and technology, which will bring options one cannot even imagine at the present (Simon, 1980). Technology is also the major driving force behind economic growth, which will ultimately benefit the poor. Concerning the climate change debate, the individualists' view of a benign natural system leads them to believe that climate change will be mitigated by known and hitherto unknown dampening feedbacks. Speculative negative feedbacks are taken into account; uncertain positive feedbacks are neglected or considered to have negligible impacts on the climate system.

The individualist emphasizes the opportunities which arise from the search for new resources and new technologies to supply and conserve energy. Energy resources turn out, over and again, to be more abundant and cheaper than expected. Policy measures like a carbon tax are unnecessary and may actually be quite harmful to the legitimate aspiration of the less developed countries to spur economic growth. Moreover, there are still too many uncertainties about the enhanced greenhouse effect and possible climate change to accept drastic measures. Energy taxes will also be ineffective because industries will move to other countries and consumers will stick to certain lifestyles whatever the costs.

Of course, in the real world actors rarely express their views in such a caricatural way. They are in constant interaction and often have strategic and public relations in mind as well. Moreover, positions may be implausible or even inconsistent when stake holders share only part of the underlying values and judgements. For example, the egalitarian concerns about nuclear reactor safety and climate change have increasingly been incorporated in hierarchist policy formulation in the form of regulatory and negotiation frameworks. Similarly, the energy business community - part of which is rather hierarchist - is advocating the need for more efficient and environmentally friendly resource use options, at the same time emphasizing the virtues of the market and the limitations of command-and-control approaches (Schmidheiny *et al.,* 1992). There is also the paradox that the egalitarian expectation of fast innovation in energy efficiency and non-carbon energy supply and imminent depletion of cheap oil and gas is at odds with their fear that the high $CO_2$ emissions of the Business-as-Usual scenarios become reality (see for example Lenssen and Flavin, 1996). Evidently, my implementation of the three perspectives into an economy-energy-climate model is only a first attempt to introduce real-world divergence in interests and values into a quantitative modelling framework.

Trisoglio *et al.* (1994) have proposed to characterize perspectives according to two dimensions: (1) how is the world seen - the world view; and (2) how it should be acted upon - the management style. A management style is correct insofar as it is based on a corresponding view on how the world functions. For example, if one believes that people will change their behaviour only in response to prices, market-oriented policies are most effective and to be preferred. Trisoglio *et al.* (1994) refer to this situation as utopian: the management style of agents corresponds with their view of the world. If, on the other hand, a management style is followed which is not based on correct understanding of the system, the situation is dystopian. The literature on utopias has a long history (see for example More, 1516; Kumar, 1987; Proops, 1989). The previously mentioned doomsday scenarios of Malthus and Meadows *et al.* can be seen as dystopias: human behaviour and (lack of) policies are discordant with nature's resource potential and resilience.[1] A rather dystopian scenario for climate change is the 'Business-as-Usual' or IS92a scenario of the IPCC (1992). This coal-based energy future with medium population and economic growth leads to a greenhouse gas emission path which probably implies serious climate change related risks. Indeed, this scenario is used as a reference future to formulate emission targets.

The utopia/dystopia approach can be used to explore a variety of images of the world's future (van Asselt and Rotmans, 1996; Rotmans and de Vries, 1997). However, in these applications it is static in the sense that an evolving dystopia does not induce adaptive behaviour. If the system collapses, the agents do not respond. Hence, the scenario outcomes are rather implausible, although they give insight in the role of uncertainties. The present approach is an important improvement in this regard, because the agents in the model are assumed to change their preferred management style if observations about the world are surprising enough, that is, if they differ enough from what they expect on the basis of their world view. Of course, I realize that this model is for illustrative purposes only and that only implementation in more detailed simulation models can support issues in climate policy.

The model-world is populated with a large number of *agents* which adhere to a mix of the three perspectives but may change their adherence and change policy if their observations do not match their expectations. These agents can be thought of as groups of decisionmakers who operate at the international level and represent institutions.[2] In this way, the system's behaviour does not deterministically follow from a set of state equations but is instead governed by the rule-based behaviour of many distributed, interacting parts. These rules influence the actions of an agent which in turn effects the actions of other agents. The resulting rule-based structure becomes grist for the evolutionary procedure that enables the system to adapt to its surroundings. The genetic algorithm (Chapter 5) is used to simulate the adaptive processes.

Translated to the Battle of Perspectives the four phase cycles of Holling (Section 4.4) explains that surprises may lead to a loss of control which provide the proximate trigger for change. When agents are confronted with the fact that current interpretations of observations fail, they may benefit from searching for more satisfactory explanations. A new perspective becomes dominant leading to a new stable situation. The related changes in agents' behaviour may lay in the structure of the existing social dynamics. However, reshaping of norms and values may cause an increasing pressure to flip the behaviour dynamics to a new kind of system. In the presented prototype I only consider one adaptive cycle in the climate policy. This means that only one transition may occur in the dominating position within the perspective triangle, and that the corners of the triangle do not change in time.

## 8.3. THE MODEL

For the purpose of this study, a simple dynamic system is employed which describes the basic dynamics of the economy and the climate system. The model is based on existing economy-climate models, such as those found in Nordhaus (1992, 1993, 1994); Manne *et al.* (1994); Hammitt *et al.* (1992) and Lempert *et al.* (1996). I recognize that this model yields a highly simplified representation of the problem, but its dynamic framework serves well to illustrate the 'Battle of Perspectives'.

There are three parts to the model: economy, energy/emissions and climate. The description of the economy is based on a single equation for aggregate economic output:

$$Y(t) = cS(t) \cdot a(t) \cdot K(t)^{\gamma} \cdot P(t)^{1-\gamma} \qquad \text{\$/yr (8.1)}$$

This is a standard constant-returns-to-scale, Cobb-Douglas production function with two production factors: capital $K(t)$ and labour $L(t)$ which is assumed to be proportional to population, $P(t)$. It also contains technical progress in the form of an exogenous factor $a(t)$. To account for the economic consequences of either climate change related damage or emission reduction measures, the scale factor $S(t)$ is introduced. Both $a(t)$ and $S(t)$ are normalized to 1 for the base-year 1995. For the world population I use an exogenous projection of 11.3 billion people in 2100, published in Bulatao *et al.* (1990). Technological change is assumed to increase exponentially but at a declining rate, following Nordhaus (1994). Gauging the equation to the world data for

1990 in 1990 US\$ yields for the constant $c$ in equation (8.1) the value of 0.0132. The elasticity of output with respect to capital, $\gamma$, is taken to be 0.25. The scale factor $S(t)$ is discussed later on.

Technological changes are regarded as being exogenous, although such development is assumed to proceed at a declining rate

$$\frac{da}{dt} = \exp(\delta_a^{rate} \cdot t) \cdot a \; , \qquad \frac{d\,\delta_a^{rate}}{dt} \; = \; -\delta_a \cdot \delta_a^{rate} \tag{8.2}$$

Economic output is produced by an aggregate capital stock, $K(t)$, which has an average lifetime of 10 year. In combination with a savings rate $I(t)$, that is, the fraction of economic output $Y(t)$ re-invested in the capital stock $K(t)$ in period t, the balance equation for the capital stock $K(t)$ is given by:

$$\frac{dK}{dt} \; = \; I \cdot Y \; - \; \delta_k \cdot K \qquad\qquad \text{\$/yr (8.3)}$$

with $\delta_k$ the rate of depreciation of the capital stock and equal to the inverse of the average lifetime. Total consumption, $C$, is equal to economic output, $Y$, minus gross investments, $I*Y$:

$$C(t) \; = \; (1 - I(t)) \cdot Y(t) \qquad\qquad \text{\$/yr (8.4)}$$

The second part of the model describes the energy system. It is kept quite simple. The economy uses energy at an intensity $e$, that is, the amount of fuel required per unit of economic output. This energy-intensity $e$ is assumed to decline logistically to some lower bound $e_{min}$. The rate at which energy efficiency improvements are introduced and hence the rate at which $e$ declines is given by the parameter $L_e$ which indicates the number of years it takes to halve the initial (1995) value of $e$. This phenomenon is called the energy efficiency transition. The pace of the energy efficiency transition is given with $L_e$ which ranges from 40 to 60 years.

The energy is supplied to the economy as a mix of fuels of which a fraction $F(t)$ consists of fossil fuels. These give on combustion a fixed amount of $CO_2$ emissions per unit of energy. Here, too, a transition away from fossil fuels is assumed in the form of a logistic decline of $F(t)$. The rate of change is determined by the parameter $L_f$ which indicates the number of years it takes to reduce the initial (1995) value of $F(t)$ with 50 per cent. I refer to this as the fossil fuel transition. In the simulation experiments, the value of $L_f$ ranges from 20 to 1000 and is used as a control variable.

Using these formulations, the emission of $CO_2$ is given by:

$$E(t) = \alpha F(t) \cdot \varepsilon(t) \cdot Y(t) \qquad\qquad \text{GtC/yr} \quad (8.5)$$

The $CO_2$ emissions $E$ are the result of a change in economic activity $Y(t)$, the energy conservation transition in the form of a declining energy-intensity $e(t)$ and the transition towards alternative fuels in the form of a declining value of $F(t)$. Equating $Y(t)$ to the Gross World Output (GWP) expressed in 1990 US\$, the coefficient $\alpha$ (equation (8.5)) gets the value of 0.32 GtC/bil\$.

$F(t)$ is one minus the percentage of emission reductions and is defined as a logistic function, where $R$ is the number of years which would be required to reduce the share of fossil fuels within the energy mix by 50 per cent, and $\varepsilon$, in conformance with Lempert *et al.* (1996), is taken as being 0.01, reflecting an autonomous trend in decarbonization.
Thus:

$$(8.6)$$

$$F(t) = \frac{1}{1-\varepsilon} \cdot \frac{1}{1 + \exp(\rho_M(t)\_(\frac{R(t)}{R(t-1)}(t-1995) - R(t)))}$$

$$\text{where} \quad \rho_M(t) = \frac{-1}{R(t)} \cdot \ln(\frac{\varepsilon}{1-\varepsilon})$$

The energy intensity decline is described by a logistic function, where $\delta$ is the contribution of available low-cost conservation measures and where the number of years required to double energy efficiency is assumed to be 50 years:

$$(8.7)$$

$$\sigma(t) = (1-\delta) + \frac{1}{1-\varepsilon} \cdot \frac{\delta}{1 + \exp(p_\sigma \cdot (t - 1995 - 50))}$$

$$\text{where} \quad p_\sigma = \frac{-1}{50} \cdot \ln(\frac{\varepsilon}{1-\varepsilon})$$

The third part of the model consists of a greatly simplified climate model. The change in atmospheric $CO_2$ concentration ($pCO_2$ in ppmv) is modelled using the reduced-form carbon cycle model developed by Maier-Reimer and Hasselmann

(1987). Carbon emissions ($E$) are divided into 5 classes (fractions $c_{1-5}$), four of which have different atmospheric lifetimes $al_{1-4}$. Thus:

$$pCO_2(t) = pCO_2(t_0) + \int_{t_0}^{t} 0.47 \cdot E(\tau)\{c_1 + \Sigma_{i=2}^{5} c_i \cdot \exp[\frac{\tau - t}{al_{i-1}}]\}d\tau \tag{8.8}$$

where $c_{1-5}$=0.13, 0.20, 0.32, 0.25, and 0.1, and $al_{1-4}$=363, 74, 17, and 2 yrs.

Equation (8.8) was fitted by least squares to the computed response of a full-scale ocean carbon cycle model and yields a good approximation for small changes, although it underestimates the amplitude and time-scale of the response for higher concentration levels (Maier-Reimer and Hasselmann, 1987).

The radiative forcing of $CO_2$ is modelled in conformance with the IPCC (1990) in the following way:

$$\Delta Q_{CO_2}(t) = \frac{\Delta Q_{2XCO2}}{\ln(2.0)} \cdot \ln(\frac{pCO_2(t)}{pCO_2(t_0)}) \tag{8.9}$$

where $\Delta Q_{2xCO2}$ is the radiative forcing associated with a doubled $CO_2$ concentration (4.3 W/m$^2$)

Aggregated radiative forcing is assumed to have the following impact on the change in the global mean surface temperature ($\Delta T^p$):

$$\Delta T^p(t) = \frac{\Delta T_{2XCO2}}{\Delta Q_{2XCO2}} \cdot \Delta Q_{CO_2}(t) \tag{8.10}$$

where $\Delta T_{2xCO2}$ is the global mean surface temperature change in the event of a doubled $CO_2$ concentration (best guess 2.5°C, see Section 8.5.2). Since oceans take a long time to warm up, the actual temperature increase ($\Delta T$) will lag behind the potential increase, $\Delta T^p$, which is modelled as follows:

$$\frac{d\Delta T}{dt} = \beta \cdot (\Delta T^p - \Delta T) \qquad \text{°C/yr} \tag{8.11}$$

where $\beta$ is assumed to be 0.05. This causes a delay time in the order of 20 years.

It is assumed that a rise in the average surface temperature brings costs with in the form of damage and/or adaptation measures. These are accounted for in the form of economic output reduction. On the other hand, these costs can be avoided or lowered by preventive measures in the form of emission reduction measures. In the model, this is done by accelerating the transition away from fossil fuels and it has a cost, too.

The scaling factor $S(t)$ in the expression for the economic output $Y(t)$ (equation (8.1)) takes these two factors into account. The (market) damage and/or adaptation costs are quantified as a relation between global temperature $\Delta T(t)$ increase and income loss. The costs of reducing emissions of greenhouse gases are assumed to be a function of $F$, the fraction of fossil fuels in the energy mix. Now, $S(t)$ is defined as the ratio of one minus the percentage of abatement costs to one plus the percentage of damage costs:

$$S(t) = \frac{1 - b_1 \cdot (1 - F(t))^{b_2}}{1 + \theta_1 \cdot \Delta T(t)^{\theta_2}} \tag{8.12}$$

with $\theta_1$ representing the scale of damage and/or adaptation, $\theta_2$ the non-linearity in the damage function, and $b_1$ and $b_2$ the scale and non-linearity of the emission reduction cost function.

## 8.4. MODELLING WORLD VIEWS AND MANAGEMENT STYLES

### 8.4.1 Experimental Set-up

The agents are assumed to represent decision makers on an international level, who are responsible for climate change policy and control the level of investments and emission reductions. Each agent adheres to a world view which is located within the perspective triangle. By considering a set of similar agents who adopt various perspectives with respect to the climate change problem, the model is able to simulate the agents' adaptation of their behaviour in terms of policy measures. Of course, I do not claim that real-world agents actually learn and adapt in this highly simplified way. I do, however, conjecture that there is 'weak isomorphism' between the 'Battle of Perspectives' and the ways in which real-world agents adapt to their changing environment.

Figure 8.1 gives an overview of how the model experiments are set up. The population of agents is distributed across the triangle of perspectives. The real world is assumed to function according to one of the three world views - in this context the 'correct' world view. This real world is observed by the agents in the form of a few indicators (atmospheric $CO_2$ concentration ($pCO_2$) and actual temperature rise $\Delta T$). If the expected and the observed value of the indicator (in this case the temperature rise $\Delta T$) differ more than a certain tolerance level, agents may change world view - they adapt to this 'surprise'. Hence, the dominance of world views, and consequently the resulting management style, change. Besides the world view, the decisions on the investment fraction (I) and the emission reduction (L$_f$) depend on the indicators representing the state of the economy and the climate. In this paragraph I discuss the way in which I have implemented the world view and management style in the Economy-Energy-Climate model.

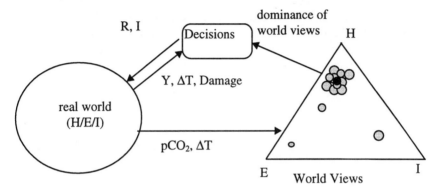

*Figure 8.1:   Experimental set-up*

### 8.4.2  World View

The model described in Section 8.3 is assumed to represent the global system. The values of several parameters within the model are assumed to differ for the three perspectives. In conformity with the construction of the uncertainty space by Lempert *et al.* (1996) and sensitivity analysis by Nordhaus (1994), four items are chosen to be uncertain and controversial and hence made world view-dependent:

- the sensitivity of the temperature for increasing $CO_2$ concentration ('climate sensitivity');
- the pace of technological improvements in the economy and of the energy conservation transition;
- the economic costs to reduce $CO_2$ emission ('mitigation costs'); and
- the economic damage incurred to the economy by climate change ('damage costs').

It should be stressed that only parameter values are changed; a more comprehensive approach would include the fact that different world views may actually use different models to describe the same system. For practical reasons, this is hitherto excluded.

In practical terms, this has led to world view-dependent implementation for 7 parameters, as is shown in Table 8.1 and Figures 8.2. The rate of technological change $a(t)$ is shown for the three perspectives in Figure 8.2a. The pace of the energy efficiency transition is determined by $L_e$ and shown in Figure 8.2b for the three world views. The values chosen for the climate sensitivity parameter $\Delta T_{2xCO2}$ , for the damage cost parameters $\theta_1$ and $\theta_2$ and for the emission reduction cost parameters $b_1$ and $b_2$ are given in Table 8.1 for the three perspectives. $L_f$ is used as a control variable. Figure 8.2c shows the development of the fossil fuel fraction for various $L_f$ values. Of course, these implementations are not rigid and unambiguous. Within a single world view, there are still quite distinct interpretations of what happened in the past and what is to be expected for the future.

*Table 8.1: Parameter values for the world view in the three perspectives*

|  | Individualist | Hierarchist | Egalitarian |
|---|---|---|---|
| Technological development | high | moderate | low |
| Climate sensitivity | low | best-guess | high |
| $\Delta T_{2xCO2}$ | 0.5 | 2.5 | 5.5 |
| Damage costs | low | moderate | high |
| $\theta_1$ | 0 | 0.0014 | 0.004 |
| $\theta_2$ | 0 | 2 |  |
| Mitigation costs | high | moderate | low |
| $b_1$ | 0.25 | 0.11 | 0.05 |
| $b_2$ | 3.5 | 2.9 | 2.3 |

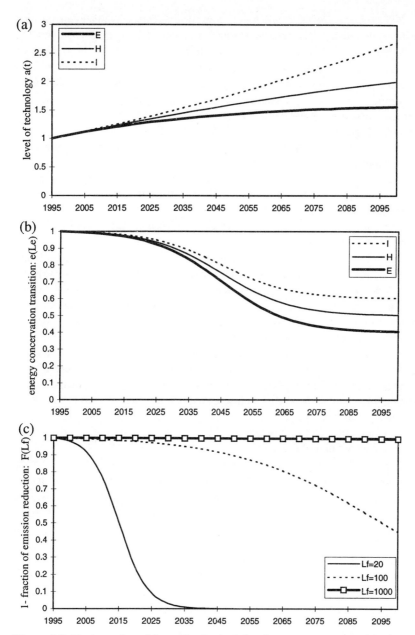

*Figure 8.2: Trajectories of the technological development parameter (a), the energy efficiency transition (b) and the fossil fuel transition (c) as implemented for the three perspectives*

*Hierarchists* are assumed to follow prominent scientific experts and institutions (such as the Intergovernmental Panel on Climate Change (IPCC)) with respect to climate-related uncertainties. They adopt the best guess or central estimate of the IPCC, 2.5°C for $\Delta T_{2xCO2}$ (IPCC, 1990, 1992). With regard to damage costs, the estimate given by Nordhaus (1994) is followed: a quadratic relation between temperature increase and damage cost results in a 1.3 per cent loss of economic growth if temperature increases by 3°C. Expectations of technological progress in the economy and with regard to energy efficiency are based on historical trends. The hierarchist is assumed to stimulate efficiency of economic production and, therefore, a moderate value of $L_e$ is assumed. Furthermore, as a best-guess estimate of the mitigation cost, the value proposed by Nordhaus (1994) is used who based his estimates on a survey of energy models (Nordhaus, 1991).

The *egalitarian* myth of nature suggests that minor changes disproportionately influence the behaviour of the system. Therefore, a value of 5.5°C for $\Delta T_{2xCO2}$ is adopted, this being one of the highest estimates to be found in the literature (Dickinson, 1986). The egalitarian myth of nature supports the use of high cost estimates of the impacts of climate change on the human system. I assume they use a highly non-linear damage curve, which causes a 32 per cent loss of economic output if temperature increases by 3°C in the course of the next century. This value is based on the high end of the range of estimates offered by Nordhaus (1994). Egalitarians are assumed to have modest expectations about the role of technology in improving economic productivity (Figure 8.2a). They do expect, however, that the threat of climate change will, in combination with carbon taxes, induce technologies which accelerate the energy efficiency transition ($L_e$) and the transition away from fossil fuels ($L_f$). They also assume that this decarbonisation of the economy can be achieved at quite modest cost per unit of reduction.

*Individualists* are assumed to use the lowest estimate of $\Delta T_{2xCO2}$ in the literature: a value of 0.5°C for $\Delta T_{2xCO2}$ (Lindzen, 1990). They also belief that no economic damage will result from climate change. If climate change occurs, technical solutions will compensate for any negative effects. I assume they expect - and aspire for - a rapid pace of technology which leads to significant improvements of economic productivity ($a(t)$). In their view, the threat of climate change is unfounded or small, cheap options to improve energy efficiency are quickly used up, and the costs to develop alternatives to fossil fuels will be quite high. Hence, the energy-intensity and the carbon-intensity of the economy will fall only slowly, also because there are vast low-cost fossil fuel reserves and there is no incentive to leave them in the ground.

### 8.4.3 Management Style

The management styles refers to the crucial decisions with regard to the economy-energy-climate system. Here, these decisions are modelled as a set of simple rules. The individual agents adhere to a management style which corresponds with their world view and which lies within the perspective triangle. During the simulation period, the preferred management style of each perspective is determined every year. The weighted average of the perspective adhered to by the individual agents determines the policy that is implemented c.q. the values of investment ratio I and fossil fuel transition parameter $L_f$. Thus:

$$I = \frac{1}{N} \sum_{i=1}^{N} a_i^E \cdot I^E + \frac{1}{N} \sum_{i=1}^{N} a_i^I \cdot I^I + \frac{1}{N} \sum_{i=1}^{N} a_i^H \cdot I^H$$

$$\text{(8.13)}$$

$$R = \frac{1}{N} \sum_{i=1}^{N} a_i^E \cdot R^E + \frac{1}{N} \sum_{i=1}^{N} a_i^I \cdot R^I + \frac{1}{N} \sum_{i=1}^{N} a_i^H \cdot R^H$$

The decisions forming a management style are made on the basis of discrepancies between expected and observed behaviour of the system. The assumptions which are made in framing decision rules are mainly based on Schwartz and Thompson (1990), Thompson *et al.* (1990) and Rayner (1991). I proceed with a description of the decision rules which make up a management style; the three management styles are summarized in Table 8.2.

*Table 8.2: Decision rules characterizing the three management styles*

|  | Individualist | Hierarchist | Egalitarian |
|---|---|---|---|
| Investment decisions | at least 2%/yr growth of Y | stable economic growth of 1.5%/yr | no expansion of capital stock. |
| Indicator for climate policy | damage cost | temperature | emissions |
| Climate policy | if damage > 1% of Y than decrease $L_f$ ; otherwise $L_f$ =1000 | if temperature rise decrease $L_f$ ; otherwise $L_f$ =100 | 50% reduction of fossil fuels in 20 years: $L_f$ =20 |

The preferred management style of *hierarchists* is one of control and reliance on experts. They are keenly aware of the social instability which may result from stagnating economic growth. In the trade-off between the stimulation of economic growth and diminishing the risk of long-term climate change, they will be led by cost-benefit analyses. In this model, this is operationalized by assuming that hierarchist institutions aim for a desired growth rate of economic output, $dY_D$, which in a world without climate change risks would give a smooth expansion of the economy:

$$I^H(t) = 0.9 \cdot I(t-1) + 0.1 \cdot \frac{d\,Y_D}{dY(t-1)} \cdot I(t-1) \qquad (8.14)$$

With this formulation, the preferred level of investments is a function of the level of investments of the previous year and abrupt changes in the investment levels are avoided. Investments will grow at the same rate as $Y/a$ unless part of the output is lost through climate change damage or is spent on emission reduction. If the world behaves according to the hierarchist world view, model experiments indicate that the desired economic growth level can be about 1.5 per cent per year. If it exceeds this value, economic output will start to fall before the year 2100, the time horizon of the simulations. Hence, I have set $dY_D$=1.5 per cent per year.

*Hierarchists* are aware of the social and economic risks involved if the climate changes. However, as long as the observed temperature increase is below 0.5°C, hierarchist institutions are assumed not to react and the fossil fuel transition is rather slow ($L_f$=100 years; Figure 8.2c). They are willing to act as soon as the rate of temperature change exceeds this threshold level. When the observed temperature increase relative to 1995, $dT_{obs}$, exceeds the 0.5°C increment, the substitution of fossil fuels by non-carbon based alternatives will be accelerated, Below the 1.0 °C level, the transition is only slightly speeded up; above it but below the 1.5 °C level, it is accelerated with nearly 1 year per year. In formula form:

$$ (8.15) $$

$$ if\ <\ dT_{obs}\ <\ 0.5\ then\ L_f = 100 $$

$$ if\ (0.5 < dT_{obs} < 1.0)\ then\ L_f(t) = 20 + (\ L_f(t-1) - 20) \cdot 0.995 $$

$$ if\ (1.0 < dT_{obs} < 1.5)\ then\ L_f(t) = 20 + (\ L_f(t-1) - 20) \cdot 0.99 $$

$$ if\ dT_{obs} > 1.5\ then\ L_f(t) = 20 + (\ L_f(t-1) - 20) \cdot 0.98 $$

I assume an upper level of a temperature increase of 2°C relative to 1900, a number based on the UNEP's Advisory Group on Greenhouse Gases (AGGG, 1990). It is also assumed that $L_f$ cannot become less than 20 years. The particular set of decision rules is determined by model experiments in which the world view is hierarchist ('the hierarchist utopia') and with a maximum temperature of 1.5°C (Section 8.4.4).

From an *egalitarian* perspective the management style should be based on the precautionary principle. In order to guard the society against a full-blown catastrophe in the long term, drastic structural social, cultural and institutional changes are necessary, notwithstanding short-term disadvantages and costs.

With respect to climate policy, this implies a rapid transition towards a fossil free society. In the model, I assume that $L_f = 20$ years. In line with the emphasis on more evenly distributed wealth and income and on less materialistic values, the egalitarian management style aims at zero economic growth. Indeed, the only growth of economic output results from population growth and technological progress (a; Table 8.1 and Figure 8.2a). This is done in the model with the rule that investments equal the depreciation rate of existing capital goods (compare equation (8.2)):

$$I^E(t) = \frac{\delta_k \cdot K(t-1)}{Y(t-1)} \qquad (8.16)$$

*Individualists* prefer the market mechanism as the management instrument par excellence. This often implies an adaptive management style. Disturbance of the climate system will provide new opportunities for smart entrepreneurs; government-based climate policies are not needed or even harmful. The individualist outlook supports a high rate of economic growth. Only if the monetary damage becomes a noticeable fraction of economic output, they will start to implement energy policy measures. The basic decision rule as implemented is, in formula form:

$$\text{if } dY(t) < \min[dY] \text{ then } I^I(t) = \min(1, \min[dY] \cdot \frac{I(t-1)}{dY(t-1)}) \qquad (8.17)$$

$$\text{else } I(t) = I(t-1)$$

where $\min[dY]$ is the minimum economic growth preferred by the individualist. A simple adaptive strategy is assumed: if economic growth falls below a certain desired minimum level, investments are increased. The value of the minimum growth rate is determined by model experiments with an individualist world view ('the individualist utopia', compare Section 8.4.4). In such a world, the value of $\min[dY]$ has to be set at 2 per cent per year to avoid a collapse in consumption per capita before the end of next century. As to emission reduction, the individualist will follow an adaptive strategy which is based on damage costs: if damage costs exceed a certain threshold value, in this model set at 1 per cent of economic output, the fossil fuel transition is accelerated quite effectively towards the rate of minimum half-life time of 20 years. This approach is somewhat similar to that adopted by Lempert *et al.* (1996). Thus:

$$L_f^I(t) = 20 + (L_f^I(t-1) - 20) \cdot 0.99 \qquad (8.18)$$

As long as no significant economic damage is detected, the half-life time of a fossil transition is assumed to be the longer period of 1000 years.

### 8.4.4 Utopias and Dystopias

Let us first look at the situation when the world is inhabited by agents which have one, shared perspective on how the world functions and how it should be managed. Indeed, this assumption of a single 'global commoner' is made in almost all studies on climate change. Such a future is indicated as XY with X denoting the world view, Y the management style and X, Y either the hierarchist (H), the Egalitarian (E) or the Individualist (I), the three so-called utopias are HH, EE and II. I briefly discuss these utopias because they have been instrumental in designing and implementing the management styles (Section 8.4.3).

A utopia is characterized by the fact that the world view is correct and that the management style of the single agent is in agreement with this world view. Such an agent adopts a perspective which is located in one of the corners of the triangle of perspectives. The development paths of the three utopias are given in Figure 8.3 for three variables: economic output (Y), fossil $CO_2$ emissions (E) and temperature change ($\Delta T$). In the *egalitarian* utopia, economic growth is approximately 1 per cent per year and the $CO_2$ emissions from fossil fuel combustion start falling after 2005 because of the policy to accelerate the fossil fuel transition. As a result, there is only a modest temperature increase of 0.5°C although the egalitarian world view holds that the climate system is quite sensitive.

In the *hierarchist* utopia, the economy grows at a stable rate of 1.5 per cent per year. The $CO_2$ emissions keep increasing and so does the temperature change. However, the hierarchist management style responds to the rising temperature by accelerating the phasing out of fossil fuels and the temperature increase can be stabilized at about 1.5°C above present values. This is assumed to be in the upper range of what is considered acceptable in many official studies. In the *individualist* utopia, economic growth is greater than 2 per cent per year throughout next century. Because the individualist expects only a modest decline in energy intensity, $CO_2$ emissions soar to over 40 GtC in 2100. In the individualist world view, the climate system is also believed to be quite insensitive to human disturbances and hence these high emissions cause only a small increase in the global temperature of 0.5°C in 100 years. This temperature change has no significant impact on economic activities, so that there is no policy response and the use of fossil fuels is not restricted.

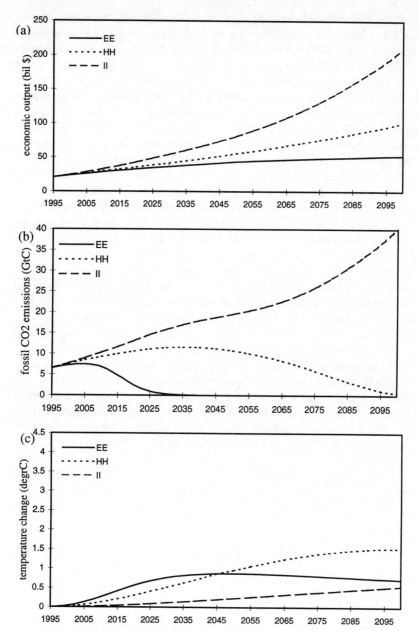

*Figure 8.3: Utopia projections if the world functions according to the world view of an egalitarian (__), hierarchist (...) or individualist (--), and the agents do not learn and adapt*

Interesting situations emerge if the world view and the management style are not in agreement - dystopias. Figure 8.4 presents for the same three model variables in the two most interesting dystopias. The first is when the correct world view is egalitarian, that is, the climate system is quite sensitive, but economic aspirations and feedbacks to temperature rise are based on an individualist management style (scenario EI). In this situation with the system functioning according to the egalitarian world view, an individualist management style leads to a collapse in economic development due to high economic growth aspirations together with severe impacts of climate change. The emission reduction measures are implemented at too late a juncture to avoid a temperature increase in excess of 4°C. This dystopia is the one which has been sketched regularly by environmentalist groups who fear that the prevailing economic growth aspirations will spell environmental catastrophe.

The second case is when the egalitarian management style is adopted by the governing agent, and subsequently turns out to be unnecessary because the climate system is quite robust with respect to human activities (IE). An egalitarian management style implies low economic growth and an acceleration of the fossil fuel transition at a cost. The resulting reduction of $CO_2$ emissions leads to a stabilization of the temperature increase. Because the climate turns out to be rather insensitive, the rise in temperature is confined to a mere 0.1°C (Figure 8.4). This combination of an individualist world view and an egalitarian management style can be seen as a world in which environmentalists gain enough popular support to dictate growth-restraining policies. Individualist-oriented business people will claim that climate change is still scientifically controversial and fear that all these measures are a waste of money. In this dystopia, they turn out to be right: economic growth is suppressed whereas no or acceptable climate risks would have been run in a high-growth development path.

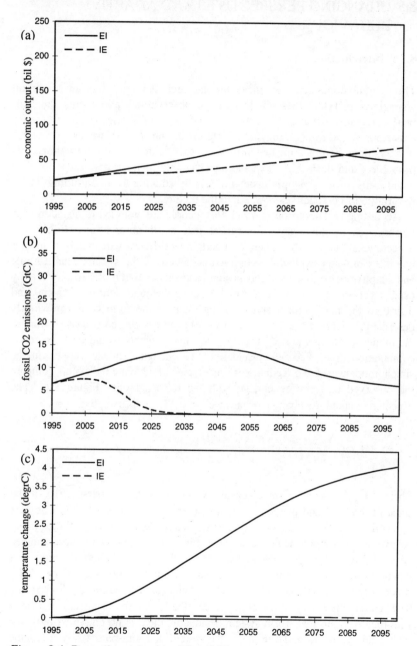

*Figure 8.4: Dystopia projections EI and IE*

## 8.5  CHANGING PERSPECTIVES AND ADAPTIVE BEHAVIOUR

### 8.5.1  Introduction

The 'global commoner' in these utopias and dystopias has an important characteristic: [s]he does not learn from observations about how the real-world actually behaves. In the case of a utopia, the world fits ones expectations and no learning and adaptation are needed. However, in the case of a dystopia there is a mismatch between expectations and observations. It is probable - and desirable - that the agent is able to learn and adapt so as to avoid a disastrous dystopia instead of rigidly sticking to its unfolding. Here, the 'Battle of Perspectives' come into the picture.

According to Thompson *et al.* (1990), people are assumed to abandon their perspectives in the event of surprise, that is, if observations differ from expectations. People who adhere to a certain world view will switch to another one if it can better explain the observed behaviour of the system. This learning and adaptive behaviour of agents is simulated in the 'Battle of Perspectives' by using a genetic algorithm. To this end, I define the equivalent of 50 agents and distribute the management styles among them in the form of the previously described decision rules. The number of 50 agents is chosen because I want to the model to be interactively used and too many agents would cost too much computation time. Too few would not give enough requisite variety. In the simple modelworld, the feedback is implemented by having the agents compare the observed temperature change with the expected one (Figure 8.1). The expected temperature change for perspective i, $\Delta T_{exp,i}$, is given by:

$$\Delta T_{exp,i}(t) = \frac{\Delta T_{2xCO2}}{\ln(2)} \cdot \ln\left(\frac{pCO2_{obs}(t)}{pCO2_{1995}}\right) \qquad (8.19)$$

where $\Delta T_{2xcCO2}$ is the climate sensitivity according to the perspective of the agent (Table 8.1) and $pCO2_{obs}$ is the measured concentration of $CO_2$. The next step is that I define a fitness function which is a measure of how well the system behaviour for a given management style fits with the real-world observations. Given the way I have implemented the feedback, this fitness function is a function of the expected temperature change resulting from the observed $CO_2$ concentration and the observed temperature change. The larger the discrepancy between the observed and the expected $\Delta T$, the less fit the management style is with regard to the real-world system. Evidently, there is no empirical basis for such a fitness function. To initialize the system in a transparent way, I assume that one of the 'extreme' agents has the correct model of the system.

For those agents who hold the correct view of the climate system, the observed temperature change will be approximately equal to the expected global mean temperature change. If their world view is incorrect, the observed and the expected value will diverge. As long as this difference between the two is less than a tolerance level, t , the fitness of the agents' perspective is assumed to be maximal and the agents have no reason to alter their perspective. This tolerance level is included to take account of the fact that perfect insight is not possible. I refer to it as 'ignorance'. In the model simulations, the existence of a certain ignorance causes a delay in the learning and adaptive behaviour of the agents. In the event of a difference between the observed and the expected temperature change which exceeds this tolerance level, the agents are surprised and motivated to alter their perspective.

$$f_i \;=\; \exp\!\left(-abs(\Delta T_{exp,\,i} - \Delta T_{obs} - \tau)^2\right) \tag{8.20}$$

The fitness function used is shown in Figure 8.5. If the observed value $\Delta T_{obs}$ is smaller than the expected value minus the tolerance level ($\Delta T_{obs} < \Delta T_{exp,i} - t$) or larger than the expected value plus the tolerance level ($\Delta T_{obs} > \Delta T_{exp,i} + t$), the fitness of the corresponding world view and management style decreases:

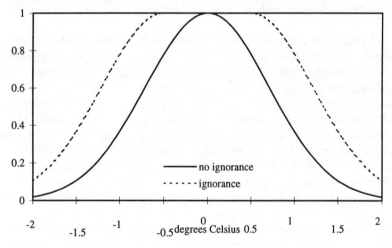

*Figure 8.5: Fitness function of agents' perspective related to the mismatch in expectations and observations. For ignorance tol = 0.5 is used and for no-ignorance tol = 0 is used*

The genetic algorithm and the dynamic system are integrated in the following manner. In scenario analysis a model as described in Section 8.3 simulates the effects of assumptions made for the control rates I and $L_f$. In an optimization approach, the optimal values of the control rates I and $L_f$ are determined. In this 'Battle of Perspectives', the control rates are a function of the state variables. The values I and $L_f$ are the (weighted) averages of $I_i$ and $L_{fi}$, the agent-specific values for the control variables. These values may change, in time, due to changes in the system. For example, if the dominant perspective of the agents concerned is individualist at the start, it may change in reaction to a persistent series of surprises into a more hierarchist or egalitarian perspective.

The experiments are performed for the three sets of assumptions on how the real-world climate system functions: hierarchist, egalitarian and individualist. For each experiment, 100 runs are performed because of the (stochastic) adaptation of the agents' perspectives. Assuming each of the 100 runs as an equally probable future, the average outcome can be considered as an expectation. The starting situation is comparable with the utopias and dystopias discussed in the previous section: a dominating management style X in a world which functions according to perspective Y. However, the agents' perspectives may now change in time, looking for the best explanation of the observations, and none of the perspectives fully determine the climate change policy A tolerance level of 0.5°C is used as a measure for ignorance.

### 8.5.2 Model Experiments

I will discuss the dystopian cases of Section 8.4.4, but now including adaptive behaviour of the agents. In Figure 8.6 the adaptation dynamics is depicted in terms of the changing distribution of agents among the three perspectives. Although the dominance between the perspectives change, there will always be room for each of them. The changing perspective prevents the system from following the extreme trajectories of the dystopias (compare Figure 8.4).

In the case of a non-adaptive individualist management style and a world functioning according to the egalitarian world view (EI), the investments to meet the high growth aspirations become excessively high as more and more output is lost to damage from climate change (Figure 8.7a). However, in case of adaptation, this is not happening because the phasing out of fossil fuels is accelerated and $CO_2$ is significantly curbed (Figure 8.7b; Figure 8.8b vs. Figure 8.4b). As a consequence, economic output peaks at a 50 per cent lower level. Despite these adaptive measures, the resulting drop in the anticipated temperature rise of 1°C by 2100 still does not bring the system in the low risk area: the global average temperature increase still amounts to almost 3°C at the end of next century (Figure 8.8c vs. Figure 8.4c). This simulation shows that a world with adaptive agents leads to significantly lower $CO_2$ emissions, but the dynamics as implemented in the model are too slow to bring the temperature change and the resulting climate change risks down to the levels of the egalitarian utopia (compare Figure 8.3).

The other dystopia represents the combination of an egalitarian management style and an individualist world view (IE). Because of adaptation, the initial desire for a fast but costly change to a fossil free society becomes less dominant as the stringent egalitarian measures are increasingly proven to be unnecessary. In such a world which functions according to the individualist world view, there will be an almost twice as high economic output and also a higher temperature increase compared with the dystopian case (Figure 8.8a vs. Figure 8.4a). This scenario is a real 'middle-of-the-road' course: the high growth levels of the individualist utopia are not reached, but the temperature rise remains significantly below the level of the egalitarian utopia (compare Figure 8.3a-c).

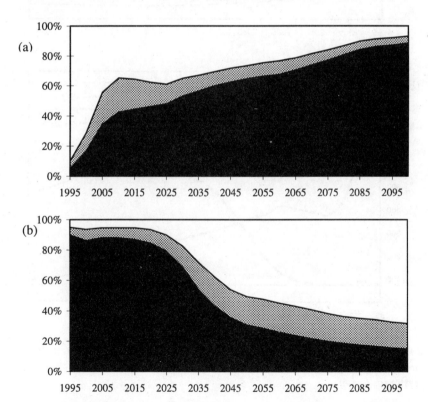

*Figure 8.6: Changes of perspectives in case adaptive agents are confronted with an EI (a) or an IE (b) dystopia:*

☐ *= individualist;* ▨ *= hierarchist;* ■ *= egalitarian*

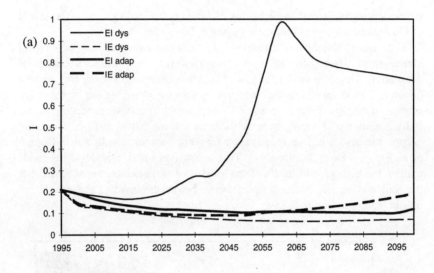

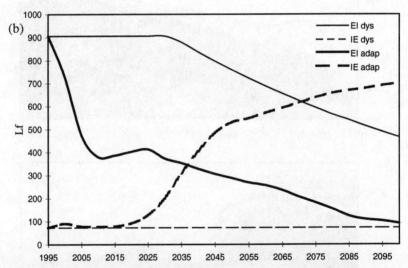

*Figure 8.7: The values of responses I (savings rate) and $L_f$ (half-time fossil fuel transition) for the dystopias (dys) and for the case agents adapt to dystopias (adap)*

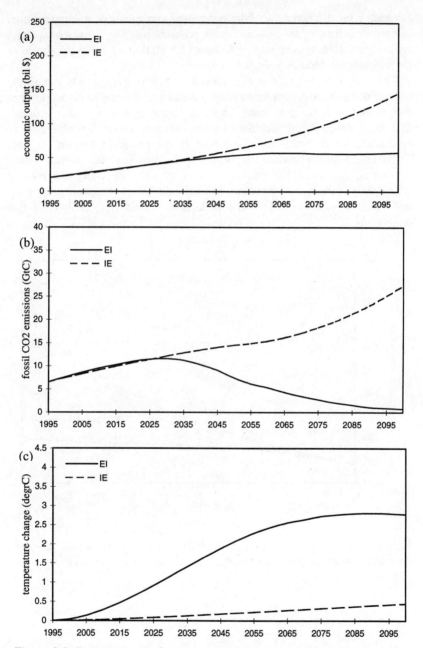

*Figure 8.8: Projections if adaptive agents are confronted with an EI or IE dystopia*

For each type of functioning of the system, the maximum and minimum values of various indicators are recorded given different possible initial management styles. Thus, each system is run 300 times (3 * 100), resulting in the spread of the indicators as depicted in Figures 8.9.

The ranges of projections of economic output overlap largely during the coming decades. A system functioning according to the egalitarian world view will, at the end of the next century, differ significantly from the other 'worlds'. The same difference is identified in emission projections for which, in an egalitarian world, emissions will reduce below present values at the end. Temperature projections differ significantly between the world views. Egalitarian and hierarchic projections overlap when emissions are reduced successfully in the egalitarian world. The individualistic temperature projections will remain significantly below other projections, in spite of their high emission projections.

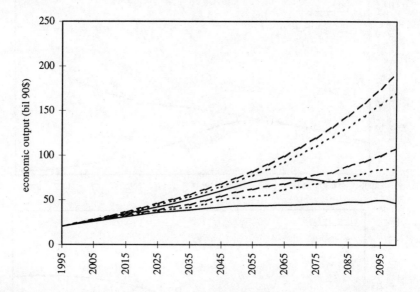

*Figure 8.9a: Range of projected economic output if the world functions according to the world view of the egalitarian (__), hierarchist (...) and individualist (--)*

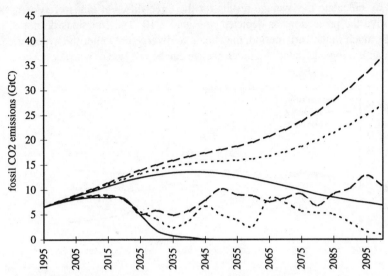

*Figure 8.9b: Range of projected CO₂ emissions if the world functions according to the world view of the egalitarian (__), hierarchist (...) and individualist (--)*

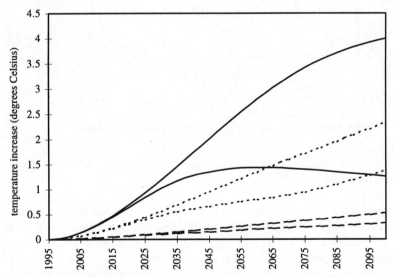

*Figure 8.9c: Range of projected temperature change if the world functions according to the world view of the egalitarian (__), hierarchist (...) and individualist (--)*

If we calculate the average results for the three different kinds of systems we derive the projections as depicted in Figure 8.10. The emissions do not differ that much in the early period, they begin to diverge only after the hypothesis on an anthropogenic induced climate change can be rejected or actually occurs.

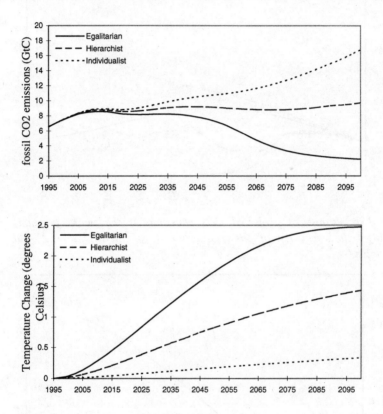

*Figure 8.10: Expected behaviour of the system for three sets of assumptions on the functioning of the system*

This analysis shows that long delays in the social, economic and environmental systems results in a non-utopian world. If climate change occurs, it is likely that the response to it will be too late, if it does not occur a lot of economic opportunities are lost. Although agents learn from surprises, the framework is constructed in such a way that the real picture of the system is within the triangle of perspectives. Within the model, reality can be known. However, insights change in time, and new insights emerge from the interaction between agents and the system. Therefore, there is a need for a changing triangle of perspectives, in which the corners, representing the extreme perspectives, change in time, but continue to explain historical facts. This moving triangle is a step too far for this moment, but an experiment will be analysed in which agents are confronted with a surprise.

### 8.5.3 Surprises

Climate change researchers are regularly confronted with new surprises. For example, in recent years new scientific findings (IPCC, 1992, 1996a,b,c) have shown that: (a) negative radiative forcing due to ozone depletion could counteract positive radiative forcing associated with chlorofluorocarbons (CFCs); (b) there is a possible cooling effect due to aerosols resulting from sulphurous emissions; (c) the rates of increase in the atmospheric concentration of most greenhouse gases have slowed down.

Imagine a world in which serious global warming may occur due to human activities. Suppose, furthermore, that this is a world in which the egalitarian perspective dominates at the start and agents do not ignore differences between observations and measurements. Now, by the middle of the next century, it is found that the global mean temperature has been suppressed by a temporary cooling effect due to the emissions of sulphur oxide. As a result, the expected temperature for all three perspectives is lower than what should be expected on the basis of a correct world view including the cooling effect. When the 'mask' falls off in the middle of the next century, the various agents are confronted with a surprise. How well would this world adapt to this surprise?

The cooling surprise would lead to a slowing-down of emission reduction, due to greater dominance of the hierarchist and individualist perspectives (Figure 8.11). This results in an additional increase of about 1°C by 2100, because this increase is not recognized before the middle of the next century. Initially, the hierarchist and individualist perspective gain more followers than without the surprise; later on, when the cooling effect is acknowledged, the proportion of those who adhere to the egalitarian perspective increases. However, in the agent implementation and choosing the year 2050 as the date of discovery, this adaptive response is too slow to a significantly higher temperature rise than would have occurred without the surprise. This experiment illustrates that a delayed response not only leads to a later reduction of emissions, but also that due to a lock-in of an individualist management style, the needed emission reductions are implemented more slowly and lead to an additional response delay.

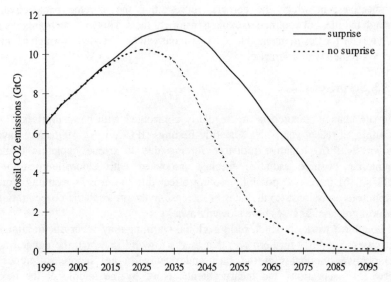

*Figure 8.11a: Average projections of fossil CO₂ emissions if the agents are confronted with a (cooling) surprise or not*

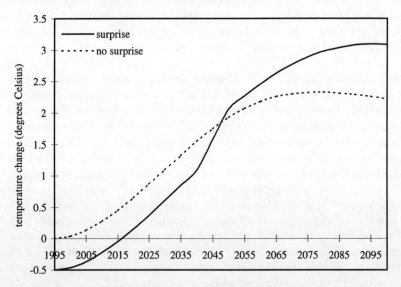

*Figure 8.11b: Average projections of temperature change if the agents are confronted with a (cooling) surprise or not*

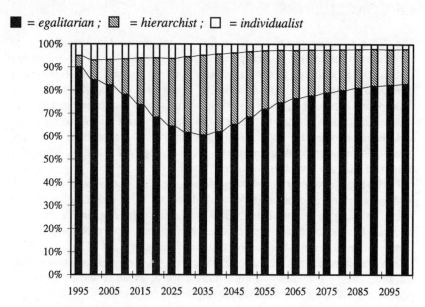

Figure 8.11c: Perspective change in case agents are not confronted with a surprise

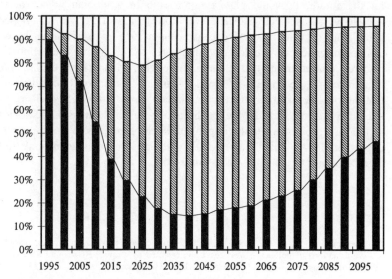

Figure 8.11d: Perspective change in case agents are confronted with a surprise

## 8.6 CONCLUSIONS

The 'Battle of Perspectives' is meant as an illustration of the use of evolutionary modelling in incorporating human behaviour within integrated assessment modelling. It simulates within the framework of utopian and dystopian scenarios the role of adaptive change by agents who learn from their observations of the real world. Obviously, the results are tentative in view of the many uncertainties inherent to the implementation of world views and decision rules for the chosen three characteristic agents. I do feel, however, that some basic aspects of the learning and adaptive behaviour presented here are operating in the real world.

Given these caveats, the following conclusions can be drawn. My approach enables a more explicit treatment of the notions of social change and scientific surprise events than earlier modelling activities in the field of integrated assessment for global climate change. Instead of projecting images of the future in terms of scenarios with exogenous or optimal policies, I am able to demonstrate the possible relevance of learning and adaptation. The Cultural Theory provides a helpful framework to organize the experiments; genetic algorithms are a useful tool to implement the approach.

The results show that, in a world in which climate change is the only problem to worry about, the learning of agents from observations in the form of a changing mix of aspirations and policies could make quite a difference for the future. It would play a minor role in a utopian world in which knowledge is perfect. However, in the real world with its imperfect knowledge, it could be of decisive importance in a situation in which dystopian tendencies would bring the world close towards catastrophe. This research demonstrates that a more thorough understanding of the role of ignorance and the features of social dynamics, as displayed nowadays in the international negotiations to reach a climate treaty, could add realism to and reduce the uncertainty in the plethora of published emission scenarios. It would also provide a healthy impetus to social scientists to participate in the important debate about how to anticipate and respond adequately to this possibly major threat which faces humankind.

## NOTES

1. Meadows *et al.* (1972, 1991) also present scenarios which avoid catastrophe by combinations of policies - these can be interpreted as utopias. Bossel and Strobel (1978) simulate utopias by inclusion of explicit adaptive behaviour.

2. A far-reaching simplification in this book is the ignorance of the many decisions of consumers on the micro-level, and the assumption that institutional actors may control behaviour at the micro-level.

# 9. Managing Malaria

## 9.1 INTRODUCTION

Malaria is one of the world's most important vector-borne diseases; there are few infectious diseases which have as great an impact on the social and economic development of societies. Out of a world population of approximately 5,300 million people in 1990, some 2,200 million were regarded as being at risk of contracting malaria, while some 270 million people were actually infected with the malaria parasite. At present, the distribution of malaria is mainly restricted to the tropics and sub-tropics, although before the Second World War, malaria was a relatively common disease in many temperate areas of the world.

Although the effective use of DDT and other insecticides after 1945 led to a significant global decrease in the prevalence of malaria and to its eradication or near-eradication in temperate zones and in some tropical areas, the rate of decrease has now slowed down considerably and a resurgence of malaria has occurred in several countries (Krogstad, 1996; WHO, 1996). The development of resistance to insecticides is considered to be one of the main obstacles in using insecticides for vector control in any strategy of malaria control/eradication. Resistance to insecticides is most pronounced in regions of Africa, Central America, and West and Southeast Asia (Pant, 1988).

A further obstacle is the development of resistance to anti-malarial drugs in *P. falciparum*, the malaria parasite responsible for most deaths. For many centuries, malaria has been treated with an extract from the bark of the cinchona tree, namely quinine, while a new (synthetic) drug, chloroquine, which became available at the end of Second World War, was found capable of preventing and curing malaria, especially since it was less toxic and effective in less frequent doses. By the 1960s, however, plasmodia resistant to chloroquine had emerged, and *P. falciparum* which are resistant to the drug are currently found throughout extensive regions of Africa, Southeast Asia, and South America (Figure 9.1) (Clyde, 1987; Payne, 1987; WHO, 1991). The increased selection and progressive dispersal of parasites resistant to antimalarial drugs is mainly caused by the fact that these preparations are increasingly being used as prophylactics and for self-medication, usually in insufficient doses. The problem of drug resistance has become particularly alarming in Africa, and its continual

194

exacerbation hampers efforts to provide adequate treatment of the disease (Nájera *et al.*, 1992).

It is evident that malaria patterns have, hitherto, depended to a large extent on the effectiveness of control efforts, together with socio economic development. Although new drugs are being developed and work is progressing on various potential malaria vaccines, given the increasing resistance of the malaria mosquito to insecticides, on one hand, and of its parasite to antimalarial drugs, on the other, the treatment of malaria seems likely to be more problematic in the future. A further factor which may influence future malaria trends, and to which attention has only recently been paid, is the projected effect of a human-induced climate change on the transmission dynamics of malaria (Bradley, 1993; Matsuoka and Kai, 1994; Martin and Lefebvre, 1995; Martens *et al.*, 1994, 1995 a,b; Martens, 1997). Anthropogenic climate change may directly affect both the behaviour and geographical distribution of the malaria mosquito and the life cycle of the parasite, and, thus, may have implications for the incidence of the disease.

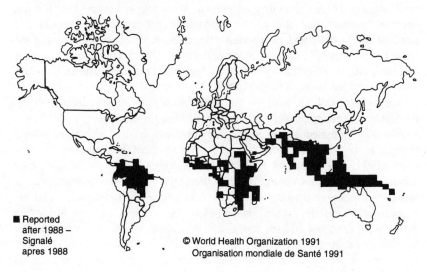

■ Reported
after 1988 –
Signalé
apres 1988

© World Health Organization 1991
Organisation mondiale de Santé 1991

*Figure 9.1: Current world-wide distribution where chloroquine-resistant Plasmodium falciparum has been reported (WHO, 1991)*

Although models are not intended to replicate all components of a real system, they do prove useful in studying the population dynamics of infectious diseases (Aron and Silverman, 1994). Experimental approaches in the laboratory and in the field are important, but cannot capture the full range of possible host-parasite interactions. Furthermore, modelling experience leads to the formulation of hypotheses which may inspire experimental research, an example of which would be the model-based hypothesis that inbreeding may accelerate the build-up of drug resistance, which has recently been confirmed empirically in Papua New Guinea (Paul *et al.*, 1995). Over and above enhancing scientific understanding, an important role of malaria models is to support decision-making in the management of malaria control operations. A well-known example of a malaria model used for the planning of malaria control was developed during the Garki project (Molineaux and Gramiccia, 1980). However, in this model resistance development, although acknowledged as a potential important effect, was not explicitly taken into account. Since the ability of organisms to develop resistance to human interventions has become an important issue in managing malaria, current modelling efforts incorporate the adaptation process by adopting either a deterministic or a stochastic approach (for example Nájera, 1974; Collet and Lye, 1987; Anderson and May, 1991).

Although the above techniques have been useful, new mathematical tools based on evolutionary processes have appeared during the last decade which are eminently suitable for modelling adaptation. According to Levins (1995), it has become apparent that the classic deterministic approach is incapable of confronting the rapid and unexpected changes on the horizon. In assessing the impact of both global and local changes, the modelling of adaptation to changes and modelling of evolutionary processes themselves provide a crucial tool with which to scan the future. The aim of this chapter is to discuss the deployment of evolutionary modelling tools in scanning future risks of the occurrence of malaria and assessing possible means of controlling those risks.

A model designed to enhance quantitative projections of climate-related changes in the potential distribution of malaria has been developed by Martens *et al.* (1994; 1995 a,b) and Martens (1997). Although this model does take account of how climate change directly affects the mosquito population, that is mosquito development, feeding-frequency, longevity of the mosquito, and the climatic effect on the incubation period of the malarial parasite inside the mosquito, it does not address artificial interventions by humans and how this may affect the increased malaria risk associated with climate changes. In order to allow for both anti-malarial control measures *and* the adaptation of mosquitoes and parasites to such malaria control policies, the simulation model created by Martens *et al.* (which describes the transmission dynamics between human and mosquito populations) is combined with genetic algorithms (Janssen and Martens, 1996; 1997). The latter involves a general and robust evolutionary modelling approach which is based on the mechanics of the survival of the fittest, whereby the inclusion of the notion of variability within the population renders the genetic algorithm a suitable tool for simulating the adaptive behaviour of a population within a changing environment. In this chapter, a simplistic, idealized model of the resistance cycles associated with insecticide and drug use in malaria control programs is presented, together with the impact of climate changes. Although this approach is adopted solely for heuristic purposes, it, nevertheless, does succeed in elucidating the mechanism of resistance development, interactions associated with climate change, and consequences for the implementation of strategies in malaria management.

## 9.2. MALARIA

### 9.2.1 Introduction

Malaria is caused by one or more of four species of parasites of the genus *Plasmodium*, whereby the vector responsible for malaria transmission is the mosquito of the genus *Anopheles*. The life cycle of the malaria parasite involves transmission both from mosquito to man and from man to mosquito, effected by the bite of a female mosquito (see Figure 9.2). The parasite multiplies within the mosquito by means of sexual reproduction, and, following an incubation period of several days (depending on the temperature and the species of parasite), malarial parasites can be found in the salivary glands of the insect. When an infected mosquito bites a human host, saliva is also injected and parasites are, thus, transferred to (hitherto uninfected) people, whereupon asexual multiplication takes place in the human host. Following an infective bite, there is an incubation period in the human patient which varies between 10 and 40 days, depending on the species of parasite. The incubation period culminates in a severe attack which is caused by the destruction of infected blood cells and the release of toxins into the bloodstream. Infections involving *P. falciparum* are often associated with fatal complications (for example anaemia and cerebral malaria).

Although malaria may manifest itself throughout the world, its incidence shows marked regional variations, these being dependent on four groups of interacting factors, namely: the human host, the malarial parasite, the mosquito as vector, and the environment, whereby the latter term is here understood to subsume physical, biological, and socio-economic elements. These factors will be discussed, in turn, in the sections which follow.

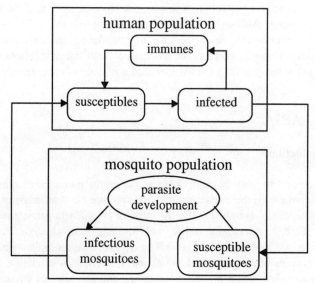

*Figure 9.2:   Transmission cycle of the malaria parasite*

### 9.2.2 The Human Host

Two main factors determine an individual's propensity to succumb to malarial infection: on the one hand, genetic factors affect the ability of the parasite to penetrate and maintain itself within the red blood cell; on the other, some degree of immunity may have been acquired by virtue of a previous history of infection. Among the genetic factors associated with protection against malarial infection are the sickle-cell trait and the Duffy factor (Molineaux, 1988), while those who have survived an attack of malaria acquire some degree of immunity to the disease. The number of parasites in the blood is lower and the infection may present few, if any, clinical symptoms. Consequently, in areas where malaria is rife, deaths from the disease occur mainly in the category of children aged between six months and five years. The high collective levels of acquired immunity of populations in these stable endemic areas reduce the likelihood that malaria epidemics will occur.

### 9.2.3. The Parasite

There are four species of the malaria parasite of the genus *Plasmodium*, namely: *P. falciparum*, the most common species in tropical areas and the most dangerous clinically; *P. vivax*, which has the broadest geographic range including many temperate zones; and *P. ovale* and *P. malariae*, which are less prevalent (Clyde, 1987). Virulence varies greatly from species to species. The ranking in decreasing order of virulence is as follows: *P. falciparum, P. vivax, P. malaria* and *P. ovale*. When left untreated, *P. falciparum* does not survive in the human body for longer than two to three years, whereas infection by *P. vivax* may last between two and more than 11 years. The duration of infection by *P. ovale* and by *P. malariae* may last from 1 year up to 53 years.

### 9.2.4 The Mosquito

Malaria is transmitted to humans by female mosquitoes of the genus *Anopheles*. This mosquito belongs to a very large genus which includes hundreds of species throughout the world, although only 60 of these are actual or potential malarial vectors. There are four distinct stages in the life cycle of the mosquito, namely: the egg, larval, pupal and adult stages. In order to produce eggs, a female mosquito must take a blood meal, and the eggs are normally laid after the blood meal has been digested. Development and survival during the larval and adult stages of the *Anophelines* depends on whether temperature, humidity, and rainfall are favourable. Temperature governs the growth rate of a mosquito population by determining the time needed for one generation to develop; the optimum temperature for most malaria vectors is found in the range 20-30°C. Relative humidities in excess of 60 per cent are preferred by vectors, and while moderate rainfall may prove beneficial to mosquito breeding, excessive rainfall may flush away the mosquito larvae.

### 9.2.5 The Environment

The physical, biological, and socio-economic aspects of the environment play an essential role in the epidemiology of malaria. Some of the physical factors have already been mentioned above. Among the biological factors which play a role in malaria transmission are the presence of predators and the presence of domestic animals. Cattle may be employed as sources of blood and hence divert mosquitoes from feeding on people. When considering the connections between malaria and socio-economic variables, two apparently contradictory relations can be identified. First, in the long run, social and economic development is associated with a downward trend in malaria, which is partly due to the increased provision of health services, both curative and preventive. Socio-economic development can also suppress malarial prevalence independently of deliberate control measures (for example via the enhancement of public hygiene, drainage, and housing) as the cases of Europe and North America would suggest (Bruce-Chwatt, 1980). On the other hand, in the short run, development projects may lead to an increased incidence of malaria, in particular where such projects are divorced from social development (for example when they involve deforestation, irrigation, colonization of new territory and so on). It is important to bear in mind that there is a direct feedback from the incidence of malaria to the socio-economic development of a country. The social and economic damage caused by malaria morbidity and mortality - for example, declines in the productivity of labour, pressure on health services - may prevent many low-income countries from achieving an efficient level of malaria control and/or an eradication program.

### 9.2.6 Climate Change Impacts

Direct effects of the anticipated changes in global and regional temperature, precipitation, humidity, and wind patterns resulting from anthropogenic climate change are factors which have an impact on the mosquito reproduction habits and on their longevity, and are, thus, associated with changes in annual vector density. In general, the rate of development of a parasite accelerates as the temperature rises. An increase in temperature may, therefore, result in the completion of the life cycle of a parasite in areas in which previous temperatures were too low for the parasite to reach maturity. Indirect effects of climate change include changes in vegetation and agricultural practices which are mainly caused by temperature changes and trends in rainfall patterns. Another indirect effect of climate change is associated with the rise in sea level and the resulting coastal flooding. The proliferation of brackish water lagoons influences the availability of habitat and either encourages or discourages vector species, depending on whether or not they prefer brackish water. Generally speaking, drought and desertification, including a migration or extension of global desert belts, could be expected to decrease malaria transmission. It is, thus, evident that major changes in the incidence of this vector-borne disease might be expected to be associated with a climate change.

### 9.2.7 The History of Modelling Malaria

The history of a mathematical approach to malaria is nearly as old as the discovery of its transmission dynamics. The earliest attempt to arrive at quantitative understanding of the dynamics of malaria transmission was made by Ross (1911). His models consist of a handful of differential equations which describe changes in the densities of susceptible and infected people and mosquitoes. In the 1950s, MacDonald (1957) added a dimension of biological realism to these early models by his careful attention to the interpretation and estimation of parameters. Although these basic models provide a useful overview of the dynamics of malarial infection, many of their predictions deviate strikingly from reality.

An obvious modification to the basic model would be the incorporation of latent periods, during which hosts are infected but are not yet capable of transmitting the disease. Furthermore, models addressing the transmission dynamics of malaria have begun to take account of the phenomenon of acquired immunity. The reason for this belated attention to immunity development is in part a consequence of the early focus in malaria models on the vector component in transmission, which is, in turn, explained by the initial aim of global eradication of malaria by means of the application of DDT. Aron and May (1982) have since then described a simple manner in which to incorporate the observed mechanism of the maintenance of immunity with continuous exposure. Although their model represents an advance over the earlier simple models, it nevertheless remains a very crude approximation of the true complexities of immunity to malarial infection.

More elaborate assumptions for the malaria parasite in the vector and in the human host are made by the Garki model (Dietz *et al.*, 1974; Molineaux *et al.*, 1978). A number of models have been developed to estimate age and time-dependent infection and recovery rates (see for example Nedelman, 1985).

### 9.2.8 Modelling Resistant Development

Most of the mathematical models which estimate the effect of eradication programs on malaria transmission have not yet included the ability of organisms to develop resistance to drugs or insecticides (for example Nájera, 1974; Tabashnik, 1986; Collet and Lye, 1987), although the evidence gathered in the field proves that this is a serious omission. With respect to resistance dynamics, a number of simulation models have contributed to our general understanding of this phenomenon and the development of strategies to reduce the development of resistance (a review of these can be found in Glass *et al.*, 1984). Most modellers have postulated that resistance is determined by a single gene, so that these models are generally not applicable when resistance is a quantitative trait (polygenic), in which the underlying genes are not identified individually. Curtis and Otoo (1986) emphasized the role of linkage between two resistance genes, resulting in a selective build-up of double resistance among insects in response to simultaneous exposure to two different insecticides, and they employed a similar approach to model the development of resistance to drugs among *Plasmodium* parasites.

Because insecticide and anti-malarial drugs are agents of selection, resistance to them can be studied using the same theoretical frameworks as those which have been applied to other types of evolutionary change. In the sections which follow, the development of resistance is charted by means of genetic algorithms, a tool to simulate complex adaptive systems.

## 9.3    MODELLING MALARIA: A COMPLEX ADAPTIVE SYSTEMS APPROACH

### 9.3.1  Introduction

The model described in this chapter is an extension of the systems approach previously adopted by Martens *et al.* (1994, 1995a,b). Martens (1997), and addresses two general malaria control options, namely: the use of insecticides to decrease mosquito densities, and the use of drugs to suppress the viability of parasites. While Martens *et al.* intended to create a global model of the effects of an anthropogenically-induced climate change on malaria risk, the model presented here aims at incorporating local dynamics, in order to derive a generic local model which takes account of human intervention in terms of insecticide and drugs use and the development of resistance to these control measures.

### 9.3.2  The Malarial System

A simple representation of the malarial system is the following. The mosquito system is represented by $x$, the vectorial capacity without taking account of the effect of temperature change. This vectorial capacity is defined as the number of potentially infective contacts inflicted by the mosquito population per infectious person per day. The human population can then easily be described by the categories susceptible ($y_1$), infected ($y_2$) and immune ($y_3$). If different age classes, births, and natural deaths are ignored, then the human population can be represented by the following three equations:

- The number of susceptible changes when immune people lose their immunity at rate ($r_3$) and if susceptible people become infected (at rate $r_1$):

$$dy_1/dt = r_3 \cdot y_3 - r_1 \cdot y_1 \qquad (9.1)$$

- The number of infected people changes when susceptible persons become infected and if infected people lose their infection at rate $r_2$ and become immune or die from infection (at rate $\mu_1$):

$$dy_2/dt = r_1 \cdot y_1 - (\mu_1 + r_2) \cdot y_2 \qquad (9.2)$$

- The number of immune people changes due to infected people who become immune and immune people who lose their immunity:

$$dy_3/dt = r_2 \cdot y_2 - r_3 \cdot y_3 \qquad (9.3)$$

The yearly rate of infection depends on the vectorial capacity, x, times number of days in a year, 365, and the portion of infected people:

$$r_1 = 365 \cdot x \cdot y_2 / (y_1 + y_2 + y_3) \qquad (9.4)$$

Assume that infection lasts for some fixed period of time $1/b_1$, in the absence of re-exposure, but that if a person is further exposed before $1/b_1$ units have elapsed, infection is sustained and another interval of duration $1/b_1$ without reinfection is required before infection is lost (Anderson and May, 1991). If infection occurs at per capita rate $r_1$, the average time spent in the immune state can be calculated as a function of $r_1$. The resulting average per capita loss of infection, is

$$\text{if } r_1 = 0 \text{ then } r_2 = b_1 \text{ else } r_2 = r_1 / (e^{r_1/b_1} - 1) \qquad (9.5)$$

The loss of immunity is simulated in the same way as the loss of infection with the use of a fixed time period $b_2$:

$$\text{if } r_1 = 0 \text{ then } r_3 = 1 / b_2 \text{ else } r_3 = r_1 / (e^{r_1 \cdot b_2} - 1) \qquad (9.6)$$

The interaction between the human population and the mosquito population determines the transition rates among susceptible, infected, and immune populations, respectively. To this end, the mosquito system is denoted by state variable x and the human system by state variable $y(t) \in R^7$. The potential of the mosquito population to transmit *P. falciparum*[1] is in the model assumed to be influenced by temperature, $T(t)$, and by the use of insecticides, $u_1(t)$. The dynamics within the human population are affected by the transmission potential of the mosquitoes and by the use of anti-malarial drugs, $u_2(t)$.

$$x(t) = f(T, u_1)$$

$$\frac{dy(t)}{dt} = g(y, x, u_2) \qquad (9.7)$$

In order to incorporate adaptation to antimalarial drugs and insecticides, this dynamic system is coupled to genetic algorithms which enable the genetic variety within the mosquito population and the parasite population (Figure 9.3). The genetic algorithms determine parameters that, in turn, determine the resistance of the mosquitoes and parasites and the optimum temperature for mosquito survival. The system can, therefore, be reformulated as

$$x(t) = f(T^a, u_1^a, T, u_1)$$

$$\frac{dy(t)}{dt} = g(y, x, u_2^a, u_2) \qquad (9.8)$$

where $T^a$, $u_1^a$ and $u_2^a$ represent fixed parameters in system (9.7). $T^a$ represent the change of the optimal temperature with respect to the reference value, $u_1^a$ and $u_2^a$ represent the degree of resistance (see Section 9.3.3). Now that they are simulated by genetic algorithms, they are subject to adaptations, if temperature changes, or if insecticides and antimalarial drugs are used. In Sections 9.3.2.1 and 9.3.2.2, this original model representation (9.8) will be described, and in Section 9.3.3 the implications of the incorporation of the genetic algorithms are discussed.

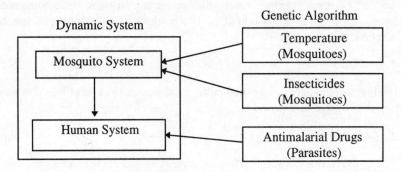

*Figure 9.3: Simplified scheme of the integration of a system dynamic model with genetic algorithms*

### 9.3.2.1 The mosquito population

The (infection-related) dynamics of the mosquito population proceed much more rapidly than do human population dynamics, so that the mosquito system can be considered as being in equilibrium with respect to changes in the human population. Therefore, the description of the mosquitoes is given in terms of an equilibrium instead of in a set of differential equations. Following Garrett-Jones (1964), the entire mosquito population is incorporated in a single state variable, namely: vectorial capacity. The formulation of vectorial capacity used by Martens *et al.* is multiplied by the relative fitness of mosquitoes to insecticides, $F^m$ (see Section 9.3.3.1) resulting in a formulation of adaptive vectorial capacity which includes the impact of the use of insecticides. Furthermore, an adaptive representation of survival probability can be used to describe the adaptation of a mosquito population to a change in temperature (see section 9.3.3.1):

$$x = \frac{\beta_1 \cdot z_1^2 \cdot z_2^{z3}}{-\ln(z_2)} \cdot F^m(u_1) \qquad (9.9)$$

where x is the adaptive vectorial capacity; $\beta_1$ incorporates variables assumed to be temperature independent (including the efficiency with which a mosquito infects a susceptible human; the propensity of the mosquito population to feed on humans; and the density of the mosquito population in relation to man). The term $z_1$ represents the man-biting habit (number of blood meals taken from humans per mosquito per day); $z_2$ is the daily survival probability of the mosquito; and $z_3$ is the incubation period of the parasite in the vector (in days).

The man-biting habit depends on the frequency with which one vector takes a blood meal and the total number of these blood meals being taken from man. The frequency of feeding depends mainly on the rapidity of digestion of a blood meal, a rate which increases as temperature rises so that at the optimum temperature, one meal is taken every 48 hours (Muirhead-Thompson, 1954). The relation between temperature and the rapidity of blood digestion is given in Detinova (1963). The resulting equation for the man-biting habit (per day) is:

$$z_1 = \frac{T - \beta_3}{\beta_2} \qquad (9.10)$$

where $\beta_2$ is the number of 'degree-days' required for the digestion of a portion of ingested blood (36.5 degree-days at relative humidity 70-90 per cent), $\beta_3$ is the minimum temperature required for the digestion of the blood meal (9.9°C) and T is the actual average temperature (in °C).

The vector's longevity determines its ability to transmit a parasite, since the female mosquito has to live long enough for the parasite to complete its development. There is presumably an optimum temperature and an optimum humidity for each species of mosquito, and it is apparent that, between certain limits, longevity decreases as temperature rises, and increases as relative humidity rises (Boyd, 1949; Molineaux, 1988). Data reported by Boyd (1949) and Horsfall (1955) on mosquito longevity indicate an optimum temperature of about 20-25°C and an optimum relative humidity of 60-90 per cent, and the assumption about the relation between the longevity of the *Anopheles* mosquito and temperature is based on these data. The maximum mean longevity is assumed to be 10 days ($z_2 = 0.9$) at temperatures of about 20°C. The assumed (non-adaptive) relationship between temperature and daily survival probability of the adult mosquito is written as follows (Martens *et al.*, 1994) (see section 9.3.3.1 for an adaptive representation):

$$z_2 = \exp\left(\frac{-1}{-4.4 + 1.31 \cdot T - 0.03 \cdot T^2}\right) \qquad (9.11)$$

The incubation period (duration of sporogony) in the vector must have elapsed before the infected vector can transmit the parasite. The duration of this latent period depends on two critical factors: species of parasite and ambient temperature. The parasites develop in the vector only within a certain temperature range, and whereas the minimum temperature for parasite development lies between 16 and 19°C in the case of *P. falciparum*, the proportion of parasites surviving decreases rapidly at temperatures over 32-34°C (Horsfall, 1955; MacDonald, 1957; Detinova, 1963). The relation between the incubation period and temperature (if higher than 16°C) can be expressed in the following equation (MacDonald, 1957):

$$z_3 = \frac{\beta_4}{T - \beta_5} \tag{9.12}$$

where $z_3$ is the incubation period of the parasite inside the vector (in days), ß$_4$ the number of 'degree-days' required for the development of the parasite (=111 degree-days for *P. falciparum* (Detinova, 1963)), T the actual average temperature (between ß$_5$ and a maximum temperature of about 40°C; in °C), and ß$_5$ the minimum temperature required for parasite development (16°C for *P. falciparum*).

### 9.3.2.2 The human population

The model used to describe the transition between the reservoirs of the human population at risk is based on a microparasite-epidemiological model as described in Aron and May (1982), Bailey (1982), Levin *et al.* (1989), and Anderson and May (1991). The human population subject to a risk of malaria is divided into three categories for each of two different age classes (i=1, children younger than 5 and i=2, people of 5 years and older). The three categories are susceptible persons ($y_1^i$), infected persons ($y_2^i$), and immune persons ($y_3^i$). The latent reservoir is omitted, because the duration of a stay in this reservoir is usually very short in comparison to the residence time in the other reservoirs. The total population is represented by $y_4$, which gets children with the birth rate $\lambda$.

The number of susceptible persons may change over time, as they become members of the infected class at a rate $r_1$. Infected individuals either die from infection at a rate $\mu_1^{(i)}$ or recover to join the immune category (at a rate $r_2$). Immune persons lose their immunity at a rate $r_3$, and those who have lost their immunity return to the reservoir of susceptible persons. All newborn babies are assumed to be members of the category of susceptibles; as they grow older, they graduate from the younger age class to the older (at a rate $\lambda_a$). People die from other causes at a rate $\mu$.

The dynamic behaviour of the human system can be described thus (see also Figure 9.4):

$$dy / dt = \mathbf{M} \cdot y$$

with $y = [y_1^{(1)}, y_1^{(2)}, y_2^{(1)}, y_2^{(2)}, y_3^{(1)}, y_3^{(2)}, y_4]$ (9.13)

and $\mathbf{M} =$

$$
\begin{bmatrix}
-r_1 - \mu - \lambda_3 & 0 & 0 & 0 & r_3 & 0 & \lambda \\
\lambda_3 & -r_1 - \mu & 0 & 0 & 0 & r_3 & 0 \\
r_1 & 0 & \begin{matrix} -\mu - \mu_1^{(1)} \\ -\lambda_a - r_2 \end{matrix} & 0 & 0 & 0 & 0 \\
0 & r_1 & \lambda_a & -\mu - \mu_1^{(2)} - r_2 & 0 & 0 & 0 \\
0 & 0 & r_2 & 0 & -r_3 - \mu - \lambda_a & 0 & 0 \\
0 & 0 & 0 & r_2 & \lambda_a & -r_3 - \mu & 0 \\
1 & 1 & 1 & 1 & 1 & 1 & 0
\end{bmatrix}
$$

where $r_1$ is the rate of infection, $r_2$ the rate of loss of infection and $r_3$ the rate of loss of immunity.

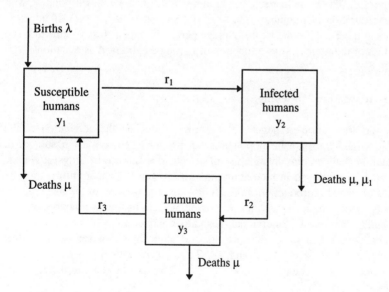

*Figure 9.4: Scheme of the dynamics within the human system*

The rate at which individuals become infected ($r_1$) depends on: the adaptive vectorial capacity (x) which represents the transmission potential of the mosquito population, the proportion of infected people in the human population, the amount of drug use and the sensitivity of malarial parasites to such drugs (that is the fitness of the parasites). $F^p(u_2)$ represents a maximum fitness which may decrease in the event of antimalarial drug use, depending on the degree of resistance (see Section 9.3.3). The use of drugs, thus, leads to a decrease in the infection rate and, consequently, an increase in the rate of losing immunity and in the rate of losing infection (formulas (9.9) and (9.10)).

$$r_1 = 365 \cdot x \cdot \frac{y_2^{(1)} + y_2^{(2)}}{y_4} \cdot F^p(u_2) \tag{9.14}$$

Rates of recovery from infection appear to increase with the increased longevity of living people in endemic areas. Assuming that re-exposure does not occur, states of infection and immunity endure for fixed periods of time. However, if a person is further exposed before such a period has elapsed, both infection and immunity are prolonged. The basic rate of loss of infection, $b_1$, is defined as the reciprocal of the average duration of infectiousness (average one year for *P. falciparum*). The basic loss rate of immunity $b_2$ is 0.67/year, corresponding with a mean duration of immunity of 1.5 years (Aron and May, 1982). If infection occurs at a per capita rate $r_1$, the average per capita rate of loss of infection ($r_2$) and loss of immunity ($r_3$) as a function of $r_1$ can be expressed as equations (9.5) and (9.6).

### 9.3.3 Adaptation Modelling

Now the application of genetic algorithms to simulate the adaptation of the mosquito and the parasite population can be described. For each subject of adaptation (temperature change, use of insecticides and use of drugs) a genetic algorithm is employed in modelling the transmission of genetic information by means of sexual reproduction. In the following sections, one of the most crucial aspects of the genetic algorithm is discussed, namely its fitness function, as used to simulate the fitness of individual mosquitoes and parasites.

The output generated by each genetic algorithm is a set of individual parameter values of $u_{1,i}{}^a$, $u_{2,i}{}^a$ and $T_i{}^a$. To conform with the system dynamic framework as described in Section 9.3.1, the average of these parameter values are used ($u_1{}^a, u_2{}^a, T^a$).

If genetic algorithms are to be used to simulate the dynamics of malaria, the validity of a number of assumptions must first be considered:

-   The values adopted for crossover probability ($p_c$) and mutation probability ($p_m$) are imaginary numbers and cannot be validated by empirical research. Although the selected numbers are at best educated guesses, they have no significant influence on the main conclusions, as will be shown in Section 9.4.7.
-   There is a lack of knowledge about the various shapes of the fitness functions, and those discussed in the following subsections, although mimicking observed patterns (for example Curtis *et al.*, 1978; Schapira, 1990), are therefore, rather subjective and should be regarded as being of illustrative value only.
-   The question of which population size is adequate for simulating the variety within a population. Too large a population would detract from the model's usefulness as an interactive learning tool. After testing various numbers, it is decided that a population of 100 individuals (mosquitoes/parasites) would be appropriate. Although it is realized that the 'real' population of mosquitoes or parasites cannot accurately be simulated by reference to such a group, nevertheless, a simulation of the aggregate adaptive behaviour of a representative heterogeneous group of mosquitoes and parasites can be made.

These problems are by no means unfamiliar within the modelling community. Taylor (1983) discussed the lack of experimental data with which one could validate the modelling approach to the issue of resistance development. The model should, therefore, be seen as a heuristic device in which expert knowledge is integrated in such a manner that interactive and transparent simulations and experiments can be performed.

### 9.3.3.1 The mosquito

With the help of the genetic algorithm, sexual reproduction is implemented using the two genetic parameters: namely the crossover probability ($p_c$) and the mutation probability ($p_m$). To simulate the adaptation of mosquitoes, a crossover probability of 0.4 and a mutation rate of 0.001 were assumed. These values are consistent with those generally used in genetic algorithm applications, and the results are not sensitive to this assumption (Section 9.4.7).

The fitness of a (biological) population is related to the chance of its members begetting descendants (Hofbauer and Sigmund, 1988). The expected lifetime of a mosquito is assumed to be a measure of individual fitness, since life expectancy might be related to the production of offspring. Having adopted this approach, I distinguish two pressures on the mosquito population, namely temperature change and insecticide use. I assume that adaptation to temperature change and to insecticides are independent of each other.

*Modelling Global Change*

*Adaptation to temperature change*  For every mosquito, a temperature level is assumed at which its expected lifetime would be maximized (Figure 9.5), but within the mosquito population there is variation of these optima among individuals. If the temperature increases over a longer period (say various years), mosquitoes for which the optimum is higher than average exhibit greater fitness. Due to the mechanisms associated with the 'survival of the fittest', the average optimum temperature for longevity will, therefore, rise.[2] The implementation of this process by means of a genetic algorithm proceeds as follows.

Within the mosquito system, the daily probability of survival is a function of temperature (see equation (9.11)). Within the population, individual temperature optima are scattered around the mean temperature. For simplicity, no distinction is made in seasonal temperature changes. The daily survival probability can, therefore, be treated as a function of the *local mean temperature*, whereupon the variable $T_i^a$ is introduced which represents the individual adaptation to temperature. This results in a daily survival probability so that the fitness function of mosquito i becomes,

$$F_{T,i} = -4.4 + 1.31 \cdot (T - T_i^a) - 0.03 \cdot (T - T_i^a)^a \tag{9.15}$$

If temperature T changes, the value of $T_i^a$ will also change since the 'survival of the fittest' keeps the mosquitoes in the optimum temperature zone.
Furthermore, the daily survival probability of the adult mosquito becomes:

$$z_2 = \exp(\frac{-1}{-4.4 + 1.31 \cdot (T - T^a) - 0.03 \cdot (T - T^a)^2}) \tag{9.16}$$

where $T^a$ is the mean of $T_i^a$.

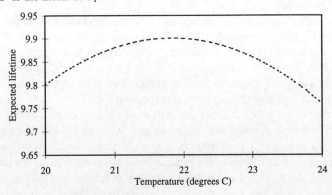

*Figure 9.5: Life expectancy (in days) as a function of temperature (equation (9.11))*

*Adaptation to insecticides* An important human-induced pressure on the mosquito population is the use of insecticides. Several models have been developed to enable us to understand and manage the evolution of insecticide resistance, and nearly all of them assume that resistance is controlled by two alleles at one locus (Taylor, 1983; Anderson and May, 1991). However, the fitness function is based on the study published by Schapira (1990) and Tabashnik (1990), although the chosen modelling approach required some simplifications.

In the simulations, I distinguish three kinds of mosquitoes, namely: susceptibles, moderately-resistant, and resistant individuals, taking them as three classes of individual sensitivity to insecticides. The assumption is that a certain dose of insecticide reduces fitness in the manner depicted in Figure 9.6, whereby it is assumed that the same dose would have a more pronounced impact on susceptible mosquitoes than on (moderately) resistant ones. The fitness function expresses the notion that the fitness of the three classes drops in a decreasing rate for a higher dose of insecticides (Curtis *et al.*, 1978; Schapira, 1990). Obviously, if alternative insecticides are applied which affect the three categories differently for some reason, for example being more effective, the results and conclusions may differ.

In addition, the simulation incorporates a 'biotic fitness' component which represent the relative fitness of the mosquito, in the event of no insecticides being used at all. A lower value for the biotic fitness of the more resistant genes explains the lower density of these genes in an insecticide-free environment. Given an initial random distribution, the following table is derived for the fitness of mosquitoes, $F^m$, to which a certain dose of insecticides $u_1$ is applied, whereby I assume that 99 per cent of the mosquitoes are susceptible, 0.9 per cent are moderately-resistant and 0.1 per cent resistant in the initial situation (values based on Tabashnik, 1990).

| | $u_{1,i}$ | relative biotic fitness $F_{bio}^m()$ | relative fitness under insecticides $F_{ins}^m()$ |
|---|---|---|---|
| susceptible | [0.0, 0.99) | 1.0 | $1-u_1/(0.002+u_1)$ |
| moderately-resistant | [0.99, 0.999) | 0.95 | $1-u_1/(0.05+u_1)$ |
| resistant | [0.999, 1.0] | 0.9 | $1-u_1/(0.15+u_1)$ |

The average fitness of the individual mosquitoes $F^m(u_{1,i})=F_{bio}^m(u_{1,i})*F_{ins}^m(u_{1,i})$, $F_{ins}^m(u_1)$, is used in the equation for vectorial capacity x.

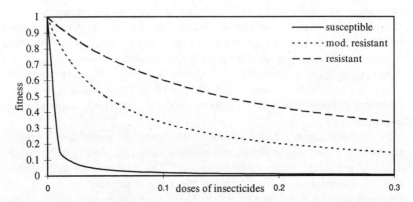

*Figure 9.6: Relative fitness of mosquitoes related to the use of insecticides. A certain dose of insecticides leads to a reduction in fitness which is more severe in the case of susceptible than resistant individuals*

### 9.3.3.2 The parasite

The dynamics of the gene pool in parasites differ from those in the mosquitoes. Since the population of parasites is spread among the human population and the mosquito population, the transmission of resistant parasites through a vector population to other human hosts limits the efficacy of adaptation in the parasite population at large. Note that a single gene pool for parasites is assumed, although several local clusters do exist (in the hosts). In view of the lack of data, I have been obliged to use the same crossover and mutation probabilities as for the mosquitoes in the reference runs.

*Adaptation to drugs*   Having established the modelling approach to the resistance among mosquitoes to the use of insecticides, the adaptation of parasites to the use of antimalarial drugs is modelled in a similar manner. Thus, a three phenotype model is simulated by distinguishing three kinds of parasites, namely: susceptibles, moderately-resistant, and resistant individuals, and taken these as three classes of individual sensitivity to the drugs involved. Given an initial random distribution, the following table is derived for the fitness of parasites to which a certain dose of drugs $u_2$ is applied, whereby it is assumed that 99 per cent of the population is susceptible, is 0.9 per cent moderately-resistant, and 0.1 per cent resistant in the initial situation:

| | $u_{2,i}$ | relative biotic fitness $F_{bio}^{P}$ | relative fitness under drugs $F_{dr}^{P}$ |
|---|---|---|---|
| susceptible | [0.0, 0.99) | 1.0 | $1-u_2/(0.002+u_2)$ |
| moderately-resistant | [0.99, 0.999) | 0.95 | $1-u_2/(0.05+u_2)$ |
| resistant | [0.999, 1.0] | 0.9 | $1-u_2/(0.15+u_2)$ |

The fitness function for a parasite, therefore, becomes

$$F^P(u_2)_i = F_{bio,i}^{P} \cdot F_{dr,i}^{P} \qquad\qquad (9.17)$$

Similarly, the fitness function for a parasite $F^P(u_2)_i$ is the product of the 'biotic' and 'drugs' fitness; the average fitness of the individual parasites, $F^P(u_2)$, is used to determine the impact of resistance on the transmission dynamics within the human population in equation (9.8) It should be noted, however, that in some places biological advantage of chloroquine-resistant *P. falciparum* has been observed (discussed by Wernsdorfer, 1994). This would imply that resistance development would proceed more rapidly than under the assumption discussed above.

### 9.3.3.3 Migration and refugees among mosquitoes and parasites
Georghiou and Taylor (1977) argued that the migration of insects tends to delay the rate of evolution of resistance. In addition, the percentage of mosquitoes or parasites not reached by the anti-malarial treatment (the so-called refugees) will inevitably influence resistance development. The complex adaptive systems approach takes account of both of these processes in the development of resistance, among mosquitoes as well as among parasites.

It would seem self-evident that, depending on landscape and infrastructure, mosquitoes are more or less able migrate from place to place, and that mosquitoes susceptible to insecticides may, thus, enter a treated area. Moreover, parasites susceptible to anti-malarial drugs can also migrate, whether they are carried by mosquitoes or humans. Migration is modelled by assuming that during each timestep a fraction of the new population is bred under the initial conditions, that is not yet adapted to the changed conditions.

Insecticides are sprayed on specific areas so that 100 per cent coverage is seldom achieved. Drugs are not taken (sufficiently) by all humans, so that a fraction of the parasites escapes from it. This phenomenon of refugees is modelled by assuming that during each timestep a part of the population, the size of which is randomly selected, has not been treated despite the control programs which have been implemented.

## 9.4   THE EXPERIMENTS

### 9.4.1 Introduction

The experiments deal with the consequences of the use of insecticides and anti-malarial drugs, together with a temperature change on the occurrence of malaria for a time horizon of one decade, using time steps of 0.1 year. Although malaria situations are extremely heterogeneous with respect to change, the two types of regions distinguished are a region of low endemicity, and a region of high endemicity. Although not the real generational longevity among the parasites and mosquitoes is specified, the time horizon is based on observed time elapsed in acquiring resistance (see Table 9.1). Furthermore, it is assumed that the initial force of infection $(r_1)$ is 2.0 per annum in highly endemic regions and 0.1 in areas of lower endemicity (Martens *et al.*, 1995a). These values were chosen since they lie within the range of the values reported in several studies on the pristine force of infection among young children. The initial settings for these systems are given in Table 9.2. Areas of lower endemicity can be characterized as exhibiting low vectorial capacity resulting in a high percentage of susceptible persons ($\approx 80\%$), and low percentages of infected ($\approx 8\%$) and immune persons ($\approx 12\%$). Areas of low endemicity *vis-à-vis P. falciparum* can be found in Southeast Asia and South America. Regions of high endemicity are characterized by a relatively high vectorial capacity. In the initial situation, there is a high percentage of immune ($\approx 68\%$) and infected persons ($\approx 27\%$). The younger age class especially suffers from a high percentage of infected persons ($\approx 45\%$). Highly endemic regions are mainly found in tropical Africa.

I now propose to report a set of results which I have derived using the complex adaptive systems approach. In the starting year, the situation is assumed to be near equilibrium. This assumption about an equilibrium state is made for analytical purposes, namely, to render the impact of control policies and temperature change on the occurrence of malaria, transparent, thereby including the adaptation of mosquitoes and parasites. Therefore, I have assumed a steady state situation in demographic, social, and economic development, although I recognize that these factors may influence future developments of malaria.

The results are presented as time series covering a period of 10 years. In view of the stochastic elements of the model, I elected to use a large number of runs (100),[3] and determine the mean and the extremes of important indicators. This procedure yields ranges of uncertainty, whereby the uncertainty does not lie in the different parameter values of the model, but rather in the stochastic characteristics and the complexity of the system.

In the interest of analytical lucidity, two broad control levels for both insecticides and antimalarial drugs are distinguished, namely: the low and the high dose. In case of a low dose, a value of $u_i$ equal to 0.002 is adopted, which represents a 50 per cent deterioration in the fitness of susceptible mosquitoes or parasites. The high dose $u_i$ is assumed to be equal to 0.05 such that the fitness of the moderately-resistant mosquito or parasite decreases by 50 per cent.

A typical outcome is shown in Figure 9.7, which shows the impact of using a low dose of insecticides. Although the input variables are the same for the 100 runs, there is a large spread in the optimal temperature for the mosquitoes, the vectorial capacity, and the incidence of malaria. Although on average the use of a low dose of insecticides leads to an increase in the incidence of malaria in the long run, it might also lead to a slow decrease of the incidence, if evolutionary adaptation among mosquitoes proceeds very slowly. In order to envisage the trends for the various sensitivity tests, I will confine myself to depicting the average scores in the following subsections.

*Table 9.1: The time which elapses before a majority (that is > 50 per cent) of the individuals in the mosquito population become resistant to the control agent (source: Anderson and May, 1991)*

| Anopheline mosquitoes (different localities) | Control agent | Time to resistance (in years) |
|---|---|---|
| An. sacharovi | DDT | 4-6 |
|  | dieldrin | 8 |
| An. maculipennis | DDT | 5 |
| An. stephansi | DDT | 7 |
|  | dieldrin | 5 |
| An. culicifacies | DDT | 8-12 |
| An. annuaris | DDT | 3-4 |
| An. sundaicus | DDT | 3 |
|  | dieldrin | 1-3 |
| An. quadrimaculatus | DDT | 2-7 |
|  | dieldrin | 2-7 |
| An. pseudopunctipennis | DDT | >20 |
|  | dieldrin | 18 weeks |

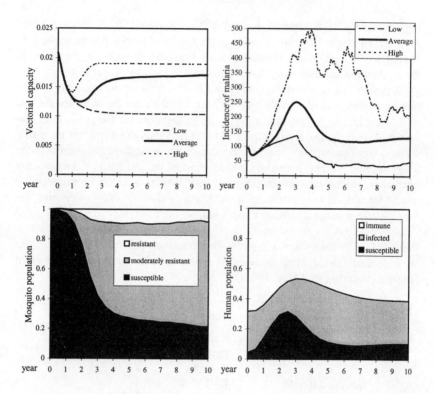

*Figure 9.7: An example of an experiment in a region of high endemicity. Depicted are the average and extremes, in the first two pictures; and fraction of resistant, moderately resistant and susceptible mosquitoes and average fraction of immune and susceptible people in the last two pictures, for a sample of 100 runs*

Table 9.2: *The initial situations were arrived at as follows: for highly endemic regions an infection rate, $r_l$, of 2.0 is assumed and for regions of lower endemicity an infection rate of 0.1. The birth rate is assumed to be equal to the natural death rate, although the additional death rates due to malaria imply a slightly declining population. The initial values for $\beta_1$, $y_1^{(i)}$, $y_2^{(i)}$ and $y_3^{(i)}$ reflect an equilibrium situation in case malaria-related deaths are not included*

|  | low endemicity | high endemicity | description |
|---|---|---|---|
| $\beta_1$ | 0.02226 | 0.13445 | temperature independent parameter |
| $\beta_2$ |  | 36.5 | degree days blood digestion |
| $\beta_3$ |  | 9.9 | minimum temperature |
| $\beta_4$ |  | 111 | degree days development parasites |
| $\beta_5$ |  | 16.0 | minimum temperature development parasites |
| T |  | 21.88 | initial local mean temperature |
| x | 0.00335 | 0.02018 | vectorial capacity |
| $\lambda$ |  | 0.02 | birth rate |
| $\lambda_a$ |  | 0.2 | aging children |
| $\mu$ |  | 0.02 | natural death rate |
| $\mu_1^1$ |  | 0.04 | fatality rate (0-5) |
| $\mu_1^2$ |  | 0.01 | fatality rate (>5) |
| $b_1$ |  | 1 | basic loss rate infection |
| $b_2$ |  | 1.5 | basic duration immunity |
| $y_1^1(0)$ | 0.077 | 0.011 | susceptible persons (0-5) |
| $y_1^2(0)$ | 0.718 | 0.034 | susceptible persons (>5) |
| $y_2^1(0)$ | 0.007 | 0.041 | infected persons (0-5) |
| $y_2^2(0)$ | 0.076 | 0.231 | infected persons (>5) |
| $y_3^1(0)$ | 0.008 | 0.039 | immune persons (0-5) |
| $y_3^2(0)$ | 0.115 | 0.644 | immune persons (>5) |

### 9.4.2 Impact of Control Programs

If the case is considered in which mosquitoes and parasites do not adapt to the use of insecticides and drugs, the new equilibrium can be calculated, given that constant levels of insecticides and/or drugs are used. Because the impact of both control programs is modelled in a similar manner, they have identical effects. The control program will lower the rate of infection as a result of rendering the mosquitoes and/or parasites less fit, and of the decrease in the percentage of infected persons. The percentage of immune persons will likewise decrease, resulting in an increase in the size of the fraction of susceptible humans.

The incidence of malaria will decrease in regions of low endemicity, as a consequence of the control programs (Figure 9.8a). In regions of high endemicity, an increase of malaria may occur if the control programs are not stringent enough, the effect being a steeper increase in susceptible humans (immune persons lose their immunity) relative to the decrease in the infection rate (Figure 9.8b).

As a result of the ability of vector and parasite to adapt to the control programs, their effectiveness decreases in such a manner that the new equilibria are located nearer to those obtaining in the absence of control programs. It might be expected that adaptation may eventually lead to higher incidence rates than those which occur in the absence of adaptation. A notable exception is the case of low doses in regions of high endemicity, since adaptation will then result in a less pronounced increase in susceptibles which will exceed the reduced decrease in the infection rate, leading to lower incidence rates.

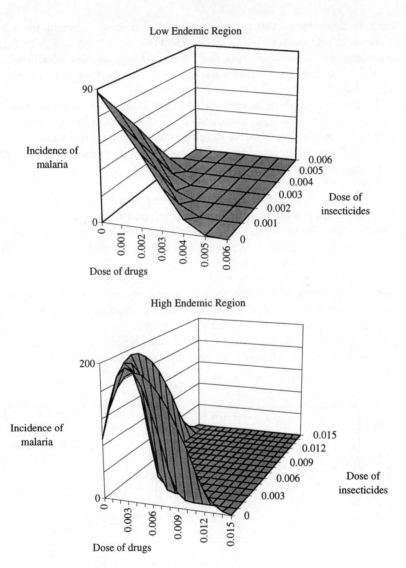

*Figure 9.8: Incidence of malaria for different levels of control in case of no adaptation (high and low endemic regions)*

In Figures 9.9a and b the averaged values over time are depicted for different levels of control programs. In regions of low endemicity, the vectorial capacity first decreases, but due to adaptation among mosquitoes subsequently increases, albeit to a level which lies somewhat below the initial level. The result is a similar pattern in the incidence of malaria, although the level continues to fall (gradually). It is, thus, evident that a combination of both drugs and insecticides at low levels is more efficient than high level use of only one of the two, a finding which reflects the enhanced development of resistance at higher doses.

In regions of high endemicity, the decrease in adaptive vectorial capacity exhibits a similar pattern to that which occurs in regions of low endemicity. It would be expected that resistance development would differ in the two regions, due to a difference in the gene pool. Nevertheless, for simplicity's sake, the same fixed population size is used within the genetic algorithm and, therefore, arrived at similar results. An improvement of the model might be the coupling of vectorial capacity and the population size of the genetic algorithm. Due to the difference in the profiles of the populations, the patterns of incidence of malaria would be quite dissimilar. Following a reduction in incidence at the outset of the control programs, incidence subsequently shows an increase due to the lower effectivity of the control measures. Due to the high fraction of susceptible humans after a successful period of control, again as a result of the flow of immune persons due to the increased rate of immunity loss, incidence may even rise to surpass the initial level. In the long run, a combination of too low levels of control does not achieve a better performance than control by a single method. Indeed, incidence peaks at a level even higher than the initial (pre-control) level due to the higher number of susceptible humans who become reinfected.

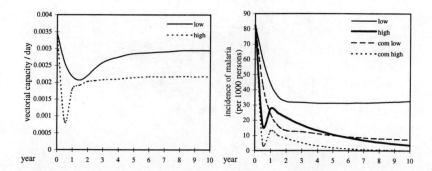

*Figure 9.9a: Adaptive vectorial capacity and incidence of malaria for different levels of control in a region of low endemicity. Scenarios low and high depict the results of a low or a high dose of insecticides. For the scenario com low, low doses of insecticides as well as drugs are combined. This also holds for com high*

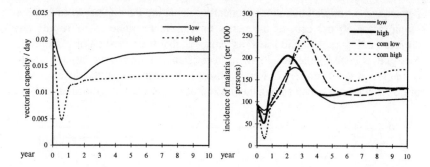

*Figure 9.9b: Adaptive vectorial capacity and incidence of malaria for different levels of control in a region of high endemicity. Scenarios low and high depict the results of a low or a high dose of insecticides. For the scenario com low, low doses of insecticides as well as drugs are combined. This also holds for com high*

### 9.4.3 Sensitivity of Malaria Incidence to Migration

Migration of mosquitoes and parasites can influence the development of resistance. Comins (1977), for example, showed that the migration of insects may greatly retard the development of insecticide resistance, and recent observations in Papua New Guinea and Tanzania support such model-based hypotheses (Paul *et al.*, 1995). Various studies (e.g. Comins, 1977; Tabashnik and Croft, 1982) found two distinct phases in the time required to develop resistance. At low doses, resistance developed more rapidly as the dose increased, paralleling the case in which migration is absent, this in contrast to the case of high doses in which resistance develops more slowly as the dose increases. In the absence of migration, the rate of resistance development is determined primarily by the rate at which susceptible genes are removed from the population. As the dose increases, susceptible genes are removed more rapidly, and resistance consequently develops apace. At low doses in the presence of migration, the pattern is similar. Where migration is present and doses are high enough to kill heterozygotes (which are intermediate between the susceptible and resistant genes, comparable with moderately-resistant in this chapter), however, mosquito mortality due to insecticides also removes resistant genes from the population. As dose increases in this range, more heterozygotes are killed, leaving relatively few resistant mosquitoes. The resistant survivors are effectively swamped by the susceptible immigrants, thereby retarding resistance development.

The impact of mosquito migration on insecticide resistance development is analysed by postulating various levels of insecticide application and various percentages of migration and subsequently calculating the number of time steps required for 50 per cent of the genes to achieve resistance. The results are depicted in Figure 9.10 and show, as expected, that the migration of susceptible mosquitoes impedes the development of resistance. Furthermore, at high levels of migration (>40 per cent inflow of susceptible mosquitoes), the development of insecticides resistance among the mosquitoes will be entirely blocked.

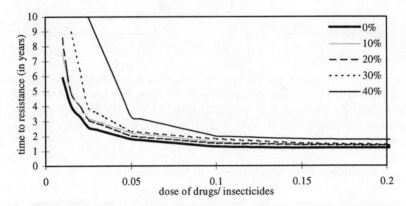

*Figure 9.10: Effect of dose on the rate of evolution of resistance featuring various percentages of migrants per time-step*

That the results do not show the two distinct phases which were found in Comins (1977) and Tabashnik and Croft (1982) is a consequence of the different fitness function[4] for the various genes. The relative fitness among the various gene combinations remains rather the same, along the line of increasing doses of insecticides. This is not the case where models, such as the one adopted by Tabashnik and Croft (1982), are concerned, since heterozygotes are not killed at low doses, but only at high ones. In fact, in such models, there is a kind of threshold value in the fitness function (survival rates for the different types of genes), while in the model a more gradual decrease of the fitness function is assumed. There was no field data known at the time of writing which would favour either of these approaches.

### 9.4.4 Sensitivity of Malaria Incidence to the Coverage Rate

In the absence of refugees from control programs (that is 100 per cent coverage), rates of insecticide resistance increase with increasing doses. If, however, a fraction of the mosquito population evades treatment by becoming 'refugees', the development of resistance is expected to be impeded. Tabashnik (1990), for example, shows that if 10 per cent of the mosquitoes are refugees evading exposure to insecticides, this may significantly impede the development of resistance.

The impact of the coverage rate is explored for the different doses applied in various control programs, and the results are depicted in Figure 9.11. For each time step, a certain fraction of the mosquito population is not reached by the control measures, and two distinct phases in the time required to develop resistance were found. In the case of low doses and low percentages of refugees, the results are about the same as in the case of zero refugees. However, when higher doses are applied, the time period required to develop resistance rapidly lengthens. The doses of control which mark the two distinct phases are different for each of the various fractions of refugees. Where higher percentages of refugees are concerned, the period of time required to develop resistance starts to become greater at an earlier juncture. Among more than 50 per cent of the refugees, resistance will not develop at all. The rate of evolution of resistance by *P. falciparum* could be retarded by selective treatment of those people with high parasitaemias.

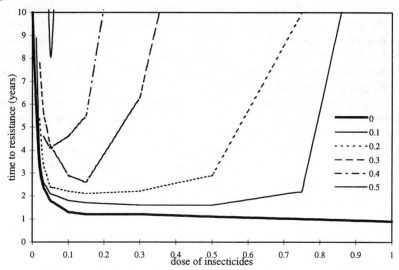

*Figure 9.11: Effects of dose on the rate of evolution of resistance featuring various percentages of refugees per time-step*

An explanation for the existence of these two distinct phases, which are also found by Tabashnik (1990), is the fact that during the period in which the mosquito evades treatment, the benefits of being resistant do not hold. In other words, mosquitoes will not benefit from being resistant in periods during which they are not being sprayed with insecticides. On the contrary, during such periods, susceptible mosquitoes enjoy a higher biotic fitness than resistant mosquitoes. By the same token, in the periods during which the mosquito population is reached by insecticides, a resistant mosquito enjoys the benefits of higher fitness. In the case of higher doses, the difference in fitness in the two cases (reached or not reached by a control program) becomes greater, resulting in the time required to develop resistance becoming longer. Furthermore, the presence of a higher fraction of refugees decreases the average time during which the population, in general, profits from the availability of resistant genes, consequently impeding the development of resistance.

### 9.4.5 Sensitivity of Malaria Incidence to Temperature Change

In this subsection, the impact of increasing temperature levels is analysed. For both the low and the high endemic regions, the change in the occurrence of malaria is simulated in the event of a temperature increase of 0.25 or 0.5°C within a decade (Figure 9.12). This temperature increase lies within the range projected by the IPCC (1991).

The impact of temperature change on the incidence of malaria would be significant. The vectorial capacity would increase, due to increasing biting rates and shorter incubation periods, which would lead to an increase of the incidence of malaria in the order of 50 to 100 per cent in regions of low endemicity. In regions of high endemicity, the incidence of malaria would fall by about 15 to 30 per cent in the event of such temperature changes, as a result of the increase in the collective immunity.

The optimal temperature for mosquito survival would increase by 0.05°C in areas of low endemicity and 0.12°C in highly endemic areas, a development which lags behind the local mean temperature increase. The impact of mosquito adaptation to temperature change compared with no adaptation is not significant. This is caused by the fact that only the life expectancy changes as a result of adaptation, and this is only one of the factors (besides the man-biting habit and the incubation period) which are related to temperature fluctuations.

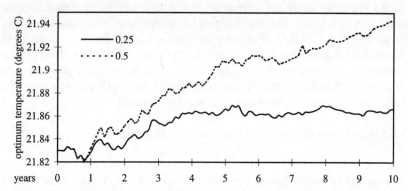

*Figure 9.12a: Optimum temperature given a 0.25 and a 0.5 °C temperature increase*

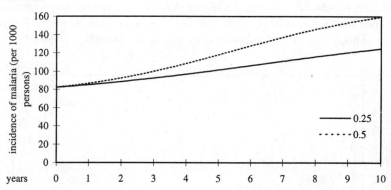

*Figure 9.12b: Incidence of malaria given a low endemic region for a 0.25 and a 0.5 °C temperature increase*

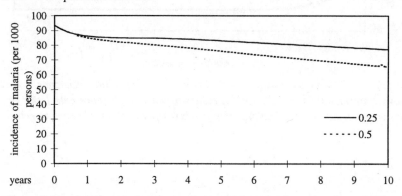

*Figure 9.12c: Incidence of malaria given a high endemic region for a 0.24 and a 0.5 ° C temperature increase*

An important factor influencing the rate of the evolution of resistance is the number of generations per year: resistance develops faster as the annual number of generations increases. Increasing temperatures will lead to a more rapid succession of generations per of unit time (Jetten and Takken, 1994). As a consequence, resistance development in the malaria mosquito population as presented in this chapter would have taken place within a shorter time span, if a temperature-dependent generation time was implemented.

### 9.4.6 Sensitivity of Malaria Incidence to Initial Resistance

The sensitivity of the initial fraction of resistant mosquitoes and parasites was investigated by an illustrative experiment. A low and a high dose of insecticides is postulated in a highly endemic region. Figure 9.13 shows that a higher level of initial resistance leads to a more rapid penetration of resistant genes in the mosquito population. Because of a higher selection pressure on the population, the time required to develop resistance decreases in an environment of higher doses. This finding corresponds with those reported in Tabashnik (1990).

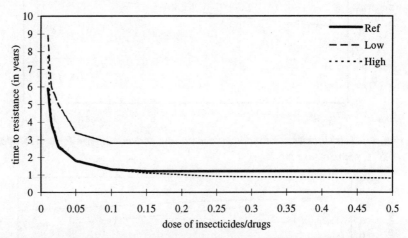

*Figure 9.13: Time to resistance for different levels of initial resistance, where low represents 0.01 per cent initial resistant genes, high represents 1 per cent initial resistant genes, while the reference is 0.1 per cent initial resistant genes*

### 9.4.7 Sensitivity of Malaria Incidence to Operators of the Genetic Algorithm

Within the range of reasonable values of the main operators of the genetic algorithm, a number of values are selected to test the sensitivity of the solutions *vis-à-vis* the chosen values. As depicted in Figures 9.14a and b, the results do not seem to be sensitive to the chosen values, although some variation does occur. This supports the chosen (unknown) values of the operations.

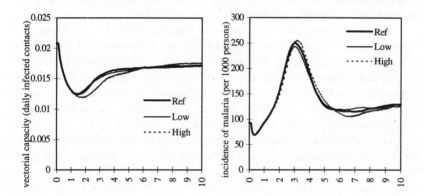

*Figure 9.14a: Vectorial capacity and incidence of malaria for different levels of crossover probability, where low represents 0.2, high 0.8 and reference a probability of 0.4*

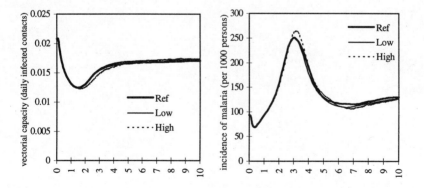

*Figure 9.14b: Vectorial capacity and incidence of malaria for different levels of the mutation probability, where low represents 0.0001, high 0.01 and reference a probability of 0.001*

### 9.4.8  Adaptive Malaria Management

In this subsection, the impact of the combined effects of climate change and resistance development on the prevalence of malaria are analysed among mosquitoes and parasites. This analysis is performed using an adaptive management style, that is one which relates the level of control programs according to the observed state of the system. Since in the model the resistance development dynamics are implemented in an identical manner for both mosquitoes and parasites, only one of the two needs to be considered in the analysis, and the mosquitoes are selected for this purpose.

The use of insecticides is related to the observed incidence of malaria, and there are two levels of application: a zero dose and a high dose. If the incidence of malaria fell below 20 per 1000 persons, the use of insecticides is assumed to be stopped, while if malaria once more exceeded this level, it would be reintroduced again (at high dose levels). Furthermore, if the incidence of malaria exceeded the level of 100 per 1000 persons, which is above the initial level, the use of insecticides would be stopped as not being effective.

The results set out in Figure 9.15 illustrate that in areas of low endemicity, the use of insecticides leads to a successful control of malaria occurrence. However, if the temperature was to increase by some 0.5°C within a single decade, the efforts to control malaria would have to be intensified significantly. In areas of high endemicity, the control of malaria fluctuates during the decade, while the incidence would continue to fluctuate around the level of 100 per 1000 persons, regardless of any temperature increase.

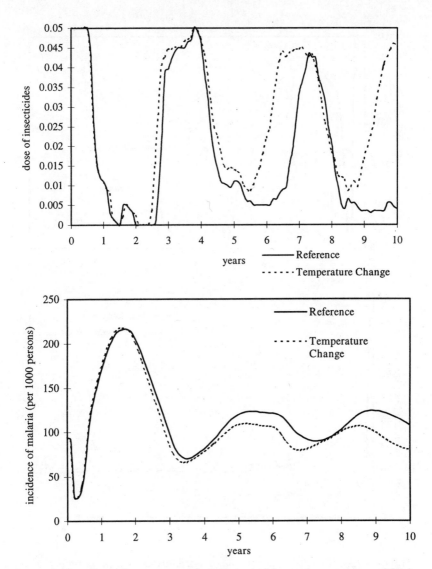

*Figure 9.15a: Control patterns and malaria incidence for a region of high endemicity in the event of an adaptive management style being adopted. The different lines show the impact of a projected climate change of the adaptive control programs*

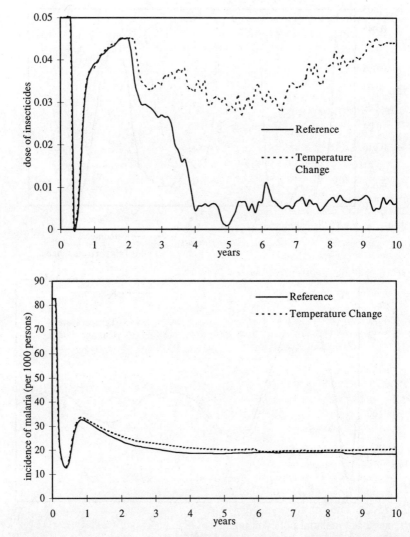

*Figure 9.15b: Control patterns and malaria incidence for a region of low endemicity in the event of an adaptive management style being adopted. The different lines show the impact of a projected climate change on the adaptive programs*

This modelling exercise, thus, shows that it would not be possible to eradicate malaria in regions of high endemicity using the assumed (that is adaptive) management style. However, in regions of low endemicity, malaria could be reduced significantly using adaptive management, although increased efforts would be needed in the event of climate change.

## 9.5. CONCLUSIONS

Models can be useful, especially if the opportunity to perform experiments in laboratories or in the field is limited. This is certainly the case where the growing problem of resistance development among malaria vectors, as well as malaria parasites, to control programs is concerned, and much remains to be elucidated. Current malaria modelling approaches, however, do not explicitly address the evolutionary character of the development of resistance. The malaria assessment model presented in this chapter is neither comprehensive nor predictive, but rather intended to include evolutionary processes of resistance development in order to provide insights into this complex adaptive system and, thus, help us to arrive at a better understanding of the possible effects of control programs.

The analysis distinguishes between two exemplary malaria regions, although malaria situations are extremely heterogeneous with respect to resistance to change. The results for the two situations described in the Chapter suggest that adequate use of insecticides and drugs may reduce the occurrence of malaria in regions of low endemicity, although increased efforts would be necessary in the event of a climate change. However, the model indicates that in regions of high endemicity, the use of insecticides and drugs may lead to an increase in incidence, due to enhanced resistance development. Projected climate change, on the other hand, may lead to a limited reduction of the occurrence of malaria due to the presence of a higher percentage of immune persons in the older age class. Given this observation, in order to retard the evolution of resistance, a combination of methods or drugs should be used, combined with a selective high dosage rate for those people or areas most vulnerable. Elements of a sustainable antimalarial policy in regions of high endemicity will probably need to rely upon a stimulation of socioeconomic development and provision of vector-proof housing. However, given the multiplicity of ecological and biological element and of the natural, adaptive defence mechanisms of the malaria parasite/vector complex, control or eradication must be planned with consideration of prevailing local conditions.

The present version of the model simulates the incidence of malaria based on the use of insecticides and medication, together with temperature change. Additional factors would need to be included before one could speak of an integrated approach to the malaria problem, whereby the inclusion of environmental management would be of particular importance. The effects of land use changes, water management, migration patterns, malnutrition, housing, and so on, on vectorial capacity would, therefore, need to be incorporated (WHO, 1992; Coimbra, 1988; Packard, 1984). As a means of accommodating such spatial differentiations, the use of cellular automata might be considered. A cellular automaton consists of an array of cells in which each cell can assume one of k discrete states at any one time. Time progresses in discrete steps, and all cells change state simultaneously as a function of their own state, together with the state of the cell in their neighbourhood, in accordance with a specified set of transition rules (for example Gardner, 1970; Tobler, 1979; White and Engelen, 1994; Engelen *et al.*, 1995). In fact, the present model simulates the dynamics of a homogenous area, whereas in a spatial model the heterogeneity of a specific area can be simulated.

The modelling approach presented here fits well in the qualitative attention currently being paid to the importance of evolutionary principles (for example Levy, 1992; Ewald, 1994). However, a great deal of empirical research is needed to improve the modelling approach. In the specific case of malaria, it is especially important that more insights into the possible shapes of the fitness functions of the parasites and the mosquitoes are acquired. This need is illustrated by the results of the impact of migration on the development of resistance at high doses, since they differ from the results of previous studies as a result of different assumptions regarding the fitness functions. Nevertheless, the fact remains that development of integrated assessment models which are based on the evolutionary and local dynamics of ecological systems may prove essential to assessing future developments in these complex adaptive systems.

## NOTES

1. I have focused on the transmission dynamics of *P. falciparum* since it is the most lethal malaria parasite and is exhibiting world-wide development of resistance to anti-malarial drugs.
2. I recognize that this account of adaptation to unfavourable temperatures is just one of the possibilities. Another would be the migration of mosquitoes to micro-habitats where temperatures are more suitable.
3. Experiments showed that a higher number of runs would not affect the mean values significantly.
4. Comins (1977) and Tabashnik and Croft (1982) do not actually employ the term 'fitness function', but I use an interpretation that is equivalent to their 'dose-mortality lines'.

# 10. Conclusions and Discussion

In this book, various methodological improvements are suggested and applied to a wide range of topics related to modelling global change. The post-modernistic attitude of integrated assessment modelling, that is the practical attitude and the explicit acknowledgement of diversity and uncertainty, aims at integrating scientific 'state-of-the-art' information for practical policy-related problems. Although integrated assessment modelling is used to advise policy makers, the lack of scientific standards and quality control may threaten for further development in this field. Furthermore, the disciplinary bias of the various research groups precludes the research society with a real integrated modelling paradigm. Therefore, I want to sketch a possible framework for integrated assessment modelling which may evolve in the coming years. But first I will summarize the major findings of this book.

## 10.1  MAJOR FINDINGS

### Methodology

#### Optimization
Optimization aims at determining the decisions to derive the best performance of a system under concern. To date, various optimization oriented models exist for climate change policy and environmental policy in general. One of the characteristics of the current generation of optimization models is that they depend upon the restrictive requirements of continuity and derivative existence. However, the awareness of the unpredictable non-linear behaviour of the global system leads to discontinue and noisy search spaces, which cannot be dealt by with traditional optimization tools. The systems can, thus, be linearized and simplified, in order to use the traditional optimization techniques, or, alternatively, new search routines can be applied to advanced complex simulation models.

In this book, two optimization case studies are discussed to investigate the latter approach. A mathematical system is constructed which combines the economics of DICE and the climate dynamics of the mathematical system version of IMAGE 1.0. Various traditional and new optimization routines are used to solve a set of optimization problems. This model, OMEGA, is used to analyse the impact of an inadequate representation of the dynamics of the climate system as reasonably understood by natural science in current optimization models for climate change. A parameterized model (like DICE) is fully calibrated on historical data, and explains, therefore, only a limited range of the system; whereas a process-oriented model (like OMEGA) describes a larger range of the system behaviour. Compared with DICE, OMEGA leads to an enhanced effort in reducing emissions for cost-benefit analysis. In the event of severe constraints on concentration levels or temperature change, far fewer emission reductions have to be made, if OMEGA instead of DICE is used. These differences could be explained by the different descriptions of the dynamics of the climate system.

In a second study, exploratory experiments with the energy-cycles part of TARGETS have been investigated. A genetic algorithm in which a set of solutions competes for 'survival', is used to solve the optimization problems. The algorithm is used as a supporting tool for the search for specific scenarios and is supposed to be a helpful tool in scenario analysis of TARGETS(-like) integrated assessment models.

**Perspectives**
Our understanding of the global Earth system is incomplete, and subjective judgements and disagreement originating from different interpretations of the blind spots can largely explain uncertainties in the images of the present and the future. I propose to capture uncertainties arising from subjective judgement and disagreement in the inclusion of various perspectives. To operationalize a perspective-based uncertainty analysis, I used the framework of Cultural Theory, although I acknowledge the weaknesses and deficiencies of the Cultural Theory. Drawing on the Cultural Theory, the perspectives are labelled 'individualist', 'hierarchist', and 'egalitarian', and are represented by distributions of preferred values of parameters in the models of two case studies on allocating $CO_2$ emission rights and projecting emission reductions of $CO_2$. Including perspectives in the uncertainty analysis helps to explain and understand the various possible images of the futures and the various ways to respond. In case of the emission right allocation, it makes clear that the difference between possible initial allocations differ so much between the perspectives that it will be hard to find a compromise in implementing a tradable emission right regime. In the case of the 'Battle of Perspectives', it illustrates various alternative response scenarios assuming different world views.

## Evolutionary approach

The present generation of integration assessment models is mainly based on the mechanistic paradigm. The Earth system is thought of as a machine which should be rationally controlled to reduce the pressures which could lead to instabilities in the 'natural' equilibrium. The evolutionary approach rejects the equilibrium approach. From a mechanistic perspective, risks may increase if the system changes, while from an evolutionary perspective, risks may increase if the system is less able to adapt to a change.

During the last decades, new evolutionary based approaches have been developed in studying complex adaptive systems: systems which organize their component parts to adapt themselves to the problems posed by their surroundings. This has provided the material for developing an integrated modelling paradigm in which I distinguish three different, but interwoven, levels of modelling reality. At the first level, the physical stocks and flows which can be simulated by sets of differential equations: a mechanistic approach. At the next level, the behavioural and informational structures of ecological, economic and social processes which can be simulated by evolutionary modelling: an organismic approach. At the third levels, the values and beliefs which might be simulated by adopting various (cultural) perspectives.

I performed two case studies in which evolutionary modelling has been applied. The first case study, the 'Battle of Perspectives', shows that an evolutionary approach enables us to include learning and adaptive behaviour in a simple climate-economy framework. In contrast with the usually employed assumption of a rational agent with (near) perfect knowledge, a heterogeneous set of agents respond to the observations. Due to the stochastic characteristics of the evolutionary processes, large uncertainty ranges are generated which derive from the unpredictability of the response of agents to the information from the system.

In the second case study, malaria is modelled as a complex adaptive system. The evolutionary modelling approach for malaria fits well in the present qualitative notice of the importance of evolutionary principles for infectious diseases. As in the 'Battle of Perspectives', a genetic algorithm was included into a system dynamics model to simulate adaptive behaviour, here of mosquitoes and parasites. Although the required data were not found to validate the model, experiments gave results which conformed with the current insights of experts. Furthermore, possible consequences of a climate change were analysed.

## Applications

### Energy-climate

Exploratory experiments have been performed with the energy-cycles part of TARGETS. From an environmental perspective, a low fossil fuel energy supply is desired. However, what kind of a transition leads to low economic costs, in order to meet the growing energy demands in a sustainable way? Based on earlier studies, a set of scenarios is constructed in which different assumptions on technological development have been implemented. The different projections in costs and effects lead to the question what to do in the short term, given the important uncertainties in the longer term, and given the ambition to meet international climate change targets. The results of hedging strategies and delayed response scenarios suggest that a short-term efficiency improvement due to an active energy policy is recommended, irrespective of the technological developments. Furthermore, if a transition to a low energy supply does not get initiated, there will be a risk of becoming locked in by the use of fossil fuels. This is due to the inertia of the energy system and the short-term cooling effect of sulphate aerosols.

Although a reduction of $SO_2$ emissions is not recommended in meeting temperature change targets, it helps to reduce the problem of acidification. The move from a $CO_2$ dominating debate to a $CO_2$-$SO_2$ dominating debate underscores the importance of an integrated assessment of the energy/environment system in which this study serves as a modest step.

### Emission rights

The industrialized countries have so far caused the major part of $CO_2$ emissions. From an egalitarian perspective, the industrialized world should take prime responsibility in responding to and supporting the developing countries in contributing their share to mitigate climate change without thwarting their development. A reduction of the risk of adverse climate change according to the 'precautionary principle' approach implies that future global emissions of greenhouse gases are constrained. Together with past emissions, a global carbon budget can be estimated, and be allocated among the population. If all world citizens living in the period 1800-2100 were allocated an equal emission quotum, this would result in a per capita emission of about 1 tC/cap yearly, assuming a future scenario according to IS92C (= a global budget of 1130 GtC). The industrial regions would have exceeded their allocated budgets for 1800-1990 by about 90 GtC (OECD) and 20 GtC (CIS). The developing countries, however, have an emission credit of about 130 GtC.

A more sophisticated allocation model is used, which takes into account historical and future development for the criteria: population size, GNP, and energy use. There are various perspectives pertaining to the allocation of a constrained global fossil $CO_2$ emission budget. In the first place, there might be differences in the scenarios concerning fossil $CO_2$ emissions, energy use, population, technology, and economic development. Second, the preferred value distribution of parameters of the model might be skewed by perspectives. Because of the political dimension of the subject and the dynamic shifting of the mixture of perspectives in time, the results show that there is no clear initial allocation of emission rights.

**Battle of Perspectives**
The concept of the 'Battle of Perspectives' is meant to illustrate a possible incorporation of agent behaviour within integrated assessment models. Agents' perspectives which determine their management style can change, if they are confronted with a persistent pattern of surprises. Although there is no claim for reality, exploratory experiments suggest that in case of successful adaptation, alternative images of the future can be generated. Futures featuring high levels of fossil $CO_2$ emissions are associated with low temperature increases, as well as low emission paths together with high temperature projections. In a speculative way, the impact of possible surprises can be analysed, which is performed for a so-called cooling surprise. Suppose temperature increase is masked by a cooling effect; this leads to a later reduction of emissions and a higher temperature increase compared with the case we had the valid observations. So, even if agents were modelled as being adaptive, the everlasting incomplete knowledge of the system makes it possible to miss the policy targets.

**Malaria**
Results suggest that adequate use of insecticides and drugs may reduce the occurrence of malaria in low endemic regions, although increased efforts are necessary in case of a climate change. However, in high endemic regions, the model indicates that the use of insecticides and drugs may lead to an increase in the incidence due to resistance development. A projected climate change, however, may lead to a limited reduction in the occurrence of malaria, due to a higher percentage of immune persons in the older age class. A 'sustainable' antimalarial policy in high endemic regions will probably be found in a stimulation of socio-economic development and vector-proof housing.

Migration of (susceptible) mosquitoes and parasites may retard the resistance development significantly. Together with the expected relevance of land use changes, a next step in developing an integrated assessment tool for malaria is the inclusion of spatial characteristics, based on, for example, cellular automata.

## 10.2   AN INTEGRATED ASSESSMENT MODELLING FRAMEWORK FOR TOMORROW

As the reader probably may have noticed, this book is a collection of ideas which are not all worked out in detail, but which address a wide range of issues in the emerging field of integrated assessment modelling. Given the findings of this book and my experience in integrated assessment modelling, I will try to sketch a possible framework of integrated assessment modelling which may improve present approaches. Until now, integrated assessment modellers are mainly acting as scientists from a specific discipline dealing with holistic problem formulations. They need to be acting more as intermediaries between different scientific disciplines and between science and policy, if they want to facilitate policy making (Peterson *et al.*, 1997). This requires the ability to deal with various paradigms and different type of models. Furthermore they have to improve the communication of complex scientific knowledge to policy relevant information.

The art of communicating insights between science and policy is finding a balance on relevance, comprehensiveness, transparency and reliability. Making a simple computer model usually evokes the reaction from the scientific community that many important aspects of the issue are ignored, and that such models tend to blur the uncertainties surrounding the issue. On the other hand, a comprehensive scientific model may be too complex for policy makers and therefore not directly useful in providing insights into the problem or supporting them in evaluating policy options. In my view, the communication between science and policy can be enhanced by using not just one type of model, but different types of models (Figure 10.1).

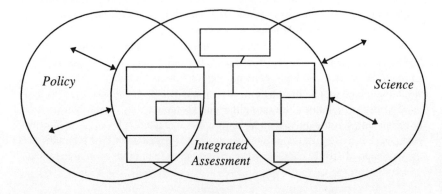

*Figure 10.1: A framework for integrated assessment modelling (boxes are different type of models)*

An important dimension of models is the level of complexity. In the cycle of developing computer models one starts usually with a simple construction. After including more and more details, one needs to simplify it again in order to communicate the results to others. In case of integrated assessment modelling this leads to heuristic tools for policy and comprehensive models to derive scientific credibility. Therefore, to assure integrated assessment modelling a sustainable future, the following three conditions should at least be met:

- Credibility building. To be accepted, any integrated assessment modelling group should co-operate with the experts in the various disciplines. Furthermore, it is recommended participating in global networks, including institutes from developing countries. For example, the global networks of the IPCC and the IGBP. Another example is the network of the collaborating centres who are participating in developing a global environmental outlook (UNEP, 1997).
- Active interaction between science and policy. An integrated assessment model can only be successfully applied if the integrated assessment modellers improve their communication, not only between various scientific disciplines, but also with various stake holders who are involved in the problem area. Examples are the Delft process (Alcamo *et al.*, 1996) and policy exercises (Parson, 1996; de Vries, 1995).
- Diversity of modelling approaches, which differ in dynamics, aggregation and time-scales. In Chapter 3 different modelling approaches have been discussed and examples are given of such models. However, integrated assessment teams usually do not apply more than one type of modelling approach. But, global change is too complex to address adequately in one type of models. The multiple dimensions of global change require different approaches. Therefore, it is essential that different models are in one framework in order to have consistency on inputs, assumptions and definitions. Thus, next to different levels of complexity, various modelling paradigms might be used in one framework. The idea is that different type of models have different purposes but support each other in the assessment of global change.

This framework of approaches provides a research group complementary ways of dealing with (participatory) integrated assessment. The framework has various advances. On the basis of a continued dialogue with policy makers and with the scientific community, the integrated assessment team may balance policy relevant questions with scientific accepted information. The inclusions of various modelling approaches, the integration of methods and theories from various disciplines, may help to address the problems of uncertainty, surprise, and evolutionary change. Of course, the actual decision making is a political process, but hopefully the proposed framework may support policy making for a sustainable co-evolution of mankind and its environment.

# References

AGGG (1990), *Targets and Indicators of Climate Change*, Rijsberman and Swart (eds), Report of Working Group II of the Advisory Group on Greenhouse Gases (AGGG), Stockholm Environmental Institute, Stockholm, Sweden.

Alcamo, J. (ed.) (1994), *Integrated Modelling of Global Climate Change: IMAGE 2.0*, Special Issue of the Journal of Water, Air and Soil Pollution.

Alcamo, J. and E. Kreileman (1996), 'Emission Scenarios and Global Climate Protection', *Global Environmental Change*, Vol. 6, no. 4, 305-34

Alcamo, J., E. Kreileman and R. Leemans (1996), 'Global Models meet Global Policy', *Global Environmental Change*, Vol. 6, no. 4, 255-9.

Alcamo, J., M. Krol and M. Posch (1995), 'An Integrated Analysis of Sulphur Emissions, Acid Deposition and Climate Change', *Water, Air and Soil Pollution*, 85, 1539-1550.

Alcamo, J., R. Shaw and L. Hordijk (eds) (1990), *The RAINS Model of Acidification: Science and Strategies in Europe*, Kluwer Academic Publishers, Dordrecht, the Netherlands.

Allen, P.M. (1990), 'Why the Future is not what it was: New Models of Evolution', *Futures*, July/August, 555-70.

Anderson, P., K.J. Arrow and D. Pines (1988), *The Economy as an Evolving Complex System*, Addison Wesley, Redwood City, CA.

Anderson, R.M. and M.M. May (1991), *Infectious Diseases of Humans: Dynamics and Control*, Oxford University Press, New York.

Anderson, S.H., R.E. Beiswenger and P.W. Purdom (1993), *Environmental Science*, Fourth Edition, Macmillan Publishing Company, New York.

Armentano, T.V. and C.W. Ralston (1980), 'The Role of Temperate Zone Forest in the Global Carbon Cycle', *Canadian Journal of Forest Research* 10, 53-60.

Aron, J.L. and B.A. Silverman (1994), 'Models and Public Health Applications', *Parasitic and Infection Diseases*, 73-81.

Aron, L.A. and R.M. May (1982), 'The Population Dynamics of Malaria', In: R.M. Anderson (ed.), *The population dynamics of infectious diseases: theory and applications*, 139-179. Chapman and Hall, London.

Arrhenius, S. (1896), 'On the Influence of the Carbonic Acid in the Air upon the Temperature of the Ground', *Philosophical Magazine*, 41, no. 251, 237-77.

Arrow, K.J. (1962), 'The Economic Implications of Learning-by-doing', *Review of Economic Studies*, 29,155-73.

Arthur, W.B. (1990), 'Positive Feedbacks in the Economy', *Scientific American*, February, 92-9.

Arthur, W.B. (1994), *Increasing Returns and Path Dependence in the Economy*, The University of Michigan Press.

Bailey, N.T.J. (1982), *The Biomathematics of Malaria*, Griffin, London.

Begon, M, J.L. Harper and C.R. Townsend (1990), *Ecology: Individuals, Populations and Communities*, Second Edition, Blackwell Science, Cambridge, USA.

Beightler, C.S., D.T. Phillips and D.J. Wilde (1979), *Foundations of Optimization*, 2nd edn, Englewoods Cliffs, NJ: Prentice-Hall.

Berk, M.M. and M.A. Janssen (1997), *The Interactive Scenario Scanner: a Tool to Support the Dialogue between Science and Policy on Scenario Development* , Report No. 481508005, RIVM, Bilthoven, the Netherlands.

Biggs, D. *et al.* (1996), *Quest - A Quasi Understandable Ecosystem Scenario Tool,* Vancouver, BC Sustainable Development Reseach Institute Canada.

Bolin, B. and R.B. Cook (1983), *The Major Biogeochemical Cycles and their Interactions*, SCOPE 21, John Wiley & Sons, New York.

Bollen, J.C., A.M.C. Toet, H.J.M. de Vries and R.A. van den Wijngaart (1995), *Modelling Regional Energy Use for Evaluating Global Climate Scenario*, RIVM report no. 481507010, Bilthoven, the Netherlands.

Bollen, J.C., A.M.C. Toet and H.J.M. de Vries (1996), *Evaluation of the Cost-Effectiveness of Implementing $CO_2$ Emission Reduction Strategies in different Regions,* Global Environmental Change, Vol. 6, no. 4, pp. 359-73.

Bongaarts, J. (1994), 'Population Policy Options in the Developing World', *Science*, No. 263, pp. 771-776.

Bossel, H. (1996), *20/20 Vision: Explorations of Sustainable Futures*, Center for Environmental System Research, University of Kassel, Germany.

Bossel, H. and M. Strobel (1978), 'Experiments with an "Intelligent" World Model', *Futures*, June, 191-210.

Boyd, M.F. (1949), 'Epidemiology: Factors Related to the Definitive Host', In: M.F. Boyd (ed.), *Malariology (volume I)*, 608-697. W.B. Saunders Company, Philadelphia and London.

Braddock, R.D., J.A. Filar, R. Zapert, J. Rotmans and M.G.J. den Elzen (1995), 'The IMAGE Model as a Mathematical System', *Applied Mathematical Modelling*, Vol. 18 May, 234-54.

Bradley, D.J. (1993), 'Human Tropical Diseases in a Changing Environment', In: *Environmental change and human health*, CIBA Foundation Symposium, 175, 147-70.

Brecke, P. (1993), 'Integrated Global Models that run on Personal Computers', *Simulation, 60*, no. 2.

Brehmer, B. (1992), 'Dynamic decision making: Human control of complex systems', *Acta Psychologica,* 81, 211-241.

Brehmer, B. and D. Dörner (1993), 'Experiments with Computer-Simulated Microworlds: Escaping both the narrow straits of the laboratory and the deep blue sea of the field study', *Computers in Human Behaviour,* Vol. 9, 171-84.

Brooke, A., D. Kendrick and A. Meeraus (1988), *GAMS: A User's Guide,* Scientific Press, Redwood City, California.

Brown, L.R. (1995), *State of the World 1995,* EarthScan, London.

Brown, L.R. (1996), *State of the World 1996,* EarthScan, London.

Bruce-Chwatt, L.J. (1980), *Essential Malariology,* Heinemann Medical, London.

Bulatao, R.A., E. Bos, P.W. Stephens and M.T.Vu (1990), *World Population Projections 1989-90 Edition: Short and Long-Term Estimates,* The John Hopkins University Press, Baltimore (published for the World Bank).

Burniaux, J.M., J.P. Martin, G. Nicoletti and J.O. Martins (1991), *GREEN: A Multi-Region Dynamic General Equilibrium Model for Quantifying the Costs of Curbing $CO_2$ Emissions: A Technical manual,'* OECD Department of Economics and Statistics, Working Paper No. 89, Paris, 1991.

Butcher, S.S., R.J. Charlson, G.H. Orians and G.V. Wolfe (1992), *Global Biogeochemical Cycles,* Academic Press, London.

Carson, R. (1962), *Silent Spring,* Penguin Books, London.

Clark, W.C. and R.E. Munn (eds) (1986), *Sustainable Development of the Biosphere,* International Institute for Applied Systems Analysis (IIASA), Cambridge University Press, London.

Clyde, D.F. (1987), 'Recent Trends in the Epidemiology and Control of Malaria', *Epidemiologic Reviews,* 9, 219-43.

Coimbra, C.E.A. (1988), 'Human Factors in the Epidemiology of Malaria in the Brazilian Amazon', *Human Organization,* Vol. 47, no. 3, 254-60.

Colby, M.E. (1991), 'Environmental Management in Development: the Evolution of Paradigms', *Ecological Economics,* no. 3, 193-213.

Collet, H.N. and M.S. Lye (1987), 'Modelling the Effect of Intervention on the Transmission of Malaria in East Malaysia', *Statistics in Medicine,* 6, 853-61.

Comins, H.N. (1977), 'The Development of Insecticide Resistance in the Presence of Migration', *Journal of Theoretical Biology,* 64, 177-97.

Costanza, R. (1996), 'Managing the DICE model', *Environmental Science and Technology,* to appear.

Costanza, R., L. Wainger, C. Folke and K.G. Mäler (1993), 'Modeling Complex Ecological Economic Systems: Toward an Evolutionary, Dynamic Understanding of People and Nature', *BioScience,* Vol. 43, No. 8, 545-55.

Coward, H. and T. Hurka (1993), *Ethics and Climate Change: The Greenhouse Effect*, Wilfrid Laurier University Press, Waterloo, Canada.

Curtis, C.F. and L.N. Otoo (1986), 'A Simple Model to the Build-up of Resistance of Mixtures of Anti-Malarial Drugs', *Transactions of the Royal Society of Medical Hygiene,* 80, 889-92.

Curtis, C.F. L.M. Cook and R.J. Wood (1978), 'Selection for and against insecticide resistance and possible methods of inhibiting the evolution of resistance in mosquitoes', *Ecological Entomology*, 3, 273-87.

Darmstadter, J. (1971), *Energy in the World Economy*, Johns Hopkins University Press, Baltimore and London.

Darwin, C. (1859), *On the Orgin of Species.*

Davidsen, P. 1988, *A Dynamic Petroleum Life-Cycle Model for the United States 1870-2050*, MIT Sloan School of Management Cambridge, Mass.

Davis, L. (ed.) (1987), *Genetic Algorithms and Simulated Annealing*, London: Pitman.

De Bruin, A.J., P.J. de Vink and J.J. van Wijk (1996), 'M - A Visual Simulation Tool', in *Simulation in the Medical Sciences*, The Society for Computer Simulation, San Diego, 181-6.

De Greef, J. and H.J.M. de. Vries (1991), *Sustainable Development as a framework for environmental polic'* (in Dutch), RIVM Report 481501001, Bilthoven, the Netherlands.

Den Elzen, M.G.J. (1993), *Global Environmental Change: an Integrated Modelling Approach*, PhD Thesis, International Books, Utrecht, the Netherlands.

Den Elzen, M.G.J., A.H.W. Beusen and J. Rotmans (1997), 'An integrated modelling approach to global carbon and nitrogen cycles: balancing their budgets', *Global Biochemical Cycles. Vol. 11, No.2, 191-215.*

Den Elzen, M.G.J., M.A. Janssen, J. Rotmans, R.J. Swart and H.J.M. de Vries (1992), 'Allocating Constrained Global Carbon Budgets: Interregional and Intergenerational Equity for a Sustainable World', *International Journal of Global Energy Issues*, Special Issue on Energy and Sustainable Development, Vol. 4, No. 4, 287-301

Detinova, T.S. (1963), *Méthodes a appliquer pour classer par groupes d'âge les diptères présentant une importance médicale*, World Health Organization, Geneva, Switzerland.

Detwiler, R.P. and C.A.S. Hall (1988), 'Tropical Forest and Global Carbon Cycle', *Science*, 239, 42-7.

Detwiler, R.P., C.A.S. Hall and P. Bodgonoff (1985), 'Land Use Changes and Carbon Exchange in the Tropics, II. Estimates for the Entire Region', *Environmental Management*, 9, 335-44.

De Vries, H.J.M. (1989), *Sustainable Resource Use - An Inquiry into Modelling and Planning*, University of Groningen (RUG-IVEM), Groningen, the Netherlands.

De Vries, H.J.M. (1994), 'Environmental Utilisation Space in Model Worlds' (in Dutch), *Milieu*, Vol. 9, no. 5, 236-43.

De Vries, H.J.M. (1995), *SusClime: a simulation game on population and development in a resource- and climate-constrained two country world*, GLOBO Report Series, no. 11, RIVM, Bilthoven. the Netherlands.

De Vries H.J.M. and M.A. Janssen (1996), *Global Energy Futures: An Integrated Perspective with the TIME Model*, GLOBO Report Series no. 18, RIVM, Bilthoven, the Netherlands

De Vries H.J.M. and R. van den Wijngaart (1995), *The Targets/IMage Energy Model (TIME)*, GLOBO Report Series no. 16, RIVM, Bilthoven, the Netherlands.

.Dickinson, R.E. (1986), 'How will Climate Change? The Climate System and Modelling of Future Climate', In: , B. Bollin, B.R. Döös, J. Jäger and R.A. Warrick (eds), *The Greenhouse Effect, Climate Change and Ecosystems*, SCOPE 13, pp. 206-70, John Wiley and Son, Chichester, UK.

Dietz, K., L. Molineaux and A. Thomas (1974), 'A Malaria Model Tested in the African Savannas', *Bulletin of the World Health Organization*, 50: 347-57.

Dörner, D. and H. Schaub (1994), 'Errors in Planning and Decision-making and the Nature of Human Information Processing', *Applied Psychology: An International Review*, 43(4), 433-53.

Dotto, L. (1994), *Ethical Choices and Global Greenhouse Warming*, The Calgary Institute for the Humanities, Calgary, Canada.

Douglas, M. and A. Wildavsky (1982), *Risk and Culture: An Essay on the Detection of Technical and Environmental Dangers*, University of California Press, Berkley.

Dowlatabadi, H. and G.M. Morgan (1993a), 'Integrated Assessment of Climate Change', *Science*, 259, 1813-14.

Dowlatabadi, H. and G.M. Morgan (1993b), 'A Model Framework for Integrated Studies of the Climate Problem', *Energy Policy*, 209-21.

Durand, J.D. (1967), 'The Modern Expansion of World Population', *Proceedings of the American Philosophical Society*, Vol. 111, No. 3, 136-159.

Durlauf, S.N. (1997), 'Insights for socioeconomic modelling', *Complexity*, Vol., no. 3, 247-8.

Ellis, J.E. and P.D. Roberts (1982), 'Measurement and Modelling Trade-offs for Integrated System Optimization and Parameter Estimation', *Large Scale Systems*, 3, 191-204.

Engelen, G., R. White, I. Uljee and P. Drazan (1995), 'Using Cellular Automata for Integrated Modelling of Socio-Environmental Systems', *Environmental Monitoring and Assessment*, 34, 203-214.

Epstein, L.M. and R.L. Axtell (1996), *Growing Artificial Societies: Social Science from the Bottom-up*, Brookings Institution, Washington, DC.

Ewald, P.W. (1994), *Evolution of Infections Diseases*, Oxford University Press.

FAO (Food and Agriculture Organization of the United Nations) (1988), *An Interim Report on the State of the Forest Resources in the Developing Countries*, FAO, Rome.

FAO (Food and Agriculture Organization of the United Nations) (1991), 'Forest Resources Assessment 1990 Project', *Forestry*, No. 7, FAO, Rome.

Farman, J.C., B.G. Gardiner and J.D. Shanklin (1985), 'Large Losses of Ozone in Antarctica Reveal Seasonal $ClO_x/NO_x$ Interaction', *Nature*, 315, 207-10.

Faucheux, S. and G. Froger (1995), 'Decision-making under Environmental Uncertainty', *Ecological Economics*, Vol. 15, 29-42.

Faucheux, S., D. Pearce and J. Proops (eds) (1996), *Models of Sustainable Development*, Edward Elgar Publishers, Cheltenham, UK, Brookfield, USA.

Ferreira, P.A.V. and T.C.D. Borges (1994), 'System Modelling and Optimization Under Vector-Valued Criteria', *Automatica*, Vol. 30, No. 2, pp. 331-6

Filar, J.A., P.S. Gaertner and M.A. Janssen (1996), 'An Application of Optimization to the Problem of Climate Change', in *Applications* C.A. Floudas and P.M. Pardalos (eds), *State of the Art of Global Optimization: Computational Methods and* 475-98, Kluwer Academic Publishers, Boston.

Fisher, A. (1988), 'One model to fit all', *Mosaic*, 19, no. 34, 53-9.

Foell, W.K., M. Amann, G. Carmichael, M. Chadwick, J.-P. Hetteling, L. Hordijk and D. Zhao (eds) (1995), *RAINS-Asia: An Assessment Model for Air-Pollution in Asia*, Final Report to the World Bank.

Forest, S. (ed.) (1993), *Proceedings of the Fifth International Conference on Genetic Algorithms*, Morgan Kaufmann Publishers, San Mateo, California.

Forrester, J.W. (1971), *World Dynamics*, Wright-Allen Press, Cambridge, Mass.

Fraser, P., S.A. Penkett, R. Hariss, Y. Makide and E. Sanhueza (1992), 'Source Gases: Concentrations, Emissions and Trends', in *Scientific Assessment of Ozone Depletion: 1991*, WMO/UNEP, WMO Global Ozone Research and Monitoring Project, Report no. 25, Chapter 1.

Frenk, J., J.L. Bobadilla, C. Stern, T. Frejka and R. Lozano (1993), 'Elements for a Theory of the Health Transition', Chapter 2 in L.C. Chen, A. Kleinman and N.C. Ware (eds), *Health and Social Change in International Perspective*, Harvard Series on population and international health, Harvard University Press, Boston.

Funtowitcz, S.O. and J.R. Ravetz (1989), *Uncertainty and Quality in Science for Policy*, Kluwer Academic Publishers, Dordrecht, the Netherlands.

Gardner, M. (1970), 'The Fantastic Combinations of John Conway's New Solitaire Game Life', *Scientific American*, 223, 120-23.

Garrett-Jones, C. (1964), 'Prognosis for Interruption of Malaria Transmission through Assessment of the Mosquito's Vectorial Capacity', *Nature*, 204, 1173-75.

Georghiou, G.P. and C.E. Taylor (1977), 'Genetic and Biological Influences in the Evolution of Insecticide Resistance', *Journal of Economic Entomology*, 70, 3, 319-23.

Glass, E.H., P.L. Adkinsson, G.A. Carlson, *et al.* (1984), *Pesticide Resistance: Strategies and Tactics for Management*, Washington, National Academy Press.

Goldberg, D. (1989),*Genetic Algorithms in Search, Optimization, and Machine Learning*, Reading, MA: Addison-Wesley.

Goudriaan, J. and P. Ketner (1984), 'A Simulation Study for the Global Carbon Cycle, including Man's Impact on the Biosphere', *Climatic Change*, 6, 167-92.

Graedel, T.E. and P.J. Crutzen (1993), *Atmospheric Change: An Earth System Perspective*, W.H. Freeman and Company, New York.

Grubb, M. (1989), *The Greenhouse Effect: Negotiating Targets*, Royal Institute of International Affairs.

Grubb, M. (1996), 'Technologies, Energy Systems, and the Timing of $CO_2$ Emissions Abatement: An Overview of Economic Issues', *Energy Policy*, Vol. 25, no. 2, 159-72.

Grubb, M. and J.K. Sebenius (1992), 'Participation, Allocation and Adaptability in International Tradable Emission Permit Systems for Greenhouse Control', in *Climate Change - Designing a Tradeable Permit System,* OECD, Paris.

Grubb, M., T. Chapuis and M.H. Duong (1995), 'The Economics of Changing Course', *Energy Policy*, Vol. 23, no. 4, 1-14.

Grübler, A. and Y. Fujii (1991), 'Inter-Generational and Spatial Equity Issues of Carbon Accounts', *Energy*, 16 (11/12), 1397-416.

Haimes, Y.Y. and D.A. Wismer (1972), 'A Computational Approach to the Combined Problem of Optimization and Parameter Identification', *Automatica*, Vol. 8, pp. 337-47.

Hammitt, J.K., R.J. Lempert and M.E. Schlesinger (1992), 'A Sequential-decision Strategy for Abating Climate Change', *Nature,* 357, 315-8.

Hao, W.M., M.H. Liu and P.J. Crutzen (1990), 'Estimates of Annual and Regional Releases of $CO_2$ and Other Trace Gases to the Atmosphere from Fires in the Tropics, Based on FAO Statistics for the Period 1975-1980', in J.G. Goldammer (ed.), *Fire in the Tropical Biota*, Springer-Verlag, Berlin, 440-62.

Hock, W. and K. Schittkowski (1983), 'A Comparative Performance Evaluation of 27 Non-linear Programming Codes', *Computing*, 30, 335-58.

Hofbauer, J. and K. Sigmund (1988), *The Theory of Evolution and Dynamical Systems*, Cambridge University Press, Cambridge, USA.

Holland, J.H. (1975), *Adaptation in Natural and Artificial Systems*, Ann Arbor, MIT University of Michigan Press.

Holland, J.H. (1992a), 'Genetic Algorithms', *Scientific American*, Vol. 267, No. 1, 44-50.

Holland, J.H. (1992b), 'Complex Adaptive Systems', *Daedalus*, Vol. 121, No. 1, 17-30.

Holland, J.H. and J.H. Miller (1991), 'Artificial Adaptive Agents in Economic Theory', *AEA papers and Proceedings*, May 1991, 365-70.

Holling, C.S. (1977), 'Myths of Ecology and Energy', in *Proceedings of the Symposium on Future Strategies for Energy Development*, 36-49, Oak Ridge, TN: Oak Ridge Association of Universities.

Holling, C.S. (1978), 'The Spruce-Budworm/Forest-Management Problem', in C.S. Holling (ed.), *Adaptive Environmental Assessment and Management*, John Wiley & Sons, Chichester - New York - Brisbane - Toronto.

Holling, C.S. (1986), 'The Resilience of Terrestrial Ecosystems: Local Surprise and Global Change', in : W.C. Clark and R.E. Munn (eds), *Sustainable Development of the Biosphere*, Cambridge University Press/IIASA Laxenburg.

Holling, C.S. (1994), 'An Ecologist View of the Malthusian Conflict', in K. Lindahl-Kiessling and H. Landberg (eds), *Population, Economic Development, and the Environment*, Oxford University Press, New York, pp. 79-103.

Holling, C.S., L.H. Gunderson and G.D. Peterson (1995), 'Comparing Ecological and Social Systems', submitted to *American Scientist*.

Hope, C., J. Anderson and P. Wenman (1993), 'Policy Analysis of the Greenhouse Effect: An Application of the PAGE Model', *Energy Policy*, 327-38.

Horgan, J. (1995), 'From Complexity to Perplexity', *Scientific American,* June, 74-9.

Horsfall, W.R. (1955), *Mosquitoes: their Bionomics and Relation to Disease,* Hafner Publishing Company, New York.

Houghton, R.A. (1991), 'Tropical Deforestation and Atmospheric $CO_2$', *Climate Change,* 19, 99-118.

Houghton, R.A. and D.L. Skole (1990), 'Carbon', in B.L. Turner, W.C. Clark, R.W. Kates, J.F. Richards, J.T. Mathews and W.B. Meyers (eds), *The Earth as Transformed by Human Action,* Cambridge University Press, pp. 393-408.

Houghton, R.A., J.E. Hobbie, J.M. Mellilo, B. Moore, B.J. Peterson, G.R. Shaver and G.M. Woodwell (1983), 'Changes in the Carbon Content of Terrestrial Biota and Soils between 1860 and 1980: A Net Release of $CO_2$ to the Atmosphere', *Ecological Monographs*, 53(3), 235-62.

Houghton, R.A., R.D. Boone, J.R. Fruci, J.E. Hobbie, J.M. Melillo, C.A. Palm, B.J. Peterson, G.R. Shaver, G.M. Woodwell, B. Moore, D.L. Skole and N. Myers (1987), 'The Flux of Carbon from Terrestrial Ecosystems to the Atmosphere in 1980 due to Changes in Land Use: Geographic Distribution of the Global Flux', *Tellus*, 39B, 122-39.

Hourcade, J.C. *et al.* (1996), 'A review of mitigation cost studies', in *IPCC, Economic and social dimensions of climate change,* Cambridge University Press.

IIASA/WEC (International Institute for Applied System Analyses/World Energy Council) (1995), *Global Energy Perspectives to 2050 and Beyond*, WEC, UK.

IMF (International Monetary Fund) (1992), *World Economic Outlook*, May 1992, Washington DC.

IPCC (Intergovernmental Panel on Climate Change) (1990), *Climate Change: The IPCC Scientific Assessment*, J.T. Houghton, G.J. Jenkins and J.J. Ephraums (eds), Cambridge University Press.

IPCC (Intergovernmental Panel on Climate Change) (1991), *Climate Change: The IPCC Response Strategies*, Island Press.

IPCC (Intergovernmental Panel on Climate Change) (1992), *Climate Change 1992: The Supplementary Report to The IPCC Scientific Assessment*, J.T. Houghton, B.A. Callander and S.K. Varney (eds), Cambridge University Press.

IPCC (Intergovernmental Panel on Climate Change) (1996a), *Climate Change 1995: The Science of Climate Change,* Cambridge University Press.

IPCC (Intergovernmental Panel on Climate Change) (1996b), *Climate Change 1995: Impacts, Adaptations and Mitigation of Climate Change: Scientific-Technical Analysis*, Cambridge University Press.

IPCC (Intergovernmental Panel on Climate Change) (1996c), *Climate Change 1995: Economic and Social Dimensions of Climate Change*, Cambridge University Press.

Jager W., M.A. Janssen and J. de Greef (1997), *Simulation of Human Agents in Integrated Assessment Models*, RIVM, Bilthoven, the Netherlands, in preparation.

Janssen, M.A. (1992), *Historical and Future Regional Emission Paths of Carbon Dioxide: Allocation and Optimization Mechanisms*, Master Thesis, Department of Operations Research, Erasmus University of Rotterdam.

Janssen, M.A. (1996), *Meeting Targets: Tools to support Integrated Assessment Modelling of Global Change*, PhD Thesis, Maastricht University, the Netherlands. ISBN 90-9009908-5.

Janssen, M.A. (1997), 'Optimization of a Non-linear Dynamical System for Global Climate Change', *European Journal of Operations Research*, Vol. 99, pp. 322-35.

Janssen, M.A. and H.J.M. de Vries (1997a), 'The Battle of Perspectives: a multi-agents model with adaptive responses to climate change', *Ecological Economics*, to appear

Janssen, M.A. and H.J.M. de Vries (1997b), 'Meeting Climate Change Policy Targets and the Role of Technological Change', submitted to *Climatic Change.*

Janssen, M.A. and W.J.M. Martens (1996), *Managing Malaria: an Evolutionary Modelling Approach*, Globo Report Series no. 12, RIVM, Bilthoven, the Netherlands.

Janssen, M.A., and W.J.M. Martens (1997*),* 'Modelling Malaria as a Complex Adaptive System', *Artificial Life*, 3, 213-37.

Janssen, M.A., and J. Rotmans (1995), 'Allocation of Fossil $CO_2$ Emission Rights Quantifying Cultural Perspectives', *Ecological Economics*, 13, 65-79.

Janssen, M.A. and O.J. Vrieze (1995*), Sequential Reduced-System Programming*, Report M 95-04, Reports in Operations Research and Systems Theory, University of Limburg, the Netherlands.

Jastrow, R., W. Nierenberg, and F. Seitz, (1990), *Scientific Perspectives on the Greenhouse Problem*, The George C. Marshall Institute, Washington, USA.

Jetten, T.H. and W. Takken (1994), *Anophelism without Malaria in Europe: a Review of the Ecology and Distribution of the Genus Anopheles in Europe*, Agricultural University Wageningen, the Netherlands.

Johansson, T., Bodlund B. and Williams R. (eds) (1989), *Electricity-efficient end-use and new generation technologies, and their planning implications*, Lund University Press, Lund.

Johnson, W.C. and D.M. Sharpe (1983), 'The Ratio of Total to Merchantable Forest Biomass and Application to the Global Carbon Budget', *Canadian Journal for Forest Research*, 13, 372-83.

Kassler (1995), *Energy for Development*, Shell Selected Papers, Shell.

Kauffman, S.A. (1991), 'Antichaos and Adaptation', *Scientific American*, August, 64-70.

Kauffman, S.A. (1993), *The Origins of Order*, Oxford University Press, New York.

Kaufmann, R.K. (1997), 'Assessing the DICE model: Uncertainty associated with the emission and retention of greenhouse gases', *Climatic Change*, 35, 435-48.

Kirkpatrick, S., C.D. Gelatt and M.P. Vecchi (1983), 'Optimization by Simulated Annealing', *Science*, 220 (4598), 671-80.

Krapivin, V.F. (1993), 'Mathematical Model for Global Ecological Investigations', *Ecological Modelling*, 67, 103-27.

Krause, F., W. Bach and J. Koomey (1989), *Energy Policy in the Greenhouse, Volume One, from Warming Fate to Warming Limit: Benchmarks for a Global Climate Convention*, IPSEP.

Krause, F., J. Koomey and A. Sanstad (1995), *Cutting Carbon Emissions: Burden or Benefit ?*, IPSEP, El Cerrito, CA.

Krogstad, D.J. (1996), 'Malaria as a Reemerging Disease', *Epidemiologic Reviews,* 18, 1, 77-89.

Kuhn, T.S. (1970), *The Structure of Scientific Revolutions*, Chicago, University of Chicago Press, second edition.

Kumar, K. (1987), *Utopia and Anti-Utopia in Modern Times*, Blackwell, Oxford.

Kwa, C. (1984), 'The Relation with Nature in Cybernetic and Evolutionary Ecology' (in Dutch), in *Kennis en Methode*, 25-40.

Kwa, C. (1994), 'Modelling Technologies of Control', *Science as Culture*,Vol. 4, no. 20, 363-91.

Langton, C.G. (ed.) (1989), *Artificial Life*, Addison-Wesley, Redwood City (CA).

Langton, C.G. (ed.) (1995), *Artificial Life*, MIT Press.

Lempert, R.J., M.E. Schlesinger and S.C. Bankes (1996), 'When We Don't Know the Costs or the Benefits: Adaptive Strategies for Abating Climate Change', *Climatic Change*, 33, 235-74.

Lenssen, N. and Flavin C. (1996), 'Sustainable energy for tomorrow's world: the case for an optimistic view of the future', *Energy Future*, 24, no. 9, 769-81.

Levin, A.S, T.G. Hallam and L.J. Gross (eds) (1989), *Applied Mathematical Ecology*, New York: Springer-Verlag.

Levins, R. (1995), 'Preparing for Uncertainty', *Ecosystem Health*, Vol. 1, No. 1, 47-57.

Levy, S.B. (1992), *The Antibiotic Paradox: How Miracle Drugs Are Destroying the Miracle*, Plenum Press, New York and London.

Lindzen, R.S. (1990), 'Some Coolness about Global Warming', *Bulletin of the American Meteorological Society*, 71, 288-99.

Lovelock, J.E. (1979), *Gaia: a New Look at Life on Earth*, Oxford University Press, Oxford.

Lovins, A.B. and H.L. Lovins (1991), 'Least-cost Climatic Stabilization', *Annual Review of Energy and the Environment*, Vol. 16.

Luenberger, D.G. (1984), *Introduction to Linear and Non-linear Programming*, Addison-Wesley, Menlo Park, CA.

MacDonald, G. (1957), *The Epidemiology and Control of Malaria*, Oxford University Press, London.

Maier-Reimer, E. and K. Hasselmann (1987), 'Transport and Storage of Carbon Dioxide in the Ocean - An Inorganic Ocean-Circulation Carbon Cycle Model', *Climate Dynamics*, 2, 63-90.

Malthus, T., (1798), *Essays on Population*.

Manne, A.S. and R.G. Richels (1991), 'Global $CO_2$ Emission Reductions: the Impacts of Rising Energy Costs', *The Energy Journal*, Vol. 12, No. 1, pp. 87-107.

Manne, A.S. and R.G. Richels (1992), *Buying Greenhouse Insurance: The Economic Costs of $CO_2$ Emission Limits*, MIT Press, Cambridge, MA.

Manne, A.S., R. Mendelsohn and R.G. Richels (1994), 'MERGE: A Model for Evaluating Regional and Global Effects of GHG Reduction Policies', in N. Nakicenovic, W.D. Nordhaus, R. Richels and F.L. Toth (eds), *Integrative Assessment of Mitigation, Impacts, and Adaptation to Climate Change*, 143-172, CP-94-0, IIASA, Laxenburg, Austria.

Marland, G. and R.M. Rotty (1984), 'Carbon Dioxide Emissions from Fossil Fuels: a Procedure for Estimation and Results for 1950-1982', *Tellus*, 36B, 232-61.

Marland, G., T.A. Boden, R.C. Griffin, S.F. Huang, P. Kanciruk and T.R. Nelson (1989), *Estimates of $CO_2$ Emissions from Fossil Fuel Burning and Cement Manufacturing Based on the United Nations Energy Statistics and the U.S. Bureau of Mines Cement Manufacturing Data*, NDP-030/RI, Carbon Dioxide Information Analysis Center, Oak Ridge National Laboratory, using updated figures NDP-030/R2.

Martens, W.J.M. (1997), *Health Impacts of Climate Change and Ozone Depletion - An Eco-Epidemiological Modelling Approach*, PhD. Thesis, University of Maastricht, the Netherlands.

Martens, W.J.M., T.H. Jetten, J. Rotmans and L.W. Niessen (1995b), 'Climate Change and Vector-borne Diseases: a Global Modelling Perspective', *Global Environmental Change,* Volume 5 (3), 195-209.

Martens, W.J.M., L.W. Niessen and J. Rotmans (1994), *Climate Change and Malaria Risk: an Integrated Modelling Approach*, RIVM Report no. 461502003, Bilthoven, the Netherlands.

Martens, W.J.M., L.W. Niessen, J. Rotmans, T.H. Jetten and A.J. McMichael (1995a), 'Potential Impact of Global Climate Change on Malaria Risk', *Environmental Health Perspectives*, Volume 103, no. 5, 458-65.

Martin, P.H. and M.J. Lefebvre (1995), 'Malaria and Climate: Sensitivity of Malaria Potential Transmission to Climate', *AMBIO*, 24,4, 200-7.

Maslow, A. (1966), *The Psychology of Science: A Reconnaissance*, Chicago, Henry Regnery.

*Modelling Global Change*

MATLAB (1992), *Optimisation Toolbox: For Use with MATLAB*, The Math Works Inc. 10.

Matsuoka, Y. and K. Kai, (1994), 'An Estimation of Climatic Change Effects on Malaria', *Journal of the Global Environment*, 1:1-15.

Meadows, D.H. and J.M. Robinson (1985), *The Electronic Oracle: Computer Models and Social Decisions*, John Wiley & Sons.

Meadows, D.H., D.L. Meadows and J. Randers (1991), *Beyond the Limits*, Earthscan Publications Ltd., London.

Meadows, D.H., D.L. Meadows, J. Randers and W.W. Behrens (1972), *The Limits to Growth*, Universe Books, New York.

Meadows, D.L., W.W. Behrens III, D.H. Meadows, R.F. Naill, J. Randers and E.K.O. Zahn (1974), *Dynamics of Growth in a Finite World*, Wright-Allen Press, Cambridge, UK.

Millenium Institute (1995), *Documentation for Threshold 21 - National Sustainable Development Model'*, Millenium Institute, Arlington, USA.

Millenium Institute (1996), *Documentation for Threshold 21 Bangladesh - National Sustainable Development Model'*, Millenium Institute, Arlington, USA.

Miller, L.H. (1985), *Global Order: Values and Power in International Politics*, Boulder, Colorado, Westview Press.

Mitchell, B.R. (1981), *European Historical Statistics: 1750-1975*, Macmillan, Facts on File, New York.

Mitchell, B.R. (1982), *International Historical Statistics: Africa and Asia*, Macmillan Press Ltd, London and Basingstoke.

Mitchell, B.R. (1983), *International Historical Statistics: The Americas and Australia*, Gale Research Co. Detroit.

Mitchell, J.F.B., T.C. Johns, J.M. Gregory and S.F.B. Tott (1995), 'Climate Response to Increasing Levels of Greenhouse Gases and Sulphate Aerosols', *Nature*, Vol. 376, 10 August, 501-4.

Molina, M.J. and F.S. Rowland (1974), 'Stratospheric Sink for Chlorofluoromethanes: Chlorine Atomcatalyzed Destruction of Ozone', *Nature,* 249, 810-2.

Molineaux, L. (1988), 'The Epidemiology of Human Malaria as an Explanation of its Distribution, Including Some Implications for its Control', in: W.H. Wernsdorfer and I. McGregor (eds), *Malaria: principles and practice of malariology (volume 2)*, 913-998, Churchill Livingstone, New York.

Molineaux, L. and G. Gramiccia (1980), *The Garki project: Research on the epidemiology and control of malaria in the Sudan savanna of west Africa*, World Health Organization, Geneva.

Molineaux, L., K. Dietz and A. Thomas (1978), *Further Epidemiological Evaluation of a Malaria Model,* Bulletin of the World Health Organization.

Molofsky, J., E.S. Menges, C.A.S. Hall, T.V. Armentano and K.A. Ault (1984), 'The Effects of Land Use Alteration on Tropical Carbon Exchange', in T.N. Veziraglu (ed.), *The Biosphere: Problems and Solutions*, Elsevier Science Publishing, Amsterdam, pp. 181-4.

Moore, B., R.D. Boone, J.E. Hobbie, R.A. Houghton, J.M. Melillo, B.J. Peterson, G.R. Shaver, C.J. Vorosmarty, G.M. Woodwell (1981), 'A Simple Model for Analysis of the Role of Terrestrial Ecosystems in the Global Carbon Budget', in B. Bolin (ed.), *Carbon Cycle Modelling*, SCOPE 16, John Wiley & Sons, New York, pp. 365-85.

More, T. (1516), *Utopia*, Cassel, London (1898).

Morgan, G.M. and M. Henrion (1990), *Uncertainty: a Guide to Dealing with Uncertainty in Quantitative Risk and Policy Analysis*, Cambridge University Press, New York.

Muirhead-Thompson, R.C. (1954), 'Factors Determining the True Reservoir of Infection of Plasmodium Falciparum and Wuchereria Bancrofti in a West African Village', *Transactions of the Royal Society of Tropical Medicine and Hygiene*, 48 (3), 208-25.

Naill, R. (1977), *Managing the energy transition - A Systems Dynamics search for alternatives to oil and gas*, Cambridge MA, Ballinger.

Nakicenovic, N. and A. Grubler (eds) (1991), *Diffusion of Technologies and Social Behaviour*, Springer-Verlag, Berlin/Heidelberg.

Nájera, J.A. (1974), 'A Critical Review of the Field Application of a Mathematical Model of Malaria Eradication', *Bulletin of the World Health Organization*, 50, 449-57.

Nájera, J.A., B.H. Liese and J. Hammer (1992), *Malaria: New Patterns and Perspectives*, World Bank Technical Paper number 183. The World Bank, Washington, DC.

Nedelman, J. (1985), 'Introduction Review: Some New Thoughs about Old Malaria Models', *Mathematical Biosciences*, 73, 159-82.

Nemhauser, G.L., A.H.G. Rinnooy Kan and M.J. Todd (1989), *Optimization*, *Handbooks in Operations Research and Management Science, Volume 1*, North Holland, the Netherlands.

Ness, G.D., W.D. Drake and S.R. Brechin (eds) (1993), *Population Environment Dynamics - Ideas and Observations*, The University of Michigan Press.

Newton, I (1687), *Principia Mathematica Philosophiae Naturalis*, Royal Society

Niessen, L.W., H.B.M. Hilderink and J. Rotmans (1997), *Roads to Health: Modelling the Health Transition*, GLOBO report Series no. 15, RIVM report no. 461502015, RIVM, Bilthoven, the Netherlands.

Nordhaus, W.D. (1991a), 'To Slow or not to Slow: The Economics of the Greenhouse Effect', *The Economic Journal*, 101, 920-37.

Nordhaus, W.D. (1991b), 'A Survey of the Costs of Reduction of Greenhouse Gases, *The Energy Journal*, 12, 1, 37-65.

Nordhaus, W.D. (1992), 'An Optimal Transition Path for Controlling Greenhouse Gases', *Science*, Vol. 258, 1315-9.

Nordhaus, W.D. (1993), 'Rolling the "DICE": An Optimal Transition Path for Controlling Greenhouse Gases', *Resource and Energy Economics*, 15, 27-50, North-Holland.

Nordhaus, W.D. (1994), *Managing the Global Commons: The Economics of Climate Change*, MIT Press, Cambridge, MA.

Nordhaus, W.D. and Z. Yang (1995), *RICE: A Regional Dynamic General Equilibrium Model of Optimal Climate-Change Policy*, February 27 1995.

Odén, S. (1968), 'The Acidification of Air and Precipitation and its Consequences in the Natural Environment', *Ecology Committee Bulletin*, no. 1, Swedish National Research Council, Stockholm, Sweden.

OECD (1989), *World Energy Statistics and Balances 1971-1987*, OECD, Paris.

OECD (1991a), *Energy Statistics and Balances of Non-OECD Countries 1988-1989*, OECD, Paris.

OECD (1991b), *Energy Balances of OECD Countries 1960-1979*, OECD, Paris.

OECD (1991c), *Energy Balances of OECD Countries 1980-1989*, OECD, Paris.

OECD (1992), *Energy Balances of OECD Countries 1989-1990*, OECD, Paris.

Omran, A.R. (1971), 'The Epidemiological Transition: a Theory of the Epidemiology of Population Change', *Milbank Memorial Fund*, 49, 509-38.

Oreskes, N., K. Shrader-Frechette and K. Belitz (1994), 'Verification, Validation, and Conformation of Numerical Models in the Earth Sciences', *Science*, 263, 641-6.

Packard, R.M. (1984), 'Maize, Cattle and Mosquitoes: The Political Economy of Malaria Epidemics in Colonial Swaziland', *Journal of African History*, 25, 99, 189-212.

Pant, C.P. (1988), 'Malaria Vector Control: Imagociding', in W.H.Wernsdorfer and I. McGregor (eds), *Malaria: Principles and Practice of Malariology* (volume 2), 1173-212, Churchill Livingstone, New York.

Parson, E.A. (1996), *A Global Climate-Change Policy Exercise: Results of a Test Run, July 27-29, 1995*, Working Paper, Wp-96-90, IIASA, Laxenburg, Austria.

Paul, R.E.L., M.J. Packer, M. Walmsley, M. Lagog, L.C. Ranford-Carwright, R. Paru and K.P. Day (1995), 'Mating Patterns in Malaria Parasite Populations of Papua New Guinea', *Science*, Vol. 269, 1709-11.

Payne, D. (1987), 'Spread of chloroquine resistance in Plasmodium falciparum', *Parasitology Today*, 3, 241-6.

Peck, S.C. and T.J. Teisberg (1992), 'CETA: A Model for Carbon Emission Trajectory Assessment', *The Energy Journal*, Vol. 13, No. 1.

Peck, S.C. and T.J. Teisberg (1993a), 'CO$_2$ Emissions Control: Comparing Policy Instruments', *Energy Policy*, 222-30.

Peck, S.C. and T.J. Teisberg (1993b), 'Global Warming Uncertainties and the Value of Information: An Analysis Using CETA', *Resource and Energy Economics*, Vol. 15, No. 1, 71-97.

Pepper, W., J. Leggett, R. Swart, J. Wasson, J. Edmonds and I. Mintzner (1992), *Emission Scenarios for the IPCC: An Update*, Unpublished Report prepared for IPCC Working Group I.

Peterson, G., S. Pope, G.A. De Leo, M.A. Janssen, J.R. Malcolm, J.M. Parody, G. Hood, and M. North (1997), 'Ecology, Ethics, and Advocacy', *Conservation Ecology*, online, 1(1): 17.

Ponting, C. (1992), *A Green History of the World*, London: Penguin.

Posch, M., J.-P. Hettelingh, J. Alcamo and M. Krol (1996), 'Integrated Scenarios of Acidification and Climate Change in Asia and Europe', *Global Environmental Change*, Vol. 6, no. 4, 375-94.

Press, W.H., B.P. Flannery, S.A. Teukolsky and W.T. Vetterling (1988), *Numerical Recipes in C: The Art of Scientific Computing*, Cambridge University Press, Cambridge.

Price, C. (1995), 'Emissions, Concentrations and Disappearing CO$_2$', *Resource and Energy Economics*, Vol. 17, no. 1, 87-97.

Proops, J.L.R. (1989), 'Ecological Economics: Rationale and Problem Areas', *Ecological Economics*, 1, 59-76.

Ramaswamy, V., M.D. Schwarzkopf and K.P. Shine (1992), 'Radiative Forcing of Climate from Halocarbon-induced Global Stratospheric Loss', *Nature*, 355, 810-12.

Ramsey, F.P. (1928), 'A Mathematical Theory of Saving', *The Economic Journal*, 543-59.

Rayner, S., (1991), 'A Cultural Perspective on the Structure and Implementation of Global Environmental Agreements', *Evaluation Review*, Vol. 15, No. 1, February 1991, 75-102.

Riebsame, W.E. (1990), 'Social Perspectives on Global Climate Change', in: S. Rayner (ed.), *Managing the Global Commons: Decision-Making and Conflict Resolution in Response to Climate Change*, 11-26, Report of the research workshop, August 1-4 1989, Knoxville Tennessee.

Risbey, J., M. Kandlikar and A. Patwardhan (1996), 'Assessing Integrated Assessments', *Climatic Change*, 34, 369-95.

Rörsch, A. and C. de Hart (1993), *Threshold 2000: Constraints and Scenarios for Sustainable Development in the Netherlands and Europe* (in Dutch), Elmar, Rijswijk, the Netherlands.

Rose, A. (1992), 'Equity Consideration of Tradable Carbon Emission Entitlements', in *Combating Global Warming: Study on a Global System of Tradable Carbon Emission Entitlements*, UNCTAD, New York.

Ross, R. (1911), *The Prevention of Malaria*, (2nd edn), Murray, London.

Rothen, S.M. (1995), *The Greenhouse Effect in Economic Modelling: A Critical Survey*, EAWAG, Dubendorf, Switzerland (draft).

Rotmans J. (1990), *IMAGE: An Integrated Model to Assess the Greenhouse Effect*, PhD Thesis, Kluwer Academic Publishers, Dordrecht, The Netherlands.

Rotmans, J. and H. Dowlatabadi (1997), 'Integrated Assessment of Climate Change: Evaluation of Models and Other Methods', in S. Rayner and E. Malone (eds), *Human Choice and Climate Change: An International Social Science Assessment*, in press.

Rotmans, J. and H.J.M. de Vries (eds) (1997), *Perspectives on Global Change: The TARGETS Approach*, Cambridge University Press.

Rotty, R.M. and G. Marland (1986), *Production of $CO_2$ from Fossil Fuel Burning by Fuel Type: 1860-1982*, Report NDP-006, Carbon Dioxide Information Analysis Center, Oak Ridge National Laboratory, USA.

Rotty, R.M. (1987), 'A Look at 1983 $CO_2$ Emissions from Fossil Fuels (with Preliminary Data from 1984)', *Tellus*, 39, 203-8.

Ruthen, R. (1993), 'Adapting to Complexity', *Scientific American*, January, 110-7.

Schapira, A. (1990), 'The Resistance of Falciparum Malaria in Africa to 4-aminoquilines and Antifolates', *Scandinavian Journal of Infectious Diseases,* Supplementum 75.

Schlesinger, W.H. (1991), *Biogeochemistry: an Analysis of Global Change*, Academic Press, United Kingdom, London.

Schmidheiney S. *et al.* (1992), *Changing course: a global business perspective on development and the environment*, MIT Press, Cambridge, MA.

Schwartz, M. and M. Thompson (1990), *Divided We Stand: Redefining Politics, Technology, and Social Choice*, New York, Harvester Wheatsheaf.

Seitz J.L. (1995), *Global Issues: An Introduction*, Blackwell Publishers Inc., Cambridge, USA.

Siegenthaler, U. and H. Oeschger (1987), 'Biospheric $CO_2$ Emissions during the Past 200 Years Reconstructed by Deconvolution of Ice Core Data', *Tellus,* 39B, 140-54.

Simon, J.L. (1980), 'Resources, population, environment: an oversupply of false bad news', *Science*, 208, 1431-7.

Sterman, J.D. (1981), *The energy transition and the economy: a system dynamics approach* (2 Vols.), MIT Alfred P. Sloan School of Management.

Sterman, J.D. (1991), 'A Sceptic's Guide to Computer Model', in G.O. Barney, W.B. Kreutzer, and M.J. Garrett (eds), *Managing a Nation: The Microcomputer Software Catalog*, Westview Press, Boulder-San Francisco-Oxford.

Tabashnik, B.E. (1986), 'Computer Simulation as a Tool for Pesticide Resistance Management', in Committee on Strategies for the Management of Pesticide Resistant Pest Populations (ed.), *Pesticide Resistance: Strategies and Tactics for Management,* National Academy Press, Washington, DC.

Tabashnik, B.E. (1990), 'Implications of Gene Amplification for Evolution and Management of Insecticide Resistance', *Journal of Economic Entomology*, Vol. 83, no. 4, 1170-6.

Tabashnik, B.E. and B.A. Croft (1982), 'Managing Pesticide Resistance in Crop-Arthropod Complexes: Interactions Between Biological and Operational Factors', *Environmental Entomology*, 11: 1137-44.

Taylor, C.E. (1983), 'Evolution of Resistance to Insecticides: the Role of Mathematical Models and Computer Simulations', in G.P. Georghiou and T. Saito (eds), *Pest Resistance to Pesticides,* 163-73, Plenum, New York,

Taylor, K.E. and J.E. Penner (1994), 'Response of the Climate System to Atmospheric Aerosols and Greenhouse Gases', *Nature*, Vol. 369, pp. 734-7.

Thompson, M. (1996), 'Cultural Theory and Integrated Assessment', submitted to *Environmental Modeling and Assessment*.

Thompson, M. and P. Taylor (1986), *The Surprise Game: An Exploration of Constrained Relativism*, Warwick Papers in Management, no. 1, Institute for Management Research and Development, Coventry: University of Warwick.

Thompson, M., R. Ellis, and A. Wildawsky (1990), *Cultural Theory*, Westview Press, Boulder, Colorado.

Timmerman, P. (1986), *Mythology and Surprise in the Sustainable Development of the Biosphere*, Cambridge University Press, Cambridge, UK.

Tobler, W. (1979), 'Cellular Geography', in S. Gale and G. Olsson (eds), *Philosophy of Geography*, 379-86.

Tolba, M.K. (1992), *Saving our Planet - Challenges and Hopes,* Chapman & Hall, London.

Toth, F.L. (1988), 'Policy Exercises: Objectives and Design Elements', *Simulation and Games*, 19, 235-55.

Tyndall, J. (1863), 'On Radiation Through the Earth's Atmosphere', *Philosophical Magazine*, 4, 200.

Trisoglio, A., R. Swart, M. Thompson, J. Rotmans, H. Dowlatabadi, A. Rahman and B. de Vries (1994), *Scenarios of Climate Change: Making the Human Factor Explicit*, Washington: Battelle Pacific Northwest Laboratories.

Trisoglio, A. (1995), *Complexity: The Challenges*, Paper presented at the workshop 'Risk, Policy and Complexity', IIASA, Laxenburg, 7-9 August 1995.

United Nations (UN) (1966), *World Population Prospects as Assessed 1963*, United Nations, New York.

United Nations (UN) (1990a), *Population Prospects 1990*, United Nations, New York.

United Nations (UN) (1990b), *National Accounts Statistics: Analysis of main Aggregates, 1987*, New York.

United Nations (1992), *Framework Convention on Climate Change*, United Nations, New York.

United Nations Conference on Trade and Development (UNCTAD) (1985), *Handbook of International Trade and Development Statistics Supplement 1985*, New York.

UNEP (United Nations Environment Programme) (1992), *The World Environment 1972-1992: Two Decades of Challenge*, M.K. Tolba and O.A. El-Kholy (eds), Chapman & Hall, London.

UNEP (United Nations Environment Programme) (1997), *Global Environmental Outlook-1*, Oxford University Press.

Van Asselt, M.B.A. and J. Rotmans (1996), 'Uncertainty in Perspective: A Cultural Perspective Based Approach', *Global Environmental Change*, 6, no. 2, 121-57.

Veblen, T. (1898), 'Why is economics not an evolutionary science?', *Quarterly Journal of Economics*, 3, 1-14.

Vercelli, A. (1994), 'Hard Uncertainty and Environment', in. F.E. Mattei (ed.), *Sustainable Growth and Uncertainty*, Proceedings of a Symposium, January 10-11, Milan, Italy.

Von Bertalanffy, L. (1968), *General System Theory*, New York.

Waldrop, M. (1992), *Complexity: The Emerging Science at the Edge of Order and Chaos*, Simon and Schuster.

Watts, J.A. (1982), 'The Carbon Dioxide Question: Data Sampler', in W.C. Clark (ed.), *Carbon Dioxide Review*, 457-60.

WCED (World Commission on Environment and Development) (1987), *Our Common Future*, Oxford, Oxford University Press.

Weaver, W. (1948), 'Science and Complexity', *American Scientist*, 36, 536-44.

Wernsdorfer, W.H. (1994), 'Epidemiology of Drug Resistance in Malaria', *Acta Tropica*, 56, 143-56.

Weyant, J., *et al.* (1996), 'Integrated Assesment', *Climate Change 1995: Economic and Social Dimensions of Climate Change. Contribution of Working Group III to the Second Assessment Report of the IPCC*, pp. 367-96, Cambridge University Press.

White, R. and G. Engelen (1994), 'Cellular Dynamics and GIS: Modelling Spatial Complexity', *Geographical Systems*, 1(2), 237-53.

White, I.D., D.N. Mottershead and S.J. Harrison (1992), *Environmental Systems: An Introductory Text*, Second Edition, Chapman & Hall, London.

WHO (World Health Organization) (1991), *Weekly Epidemiological Record*, 66(22): 162.

WHO (World Health Organization) (1992), *Vector Resistance to Pesticides*, Fifteenth Report of the WHO Expert Committee on Vector Biology and Control, WHO Technical Report Series, 818, Geneva.

WHO (World Health Organization) (1992b), *Our Planet, Our Health*, Report of the WHO Commission on Health and Environment, WHO, Geneva.

WHO (World Health Organization) (1996), *The World Health Report 1996*, WHO, Geneva.

Wigley, T.M.L. (1994), *MAGICC: Model for the Assessment of Greenhouse-gas Induced Climate Change: User's Guide and Scientific Reference Manual*, Preliminary version.

Wigley, T.M.L. (1995), 'A Successful Prediction?', *Nature*, Vol. 376, 10 August, 463-4.

Wigley, T.M.L., R. Richels and J.A. Edmonds (1996), 'Economic and Environmental Choices in the Stabilization of Atmospheric $CO_2$ Concentrations', *Nature*, Vol. 379, 240-3.

Williams, R.H. (1990), 'Low-cost Strategies for Coping with $CO_2$ Emissions Limits', *The Energy Journal*, Vol. 11, No. 3, 35-59.

Wilson, D. and J. Swisher (1993), 'Exploring the Gap: Top-down versus Bottom-up Analyses of the Costs of Mitigating Global Warming', *Energy Policy*, 249-63.

WMO (World Meteorological Organization) (1992), *Scientific Assessment of Ozone Depletion: 1991*, WMO/UNEP, WMO Global Ozone Research and Monitoring Project, Report no. 25.

Wolfe, P. (1959), 'The Simplex Method for Quadratic Programming', *Econometrica*, Vol. 27, 382-98.

World Resources Institute/Institute for Environment and Development (1991), *World Resources 1990/1991*, Washington, DC.

WRR (Dutch Scientific Council for Governmental Policy) (1994), *Sustained Risks: a Lasting Phenomenon*, Reports to the Government no. 44, SDU Uitgeverij, The Hague, the Netherlands.

Wynne, B. and S. Shackly (1994), 'Environmental Models - Truth Machines or Social Heuristics', *The Globe*, 21, 6-8.

Zapert, R. (1994), *Uncertainty Analysis of Enhanced Greenhouse Effect Models*, PhD Thesis, University of Maryland, Baltimore County, Maryland.

Zweers, W. (1984), 'Nature and Culture in an Ecological Perspective', In. *Milieucrises en filosofie, westers bewustzijn en vervreemde natuur*, 97-141, Ekologische uitgeverij, Amsterdam, the Netherlands (in Dutch).

# Index